COUNT ZINZENDORF AND THE SPIRIT OF THE MORAVIANS

"For the Kingdom of God is not just a lot of talk; it is living by God's power."
1 Corinthians 4:20

"He died for everyone so that those who receive His new life will no longer live for themselves. Instead, they will live for Christ, who died and was raised for them."
2 Corinthians 5:15

Paul Wemmer

Copyright © 2013 by Paul Wemmer

COUNT ZINZENDORF AND THE SPIRIT OF THE MORAVIANS
by Paul Wemmer

Printed in the United States of America

ISBN 9781628398373

All rights reserved solely by the author. The author guarantees all contents are original and do not infringe upon the legal rights of any other person or work. No part of this book may be reproduced in any form without the permission of the author. The views expressed in this book are not necessarily those of the publisher.

Unless otherwise indicated, all Scripture quotation are taken from the Holy Bible, New Living Translation, copyright © 1996, 2004, 2007 by Tyndale House Foundation. Used by permission of Tyndale House Publishers, Inc., Carol Stream, Illinois 60188. All rights reserved.

If you would like to write a comment or order additional books, please email the author at:

Paul4120@gmail.com

www.xulonpress.com

Endorsements

Before reading Paul Wemmer's book, I knew little about Zinzendorf (except that he had written many hymns) or about the Moravians (other than their influence on John Wesley). I was especially taken with the centrality of the sufferings of Christ in Zinzendorf's spiritual experience as seen in his emphasis on Jesus as the Man of Sorrows and on resting in His wounds, his dedication to prayer and missionary activity, his love for the Jews, the intensity of his personal suffering that drew him ever closer to his Savior, and ... well the list could be greatly extended. I also appreciated Paul's own narrative and spiritual/theological comments throughout the book.

This verse of Wesley's translation of Zinzendorf's hymn 'Seelenbräutigam, O du Gotteslamm' (written when he was only twenty or twenty-one) certainly describes his subsequent life:

Savior, where'er Thy steps I see.
Dauntless, untired, I follow thee!
O let Thy hand support me still.
And lead me to Thy holy hill!

Darrel W. Amundsen, Ph.D.
Professor Emeritus of Classics
Western Washington University

Visions, prophecies, healings and special anointings are exciting and are much abounding theses days. But may we dare to ask the Moravians to show us their priorities? They prayed continuously for almost 120 years. The result was an unprecedented zeal for missionary activities, a love for the Lamb of God, and personal holiness. They were in accord with Paul's pleading, 'Pray hard and long. Pray for your brothers and sisters. Keep your eyes open. Keep each other's spirit up so that no one falls behind or drops out' (Ephesians 6:18, The Message).

Isn't time to emulate Jesus when He was on earth? He prayed in the morning. He prayed at night. He prayed all night and He prayed when He was alone. He prayed with others and He prayed at public gatherings (Mark 1:35, Luke 6:12, John 6:15, Matthew 11:25, 14:19, 14:23). When we work, we work for somebody. When we pray, God works for us.

Pastor Jason Hubbard.
Director of the *"Light of the World Prayer Center"*
in Bellingham, WA.
www.lowpc.org

Humility is perhaps best demonstrated not by those who lack power and resources, rather by those who do. Count Zinzendorf was such a man. As a nobleman of considerable wealth and privilege, his earnest devotion to the Almighty produced a highly innovative model for ministry. Besides his well known role for incubating continuous prayer, he utilized what had been entrusted to him to build a pioneering trans-denominational and economic community for disciples of Jesus. He was the friend to commoners and the persecuted. He was an excellent example of "minister in the marketplace 24/7." Out of this ministry in Eastern Germany, the "modern" missions movement to the nations was birthed.

Endorsements

My good friend, Paul Wemmer, has done a favor for us all in compiling a concise biography of the humble nobleman Count Zinzendorf.

Thomas P. Dooley, Ph.D.
Founder & President of Path Clearer

Paul Wemmer brings alive the story of the Moravians and highlights the Christ-like character they displayed through adversity, pain, and suffering. They strove for one great cause, bathed in fervent prayer, day and night, to bring salvation to the poor and oppressed. They realized that every true labor in which godly men have engaged throughout history was founded on a deep love for the lost. This book vividly inspires the reader earnestly to pursue Christ anew, and lights for us again the forgotten but still burning 'Lamp Stand of the Moravians.'

Pastor Gary J. Senff, Master of Divinity.
Trinity Assembly of God, Pahrump, Nevada.

God uses men. God used Count Zinzendorf to kindle a prayer-fire at Herrnhut that burned for a hundred years – a fire that purified the church and sparked a revival of missions. God used Paul Wemmer, in this eye-opening account of Zinzendorf's life, to re-ignite Zinzendorf's passion for Christ in the hearts of readers. I pray that the love of Christ will re-capture your heart as you read it. It did mine!

Pastor Alvin VanderGriend.
Author of books, including the best selling book, "Love to Pray."
Co-founder of the "Denominational Prayer Leader's Network."

Dedication

This book is dedicated to the *ekklesia,* the corporate gathering of believers, the assembly of heaven's citizens here on earth, the bondservants of Christ united in purpose and in loving loyalty to their Master and King.

This book is also dedicated to my wife, Jean, our families, our children and ten grandchildren, in answer to their frequent inquiry, "Why is Opa constantly traveling to Germany?" And now, they can give an answer to each other with a smile, "Opa wants to write a book and tell it all."

Note to Readers

We have given thousands of books away free and it surprised us that so many dear readers showed so much interest. What gave us the most joy was when we received emails about starting prayer groups motivated by the enduring prayers of the Moravians.

This book is priced for minimal profit and any remuneration will be used for printing additional books.

It is made available to all those who seek to lift up the Lamb of God and our indwelling gracious Lover. "I have but one passion, and that is Jesus, only He" (Count Zinzendorf).

It is made available to all those who already want to start singing here on earth with the mighty heavenly chorus, "Worthy is the Lamb who was slaughtered – to receive power and riches and wisdom and strength and honor and glory and blessing" (Rev. 5:12).

It is for all those who want to join with our Heavenly Father in His magnificent desire to increase the supreme excellencies of the Sovereign Monarch, our Savior. After the incarnation:

Jesus received additional glory as a Perfect Savior (Hebrews 2:9-10).

Jesus received additional glory as a Perfect High Priest (Hebrews 5:9).

Jesus received additional glory by redeeming His flock (John 17:10).

Jesus received additional glory because of His church, the dazzling bride (2 Thessalonians 1:10).

Jesus received additional glory when the all-powerful Father raised His Holy passion, Jesus arose from the grave (1 Peter 1:21).

We who desire to increase the glory of Jesus will behold and contemplate the new titles given to Him after His atoning death on the cross: Jesus our compassionate Advocate, our powerful Mediator, our faithful Intercessor, our radiant Redeemer, our tender Good Shepherd, our superior Heir of all things, our merciful Judge and wise Head of His church.

"His present glory is a combination of all His glories, inherent and acquired. It is the glory of His deity, His humanity, His attributes, His offices, and His character. We are not called to share them, but to rejoice in them and to praise Him for them forever" (William MacDonald).

"The one who has Christ has everything. The one who has everything except for Christ really has nothing. And the one who has Christ plus everything else does not have any more than the one who has Christ alone" (Augustine).

"We are called to an everlasting preoccupation with God's Son" (A.W. Tozer).

"Jesus shares His Father's throne, that He is the Head of the church, possessor and bestower of all the fullness of divine grace, the coming Judge of the world, conqueror of every hostile power, intercessor for His own, and, in short, bearer of all the majesty which belongs to His kingly office" (Denney).

"And I have revealed you to them and will keep on revealing you. I will do this so that your love for me may be in them and I in them." This is Jesus' prayer in John 17:26, to **give us** the same passion for Him [Jesus] as **God has** for His Son.

Vicit agnus noster, eum sequamur

Our Lamb has conquered; let us follow Him
[Moravian Seal].

Contents

1	My Story	17
2	Call to Herrnhut	28
3	Early Years	36
4	School Days	42
5	The Wittenberg Years	51
6	Falling In Love	59
7	Life in Dresden	63
8	The Moravians in Herrnhut	70
9	Thoughts on Justification	82
10	The Great Sifting	88
11	Fire From Above	95
12	Losung: Watchword for the Day	103
13	Salt of the Earth	110
14	Exile	118
15	Moravians Overseas	129
16	Zinzendorf's Work in Exile	136
17	Missionary Journeys	146
18	The Rise and Fall of Herrnhaag	162
19	New Horizons	171
20	Homecoming	179
21	Setbacks and Triumphs	184
22	Christian Renatus	194
23	Zinzendorf's Wife: A humble helpmate	201
24	*Heimgang*, Home Going	208
25	Count Zinzendorf's *Lobrede*, oration of praise	226
26	The Moravian spirit	232
27	Helpful pointers for a victorious transformation	249
28	Addendum	262
29	Important events in Zinzendorf's life	267

1

My Story

A brief history of my life and conversion will clarify why I write so much about the Holy Spirit. I was born in the little German town of Telgte, Westphalia, in 1940, when Germany was already at war. My mother told me she prayed it would be quiet the night she called the midwife to come help deliver me, her fourth child. For her, a quiet night meant that there would be no piercing siren from the mayor's building, calling villagers to wake up and take cover in basements. Later in the war, the Allies sent streams of huge B17 bombers, but at this time only small groups of airplanes came at night, randomly dropping bombs. My earliest memories were of people in bunkers praying loudly while explosions shook the earth. Only eight miles away, bombs completely destroyed the town of Münster.

Telgte's history is steeped in religion. Catholic pilgrims travel from far away to visit a chapel venerating Mary. Brochures proclaim that over 100,000 pilgrims visit Telgte yearly. For you to really understand my Catholic upbringing, let me translate a very popular hymn to Mary, which is still in the rather extensive hymnbook in Telgte. *#960 Wunderschön prächtige:*

Wonderful, magnificent, high and mighty, full of love, blessed heavenly Lady.
As your child eternally unite me with you.
Yes, with my body and soul I trust.
Possession, blood and life I want to give you.
All, whatever I have and all that I am I give to you, Mary, with joy.

Mary would weep over the glory stolen from her Son. Her true perspective is reflected in Luke 1:47, "How my spirit rejoices in God *my Savior!*"

Jesus said, "You search the Scriptures because you think they give you eternal life. But the Scriptures point to *me!*" (John 5:39) Jesus brings to light, "He [the Holy Spirit] will bring *me glory* by telling you whatever he receives *from me*" (John 16:14) John said "...And we have seen *his glory,* the glory of the Father's one and only Son" (John 1:14). Moses cautioned us, "You must worship no other gods, for the Lord, whose very name is Jealous, is a God who is *jealous* about his relationship with you (Exodus 34:14, emphasis mine).

As a product of this environment, I became a devout Catholic, never missed a Mass, and made a vow as a young boy to pray the Rosary daily. Little did I know that one day this would all change dramatically.

I was almost eighteen and had finished my education when I stood on the deck of an ocean liner, the *M.S. Berlin*, ready to sail across the Atlantic. As I watched tugboats pull the big ship out of Bremerhaven Harbor, I was looking forward to practicing my English while on board the ship. When I was a young boy, I loved to listen to the English language. I built my own radio in a cigar box, and at night I listened to the BBC radio station in England. My radio was called a "detector," and it required an earplug to listen. What excited me the most, standing there on the ship's deck, was that I was headed for America: the land of unlimited opportunities.

My Story

Life for an immigrant was busy. Finding work, improving my English vocabulary, get a driver's license, buying my first car, a 1954 Chevrolet. Making friends.

In 1963, at the age of twenty-three, I received my "greetings" from Uncle Sam to serve in the Army. After hearing horror stories from my father and my older brother about war and dying, I was scared to become a soldier and not too enthusiastic about going to the Army induction center in Los Angeles.

My father, who was a simple farm boy, cried when I left. During WWI, he served in the German Army for two years against his will. He served an additional five years in WWII, and for two of those years he was in a prison camp.

My older brother, Reinhard, spent two years in the German Army during WWII and fought in the Battle of the Bulge. When he was discharged in 1945, he was only eighteen. Seeing this small, emaciated young boy, a friendly American soldier gave him a candy bar and told him to, "Go home to mama." When I complained about working hard as a printer and moving heavy skids of paper, Reinhard told me to be happy that nobody was shooting at me. His idea of contentment was not being in a foxhole with an enemy after him.

In 1964, while stationed at Fitzsimmons Army Hospital in Denver, I became a U.S. citizen. On the army base, an excellent teacher, who was a member of the American Daughters of the Revolution, taught an American history class. I still have a copy of the letter she filed with the Army headquarters. "Specialist P.W. distinguished himself by performing tasks beyond normal expectations." What a proud day it was when I stood before the judge in my "First Class" uniform and was sworn in as a U.S. citizen!

In 1967 I married an Austrian girl, Leopoldine. We met in Los Angeles at St. Stephan, a German Catholic church. Before long we had two children, a girl and a boy. My wife and I were both devoted to the Catholic Church. On a trip to Tijuana, Mexico, I bought a huge, eight-foot rosary. At night we sometimes sat on the floor in the living room, passing the rosary around with our children as we changed the beads from one Hail Mary to another.

With my background in printing, I became a supervisor in the Los Angeles elections department and eventually had up to twenty people working for me. My job was to oversee the printing of election materials. One day, the Registrar of Voters came by with a group of election officials from another state. He introduced me with a rather humorous comment, "Here is a German who runs the print shop as smoothly as a Swiss clock."

My wife and I bought a two-story house in Valencia, thirty miles north of Los Angeles. Life was easy. I had a secure civil service job, two beautiful children, and a good wife who was frugal and kept the house immaculate. Our two-story house cost $35,000, which my VA loan enabled us to buy with $100 down. We raised our children very strictly and very Catholic, the same way we had been raised.

One day in 1978, my wife read in the church bulletin about a weekly meeting of people called Charismatics. She thought we should see what this group was all about. I was skeptical, as I had participated in other church groups and attended retreats that hadn't helped me very much. At one retreat, called *Cursillo,* little course, they pumped us up over the weekend, but when Monday came, I felt the same. Many times I cried out to God, "Where are you?" Praying, litanies, confessions, sacraments, *Novenas* (certain prayers, nine days in a row), venerating Mary; none of it helped. God seemed far away.

After visiting the charismatic prayer group a few times, we knew that they had something we didn't have. We asked the leader how we might experience the joy that they expressed by raising hands, speaking that funny lingo, and

My Story

dancing for gladness. He answered, "Well, my dear saints, you have to believe that Jesus died on the cross for you and repent of your sins." I'd never been called a saint and it seemed strange; I wasn't even dead yet. It didn't matter, we wanted what they had. The leader lead us in a sinner's prayer which we gladly repeated, and then the whole group laid hands on us, asking the Holy Spirit to baptize us.

Nothing dramatic happened that moment, no slaying in the Spirit or speaking in tongues. Within a few days, however, we had an insatiable hunger for reading the Bible. We bought The Living Bible (superseded by the new Living Translation) and I started reading. I read at home, during my lunch hour, and at break time. I couldn't get enough. We discovered a Christian TV channel and watched programs night after night.

One day, I read Romans 3:27-28, "Can we boast, then, that we have done anything to be accepted by God? No, because our acquittal is not based on obeying the law. It is based on faith. So we are made right with God through faith and not by obeying the law." I started to cry as I realized that working for my salvation was futile. Salvation is a free gift, not something earned. This revelation was of epic importance in my life. Many like me have grown up misunderstanding what it takes to be right with God.

Soon after coming to faith in Christ, I began to think about the spiritual need in my home country of Germany. It is much like the rest of Europe, where so few people know the wonderful truth that salvation is a gift. A dream started to take shape, that one day I would take the gospel to my homeland.

As I fast forward thirty years to 2007, that dream came true. While living in Dresden, Germany, for five months, I was involved in street evangelism. Night after night, I talked to young people about Christ in the notorious area of Alaunstrasse. During the day, I initiated conversations with people on streetcars, trains, and park benches. When they were interested, I gave them a tract called, "The Most Important Decision," by William MacDonald. This booklet gives step-by-step instructions on how to be saved. The English version is titled, "Final Destiny."

After more than three hundred conversations and giving away three hundred booklets, I found only two people who could give the biblical answer to the question, "How is a person saved?" In Germany, perhaps five percent of the people still believe in God. Yet, they seemed totally at a loss when asked, "Since you believe in God and heaven, tell me how a person gets to heaven?"

One lady told me that she would go to heaven because she was baptized as a child and married in a church. Another girl I met on a streetcar said that God forgives many sins, but when they become serious then He stops forgiving. Another man told me that he didn't sin because he worked all the time.

Despite lack of faith in Christ, people in Germany still cling to the hope of heaven. This is illustrated by an accident that occurred some years ago. One hundred and one people died when a wheel came off a fast moving passenger train. A period of mourning was declared in Germany. Both a Protestant minister and a Catholic priest comforted the public by assuring them that the train victims were in heaven.

Is Jesus the only way to God? It is a controversial question. Larry King, interviewer for CNN, was so curious about this issue that over the years he often asked his guests this question. In 2005, four out of six people on King's religious panel affirmed, "There are many paths to God." A recent survey on religious faith included the question, "Can many religions lead to eternal life?" The results showed 83 percent of mainline Protestants and 79 percent of Roman Catholics answered yes.

The fact is, there is no middle ground when answering the question: "Is there only one way to God?" The reply must be either yes or no. Jesus said in John 14:6, "I AM the Way, the Truth, and the Life. No one can come to the Father except through me." He did not say, "I will SHOW you a way."

After my wife and I became Christians, we were like dry sponges soaking up the Word. Some nights I could not sleep for joy. Certain things changed immediately. Always an avid reader, I soon lost my taste for worldly books; only Christian books interested me. Systematic theology became my favorite subject. To this day, I read one or two Christian books a week. Even though I was literally hooked on aviation and had a pilot's license to fly commercial, multi-engine planes, I canceled my Aviation Book Club membership. Our lives demonstrated that the all-consuming power of a newfound affection for Jesus drives out all other icons.

When a person is born again, a desire to read and study the Word of God develops. The Word provides daily manna and it sanctifies the spirit, heart, soul, mind, emotions, willpower, and attitude. Jesus prayed to the Father for each of us, "Make them holy by your truth; teach them your word, which is truth." (John 17:17)

Before long, I was embarrassed to pray the rosary and asked the Lord to release me from my vow. Keep in mind, I wasn't reading any literature critical of the Catholic Church, but Jesus said in John 8:32, "And you will know the truth, and the truth will set you free." Going to the confession box was the next thing we thrust aside. How glad we were not to subject our children to the torturous ordeal of crawling into that dark box! Within a few months, we were free of the Catholic Church and joined the Assemblies of God Church.

In this day and age, there is a prevailing attitude of tolerance and being politically correct, but more than eighty dogmas and rules of the Catholic Church are diametrically opposed to the Word of God. (There is an excellent book about the errors of the Roman Catholic Church titled: A

Woman Rides the Beast, by Dave Hunt, P.O.B. 7019, Bend, Oregon, 97708).

In 1983, our family went through a time of incredible suffering. My wife, Leopoldine, died of breast cancer. She was only forty-seven years old and my children were fourteen and twelve. I will never forget the night when I woke my children up and told them that their Mom was in heaven. Marcus took the still-warm hand of his mother and tenderly stroked it. Somehow, I knew that God would not lead me into a situation where His grace could not sustain me.

The overarching consolation in all our troubles is found in James 1:2-4, "Dear brothers and sisters, when trouble comes your way, consider it an opportunity for great joy. For you know that when your faith is tested, your endurance has a chance to grow. So let it grow, for when your endurance is fully developed, you will be perfect and complete, needing nothing."

I had peace of mind at the funeral. She loved Jesus and told me once that she heard a beautiful voice in her sleep say, "I am the Holy Spirit and I live within you." I never doubted her for a second that she heard that voice. She was a truthful, thoughtful wife.

Some time later, the children and I went out together for a pizza. On the way home, Claudia said to Marcus, "Mom would have enjoyed going out tonight." Marcus replied, "Compared to what Mom is eating now, a pizza would taste like a burned bun." We had a good laugh.

In 1983, we moved to Washington State, where my daughter attended Western Washington University. Nine years later, I married my present wife, Jean. She readily converted. As a child, Jean attended the United Church of Canada, but she had a spiritual emptiness that continued into adulthood. Even though she searched for answers in various churches and tried different denominations, nothing satisfied her.

My Story

Shortly after we met, I explained to Jean that the way to satisfy her spiritual hunger was to accept Jesus personally as her Savior. I laid hands on her and asked the Father to baptize her with the Holy Spirit, according to Luke 11:13, "So if you sinful people know how to give good gifts to your children, how much more will your heavenly Father give the Holy Spirit to those who ask Him." She was so joyful in her new faith that after we were married, she sometimes woke me up at night singing or asking me what certain Scripture verses meant.

Like Jean, many people who attend church are spiritually unfulfilled, perhaps because of a misunderstanding about being born again. One area of confusion is assurance of salvation. Since I accepted Christ in 1978, I've never doubted I was saved. Paul tells us in Romans 8:16, "For his Spirit joins with our spirit to affirm that we are God's children." There are many assurances of our salvation in God's Word, including 1 John 5:13, "I have written this to you who believe in the name of the Son of God, so that you may **know** you have eternal life."

These biblical statements contrast starkly with Roman Catholic doctrine. Cardinal O'Conner stated in 1990, "Church [Catholic] teaching is that I do not know at any given moment what my eternal future will be. I can hope, pray, do my very best–but still do not know. Pope John Paul does not know absolutely that he will go to heaven, nor does Mother Teresa" (*The Berean Call*, July, 1996). How sad that Roman Catholics deny justification by faith alone and believe that good works are a necessary requirement. In contrast, the Word of God says, "And since it is through God's kindness, then it is not by their good works. For in that case, God's grace would not be what it really is–free and undeserved" (Romans 11:6).

Before long, I discovered that my new wife, Jean, was highly gifted in business administration. In 1995, she bought an existing Adult Family Home, and I worked along with her. In our home we had room for up to five elderly ladies, who lived with us day and night, some with Alzheimer's and some physically handicapped. Being on the job twenty-four hours a day was demanding and our responsibilities were heavy. I can't imagine running an assisted living home without much prayer for strength and wisdom.

Our experiences ranged from terrifying to hilarious. Despite our best efforts in caring for these women, one fragile lady had a bad fall and blood gushed everywhere. Then there was the morning my wife and I discovered clothes and bedding stacked in front of our bedroom door. One of our ladies insisted that Jean had died and she was moving in with me.

Over the years there were ten ladies who stayed with us until they died; not one suffered for a moment. Hospice did a great job controlling pain with morphine patches. We are convinced that it is unnecessary to hasten death through euthanasia in those who are hopelessly ill. God governs the days of our lives and determines when we die. "You saw me before I was born. Every day of my life was recorded in your book. Every moment was laid out before a single day had passed" (Psalm 139:16).

After retiring from Adult Family Home ownership in 2006, we moved to Bellingham, Washington, and bought a condo. We joined a dynamic, growing church, Christ the King. The senior pastor, Grant Fishbook, is an anointed preacher. Soon we joined a prayer group where a dear saint, Tim McClellan, prayed over us and said to me, "I see in my spirit that you should write a book." Although I had never written a book, his words stayed in my heart.

My dream of returning to my native Germany as a street evangelist persisted. From the moment I met Jean, she knew that was my deepest desire. After forty-seven years of steady employment, including the cage-like feeling of being in the U.S. Army, I wanted to fulfill my heart's desire. I longed to share with the German people the Good News that Jesus died for their sins so that they can go to heaven. But how would my dream be fulfilled? Fifty years is a long time.

2

Call to Herrnhut

Needing God's direction for Germany, I told Jean I wanted to fly alone to the International House of Prayer (IHOP) in Kansas City. This nucleus of holy ground was founded by Mike Bickle after he heard the audible voice of God telling him to establish, "The Tabernacle of David" (Acts 15:16) as a place of unceasing prayer and worship. IHOP is not a church or a denomination, but a center for intercessory prayer and spiritual warfare. For the last ten years, hundreds of people have prayed day and night at IHOP. The center occupies half of a city block and includes an apartment complex where visitors can stay. The apartment building is called Herrnhut, named after the Moravian settlement in Saxony, Germany, founded by Count Ludwig von Zinzendorf in the eighteenth century.

During my visit to IHOP, there was a group of over one hundred young people called, *"Fire in the Night,"* who prayed from midnight to six o'clock in the morning. There were always a half a dozen musicians on the stage, who rotated a performance schedule every two hours. On the walls there were Bible verses such as, "Remember, the fire must be kept burning on the altar at all times. It must never go out" (Leviticus 6:13). Observing this, I thought, "Will my

Father not give justice to his chosen people who plead with him day and night?"

The first two days, I kept thinking that a week was too long to do nothing but pray. There was no one to talk to and no break-out sessions. But as the days and nights slipped by, the sweetness of the Lord's presence increased and I began to delight in Him. Homage turned into adoration. His dazzling beauty captivated me. I shared David's heart, expressed in Psalm 27:4, "The one thing [above all things] I ask of the Lord — the thing I seek most — is to live in the house of the Lord all the days of my life, delighting in the Lord's perfections and meditating in his temple."

During that week of prayer, my desire was to seek His will. I didn't expect an immediate word about going to Germany or guidance about what to do next. The Lord is never in a hurry with His directions, but this time things happened rather quickly.

Sharon, a secretary at the front desk at IHOP, noticed my German accent and insisted that I meet a young man from Dresden, Dierk Müller. This young man grew up in East Germany under the Communist regime. After the wall came down, he traveled to South Africa, and while there was gloriously saved. When he came home, the change in this new man in Christ was so dramatic that his father and mother barely recognized their son. They told me that Dierk spoke continually about Christ. It wasn't long before Dierk resigned his banking job and started college in America, where he earned degrees in theology and biblical languages.

When Dierk and I met, he had just graduated from a Baptist Bible college in Kansas City. After eight years of studying, he was ready for a vacation. His parents had flown in for graduation, and they wanted to visit a few wonders of our country, especially the Grand Canyon. Their trip was delayed a few days because Dierk had a problem. His car was an old jalopy with no air conditioning, unless you counted the window that was permanently stuck open. His parents were in their sixties, and he intended to take them to Nevada in this clunker. Most Germans have no clue about the vastness of our country or the high desert temperatures.

"Dierk," I cried in desperation, "your parents will come home as mummies."

He informed me that they were tough because they had grown up behind the Iron Curtain and were used to deprivation.

A quick call to my wife settled things. Together we agreed to give Dierk and his parents a love offering and paid for their rental car. Reimar and Reinhilde Müller were like little kids at the car rental place. It took them a long time to decide which car suited them, but they finally settled on a Buick sedan. They had a wonderful vacation and sent us a postcard, thanking us for what they called, in German, a limousine.

Dierk and his parents urged us to come visit them in Germany. With this encouragement, my wife and I packed up and set out for Dresden, where Dierk had hopes of establishing a Bible school. In all of the former East Germany there was not one Bible school.

When we arrived in Dresden, we were warmly welcomed by the Müller family, who vacated their small bedroom for us while they slept on an air mattress in the living room. We enjoyed singing wonderful German hymns while Reimar played the piano. Although my wife speaks only a few words in German, she enjoyed the warm fellowship during the two weeks we were there. We missed seeing Dierk, as he happened to be in Norway visiting a friend he met at school in Kansas.

Dresden is perhaps the most beautiful city in Europe. Like a Phoenix rising from the ashes, it has become once again a cultural center after being devastated by fire bombs in 1945. Thousands of tourists come to admire massive cathedrals and enchanting church spires. The Balcony of Europe is a lovely terrace that overlooks the wide, peaceful Elbe River. Beautiful municipal buildings, theaters, renaissance-style facades, royal palaces, an opera house, magnificent portals and gabled buildings grace the restored city. The Green Vault is one of Europe's richest treasure chambers, holding the acquisitions of August the Strong. It contains enameled figures with over 5,000 diamonds, rubies, emeralds and pearls. August the Strong, Prince Elector of Saxony and King of Poland, was a sensuous man who died when Count Zinzendorf was thirty-three years old. He embarked on daring building projects and collected vast treasures. As a result, Dresden has magnificent architecture and the largest jewelry collection in Europe.

One of the main reasons for our trip to Germany was to learn more about Count Zinzendorf and Herrnhut, the Moravian community he established. We were fascinated by the spiritual vitality that characterized the Moravians. So, with the Müllers, we set out for Herrnhut.

After a drive of approximately one hour from Dresden, we entered the quaint little town. Winding through narrow streets we saw houses with red roofs, a Moravian church, a delightful bakery, a butcher shop, and a few stores. Rolling hills surround Herrnhut, and on one hill we saw a lookout tower. While there we met Jonathan, a young American who was connected to Youth with a Mission (YWAM). He directed us to the YWAM training facility located one mile away in a huge mansion, teeming with life. Young men and women from all over the world come to attend YWAM Discipleship Training School (DTS), a three-month preparatory course for missionaries. Thousands of these young women and men travel throughout the world, sharing the Good News.

When Jonathan heard of our plan to see Herrnhut as tourists, he wouldn't hear of it.

"No, no," he insisted, "you have to meet the Spirit-filled Moravians."

Jonathan gave us directions to the home of Raymond and Mechthild Friesen, who live right across the street from a wonderful center for spiritual renewal, the *Jesus-Haus*. Raymond is a native Canadian and Mechthild is a native of Herrnhut. Some of the residents of Herrnhut are actually direct descendents of the Moravians who founded the town.

After a delightful visit with the Friesens, we learned about an apartment available in Herrnhut. It had been reserved for an Australian couple, but they were unable to come. How perfect! The Lord seemed to be opening doors for us in Germany. We moved into the furnished apartment and ended up staying seven months. Living among the Moravians in Herrnhut was one of the most exhilarating and pleasant experiences of my life, a dream come true. Jean enjoyed our stay as well, especially since many worship services at the *Jesus-Haus* were bilingual to accommodate the many English-speaking visitors.

In Herrnhut, a lively group of Spirit-filled Christians make up the congregation of the *Jesus-Haus*. While we were there, the flock was remodeling a 200-year-old hospital building. We watched as a dozen workers busily renovated rooms, breaking down walls, and strengthening floors with steel girders. The old hospital was originally built by a renowned businessman, Dürninger, who lived at the same time as Zinzendorf. He had a very prosperous textile business and gave many people employment as weavers.

As of 2011, about forty-five rooms in the old hospital had been renovated and construction continues. The renovated building has a praise room, dining room, prayer room for Israel, healing room, congregation room, children's activity room, seminar rooms, youth rooms, guest and co-worker rooms, and small rental apartments for visitors. A big worship room is near completion. The *Jesus-Haus* congregation, also known as *Christian Center* extends an invitation to people of all denominations to come for spiritual renewal, weekend retreats, or to help with specific projects. There are also women's and men's retreats featuring special speakers. The cost for staying overnight is reasonable. The prayer room is always open, warmly welcoming all to come and enjoy the affable surroundings. The Elders of the *Jesus-Haus* in Herrnhut make everyone feel welcome.

Herrnhut has a friendly baker who is extraordinarily skilled in his craft. His family has owned the bakery since 1841. He delights even the most demanding palate with his famous German pastries, warm rolls, and dark, wholesome bread. A Herrnhut butcher sells a big *Frikadelle,* a delicious meat patty spiced with pepper and onions, for less than one Euro. And of course, who can resist the famous German sausages.

A little bit of German comes in handy but the Sunday morning church services and some midweek meetings are bilingual. Most Germans speak English and enjoy practicing with English-speaking visitors.

We were privileged to attend weekly meetings of the *Jesus-Haus* staff and Elders, and listened as they discussed future building programs, upcoming events, and plans for visitor accommodations. During one meeting, the pastor reported that resident printer Gerhard Winter donated some boxes of old books. His brother, Pastor Christian Winter, had collected the books for a future archive. Pastor Frank asked who would like to sort the books and put them on shelves. When nobody volunteered, I raised my hand. Pastor Frank was pleased to designate my wife and me as temporary librarians. We bought some shelves at the Dresden IKEA and I began to explore the old books.

To my amazement, I discovered not only books but tracts, eulogies, and letters written in the eighteenth and nineteenth centuries. I categorized them and then showed the rare discoveries to Pastor Frank. He was astonished at this unexpected treasure.

I translated and wove two books together, occasionally downloading information from the Internet to clarify certain passages. The first book was dated 1860 and was written by C. H. Pensel for the one-hundred-year memorial of Count Ludwig Zinzendorf's death. The second book was written in 1900 by Hermann Römer and published by Gustav Winter for the two-hundred-year memorial of Zinzendorf's birth. (Both old books do not give any references or citations to other historical books or papers).

Mechthild, the wife of the couple who welcomed us so warmly to Herrnhut is a granddaughter of Gustav Winter, the printer in 1900. Contained in these old books were passages from Zinzendorf's diaries as well as excerpts from the many letters he wrote during his life.

I still have a good command of the German language, as I've been an avid reader since I was a boy growing up in Germany. Still, it was sometimes difficult to translate the archaic German used in the two old books, as many of the words were spelled differently in the eighteenth century.

There are several biographies about Zinzendorf and the Moravians. Some are written in novel form, and are informative and entertaining. I am neither a biographer nor a novelist, but in the following pages I share what I gleaned from the old German books about Zinzendorf and the spirit of the Moravians. I've also included Zinzendorf's beliefs about progressive sanctification, and insight into how he pioneered the worldwide missionary movement. Finally, applicable Scripture verses are interspersed with some of my own theological insights, which you will find in smaller type.

A story about George Washington Carver may shed some light on why I find Zinzendorf's life so compelling. Carver, a black scientist and "Father of the Peanut," was granted the opportunity to make a speech before the U. S. Senate. His enthusiasm about the value of the peanut and all the products that could be extracted from it captured their attention. He spoke for several hours, and afterward they asked him how he knew so much about the peanut. He replied that if you love something, it will tell you its secrets.

Zinzendorf's passionate love for Jesus Christ fascinates me. For the last few years, I have immersed myself in studying his life. I pray as we go on this journey together, we will discover Zinzendorf's secrets. How did this man inspire generations of people to pray continuously, day and night, for over one hundred years? How did he "uncrowd" his heart to spend hours a day in prayer, even though he was so engaged, laboring to expand God's kingdom? Why were his followers so devoted to Christ that when Moravian missionaries were murdered, others volunteered to take their place? Why were they willing to make dangerous ocean voyages, risking their lives to share the Good News with those who had never heard? What made the Moravian missionaries so different from others?

My prayer is that we will all find answers to these questions, and that Zinzendorf's passion for the Lamb of God will be ignited in the heart of each person reading this book.

> "Asking God, the glorious Father of our Lord Jesus Christ, to give you spiritual wisdom and insight so that you might grow in your knowledge of God" (Ephesians 1:17).

3

Early Years

"The Lord says, 'I will guide you along the best pathway for your life. I will advise you and watch over you'" (Psalm 32:8).

Count Nikolaus Ludwig von Zinzendorf was born on May 26, 1700, in Dresden, Germany. For generations, his family lived in Austria and belonged to one of the oldest aristocracies. Over the centuries, his family served different Austrian emperors in war and in peace. Many of his ancestors received distinguished decorations and awards. Thirty-eight years before Ludwig was born, the Emperor Leopold I of Austria gave the family an even higher rank in the ladder of aristocratic titles. (The German language quite often strings up to three or four words together, depending on the emphasis, and for a non-German it is a conundrum. Zinzendorf's new family rank illustrates this). They were given the prominent title of *Reichsgrafenstand,* or a princely rank of an Empire Count Position.

At the time of Martin Luther's reformation, spiritual light was dawning in Europe, and with it came great conflict. Across Europe there were cries of *sola gratia, solo Christo, sola fide, sola scriptura,* or by grace alone, by Christ alone, by faith alone, by Scripture alone. Some Catholics opened their hearts to the saving faith in Christ and became Protestants. Even among the royalty there was a mighty revival, and Zinzendorf's grandpa was one of those who were converted. When persecution became intense, Grandpa Zinzendorf left his estate in Austria and migrated to Germany. He changed his family name from Sinsendorf to Zinzendorf. (It is reminiscent of God giving Abram the new name of Abraham when he left his home in Ur, the "h" signifying the breath of God or the Holy Spirit).

Zinzendorf's aristocratic grandfather, Maximilian, had two sons and three daughters. Both sons had high positions in the Saxon government. George Ludwig, Zinzendorf's father, held an elevated position as a minister and was highly esteemed by the *Kurfürsten,* the Prince Elector, ruler of Saxony. George Ludwig was thirty-seven years old when Nikolaus Ludwig, known as Count Ludwig von Zinzendorf, was born. Sadly, George had tuberculosis and he died shortly after Ludwig arrived. At that time, tuberculosis was a slow, fatal disease, but George had a strong faith in God. One of the books mentions that his mind was directed towards heaven as he knew his life was ending.

While translating the old source, I came across the German word *Lebendige* for the first time, which in this context means born again. This German word conveys the idea that a person was previously either dead or in a comatose state. "Once you were dead because of your disobedience and your many sins" (Ephesians 2:1). Zinzendorf's father, George, was described as among the *Lebendige.*

He must have known of Paul's writing in Colossians 3:1-2, "Since you have been raised to new life with Christ, set your sights on the realities of heaven, where Christ sits in the place of honor at God's right hand. Think about the things of heaven, not the things of earth."

Young Ludwig's mother, Charlotte Justine, was a lady of royal blood and also born again. Like most aristocrats at that time, she was cultured and highly educated.

Shortly after the birth of her son, she recorded in the family Bible:

"On Wednesday evening, May 26, 1700, the almighty God blessed me, because of His grace, with a gift of my first-born son, Nikolaus Ludwig, in Dresden. He became a fatherless orphan after six weeks, because my 'herzliebster,' sweetheart husband, his lord and father, the blessed Count von Zinzendorf, was torn from my side. The Father of Mercy governs the heart of this child that he may walk upright in the path of virtues, and may no wrong control him. Let his ways be strengthened by the Word of God, and then he will not lack any goodness here and in eternity. He will indeed experience that the King of kings and the Lord of lords has promised and said, 'I am the Father of the fatherless.'"

Some time later we find Count Ludwig Zinzendorf's handwriting under his mother's inscription, *"Factum est,"* it has happened.

Before his death, George Ludwig had a close friendship with the preeminent minister of Dresden, Philip Jakob Spener. Spener was a Pietist, and in a time of dead religion he served the revived or born again Christians. When the shepherd Spener christened little Ludwig, many aristocrats stood at the baptismal font. Spener also dedicated Ludwig to the Lord when the boy was four years old. He laid hands on him with a prayer that he be used for the expansion of God's kingdom. God certainly answered that prayer. Spener was converted through a very popular book called **True Christianity**, written by Johannes Arndt. Spener preached fiery sermons about the saving power of the Gospel. He created controversy when he wrote a book called **True**

Evangelical Churches. In Latin the book was titled *Pia Desideria*, with the subtitle, "A heartfelt desire for a God-pleasing reform of the true Evangelical church." When Protestantism divided into opposing sides, he eventually had to leave Dresden. He found refuge in Berlin under the protection of the Prince Elector of Brandenburg.

When his father died, Ludwig was only six weeks old. His mother was still quite young, so she took Ludwig to her mother in Grosshennersdorf, not far from the area of Herrnhut. At that time, the official town of Herrnhut did not actually exist.

Ludwig was blessed with his mother's care until he was four years old. At that time, she married a royal, fifty-year-old Field Marshall von Natzmer. She moved to Berlin, leaving little Ludwig in Grosshennersdorf, but she was always concerned about him. Because Berlin is 150 miles north of Grosshennersdorf, she couldn't see Ludwig often. They did correspond frequently in his later years. She was married to the Prussian general for thirty-five years before becoming a widow for the second time. She continued to live in Berlin until she died in 1763, at the age of eighty-seven, three years after Zinzendorf's death.

Ludwig spent his childhood with his grandma, Henriette Katharina von Gersdorf, a widow whose husband died when Ludwig was two years old. She was a highly esteemed lady, not only because of her husband's noble rank, but because she was intelligent, astute, morally courageous, and determined. She had a new focus in life and showered tenderness upon Ludwig. She coined the endearing pet name for him, *Lutz* or *Lutzchen,* which in German sounds like *sweet* and *adorable.* Lutz responded to her love with emotional attachment. An unmarried daughter, Aunt Henriette Sophi, who was only ten years older than Ludwig, also lived with them. She too had a far-reaching influence on the young boy. The atmosphere in the mansion was peaceful, affectionate, and godly.

Every Sunday they all went to the village church for services, and every day Aunt Henriette felt it was her duty to read aloud from the Bible or to let Lutz read. "Direct your children unto the right path, and when they are older, they will not leave it" (Proverbs 22:6). Books written by Martin Luther and other godly writers were also encouraged. Henriette prayed every morning and evening with Lutz. This loving, disciplined lifestyle made a lasting impression upon his soul. His mother once wrote in a letter, "He burns like tinder."

Later, Zinzendorf recorded part of his spiritual journey as a child, "I did not understand the grandeur and sufficiency of Christ's passion, nor did I realize my wretchedness and inability in my fallen nature." At a young age, he decided to give his life to Jesus and wrote his thoughts on this experience: "Even if nobody gives Jesus His deserved preeminence, I will attach myself unto Him and will live for Him and die with Him." With childlike devotion, he talked for hours with Jesus as a brother, telling Him all that was in his heart. In his letters, Zinzendorf often wrote that the love of Jesus Christ, His merits, and His sorrows were the passion of his soul. He wrote, "The virtues of the Savior apprehended and captured my heart. The nobility of His *Gemüt* lifts my Savior above everything else. The loftiest and most noble thought we can have in our minds as human beings is that the Creator of His creatures died for each one of us." The German word *Gemüt* means mind, soul, and heart.

While living with his grandmother, Ludwig had a tutor who quickly noticed that Lutz was quite intelligent. The boy acquired knowledge easily and was sometimes whimsical, as are some children with keen minds. His handwriting was often sloppy, much like intelligent doctors who write illegible prescriptions. The biography written in 1860 includes an interesting anecdote. Young Ludwig wrote some of his wishes or prayers on pieces of paper. He then threw them out the window into the wind, believing that God would find them and read them.

One day, Grandma promised Lutz they would play and sing his favorite hymn at the evening devotion, "You are our beloved Father because Jesus is our Brother." Lutz waited all day long eagerly with anticipation, but in the evening he was so tired from playing he slept through the sing along. When he woke up and was told the devotion was over, he displayed such a burst of anger, Grandma had *alle Mühe*, great difficulty to calm him down.

Both of the old books point to the fact that the boy's priority was his relationship with his *Heiland*, his Savior. Zinzendorf wrote, "I can say with truth that my heart was spiritually-minded as far back as I can recall. At times when vain and foolish pride of rank beset me, my heart's affection never departed from my *Heiland*."

It wasn't just his family who noticed Ludwig's devotion to God. When he was six years old, Swedish soldiers on a foray burst into his room, where Lutz happened to be at his customary devotion. They stopped the clamor and were awed as they heard the boy pray. Then they left, leaving the place intact. This incident was prophetic of the way the Count was to inspire others with the depth of his intimacy with the risen Savior the rest of his life.

4

School Days

Ludwig's education began early. His grandma was fluent in Latin and Greek and taught him both languages. She also knew a great deal of theology. When he was ten years old, both his grandma and mother decided that Lutz needed to further his education at the prestigious Halle Paedagogium. Halle is near Leipzig and about ninety miles northeast of Dresden. (All these cities are easy to reach by train today. You can buy a "Weekend Ticket," and travel with five people all day long for 40 Euros).

Grandma and mother had unlimited trust in a *Gottesmann*, man of God, August Hermann Franke. He was a Pietist and leading professor at the Halle Paedagogium. The Pietists were a group of people who pursued true faith in Christ and were opposed to the formalists and legalists of the day.

According to *Webster's Dictionary*, Pietism was, "A religious movement originating in Germany in reaction to formalism and intellectualism and stressing Bible study and personal religious experience." In other words, the Pietists emphasized having a living relationship with Jesus as Savior and a love for God's Word. They didn't attach importance to legalistic rules or faith based solely on religious affiliation. They didn't believe it sufficient to give mental assent to a creed, but what was essential was to have an experience with the living, risen Savior.

Their understanding of being born again was twofold. First, a person needs a *Busskampf*, a struggle of repentance, the grace of sorrow for your sins and the subsequent deliverance from a guilty conscience. Second, a *Durchbruch* is needed, a breakthrough, a peace of mind and the wonderful assurance of forgiveness, and the certainty of being a child of God. Although they thought orthodox theology necessary to ground the emotions, they also believed it to be dead and lifeless without a personal relationship with Christ Jesus.

August Hermann Francke established an orphanage, a home for the poor, a foreign mission society, a seminary for teachers, a printing office and a bookstore. A remarkable number of revived nobles supported him. He was a frequent guest of Zinzendorf's grandmother, Henriette. In his writings, he stressed the concept of man's natural state of depravity and corruption and the need of a conscious new birth.

The Pietists also rediscovered the doctrine of the priesthood of all believers. They shared their faith with like-minded friends in less formal meetings that they attended in addition to church. These private meetings were called in Latin, *collegia pietatis*, association of piety, or simply, Pietists. They also assailed government interference, theological controversy, and the unworthy lives of both clergy and laity. They rejected theater, dances, playing cards, and also called for moderation in food, drink, and dress. They practiced asceticism similar to that of the English Puritans.

> We might think that the Pietists had a touch of legalism. But keep in mind that with our corrupted nature we are all susceptible to legalism. We don't have to be taught to relate to God on a performance basis; it comes to us naturally. That is why all the false religions are works and duty-oriented. True disciples of Jesus come to Him on the basis of His merits, not their own. We must battle to keep foremost that God's

approval is not based on performance, certain disciplines, or involvement in Christian activities.

Paul writes in Titus 2:11, "For the grace of God has been revealed, bringing salvation to all people." Spiritual discipline will not earn salvation. Faith through grace saves us. I like the acronym based on the word, GRACE: God's Riches At Christ's Expense. Having said that, it is imperative to understand that the spiritual disciplines of prayer, Bible reading and fellowship with other believers are necessary for spiritual growth. Paul often admonishes us to diligently pursue progressive sanctification. He writes in Titus 2:12, "And we are instructed to turn from godless living and sinful pleasures. We should live in this evil world with wisdom, righteousness, and devotion to God."

Legalism does not win God's approval because salvation is not attained by grace plus works. Yes, we are saved unto good works; however, good works are not the root of our salvation but the fruit of our salvation. Legalism is the opposite of grace. To use license to heedlessly sin is a perversion of grace and reflects immaturity in our walk of sanctification. When a pastor lovingly confronted a young man about his live-in girlfriend, he justified his behavior by saying, "You are right; I am just a carnal Christian." When a professing believer is characterized by persistent sin and shows no shame and repentance, there should be concern whether there ever was a true conversion. Paul gives a warning about taking advantage of God's grace, "Don't be fooled by those who try to excuse these sins, for the anger of God will fall on all who disobey him" (Ephesians 5:6).

Zinzendorf's mother took her little Lutz to start school in Halle. She spoke with Professor Franke about her son, "Ludwig is very bright, but he may have the propensity to become prideful because of his intelligence. He may have to be reined in a little bit." The memorial book written in 1860 relates that two boys overheard this conversation and persuaded the other students to bully Ludwig. For the ten-year-old boy, this initiated years of suffering.

School Days

Ludwig was picked on right from the beginning. Imagine the sheltered life and godly environment in Grosshennersdorf, compared to the rough life of a boarding school. Boys taunted him, saying, "Here is the boy who is too smart; pride is written on his forehead." They tripped him, scattered his books, and by the time he picked them up he was late for class. Unfortunately, corporal punishment for such an offense was common. When classmates peppered his soup, Ludwig coughed so hard he sprayed the liquid all over the table. His punishment was to stand outside the dining hall. He was given menial tasks, and one day somebody wrote on the bulletin board, "Next week the Count will get the stick." The ultimate humiliation came when he had to stand in an alley wearing donkey ears and a sign on his chest proclaiming, *Fauler Esel*. Even today in the German language this is a degrading epithet, lazy donkey. Years later he wrote, "With a few exceptions my school fellows hated me throughout my stay in Halle."

Ludwig's *Hofmeister* or tutor was Daniel Crisenius. He was a worldly man, cunning and crafty. He showed his shrewdness by blackmailing Ludwig to extort money from home. The Zinzendorf family knew nothing about this situation. When Ludwig wrote home and complained about school, Daniel intercepted his letters, destroying them whenever something negative was written. Unfortunately, Professor Franke had a good opinion of Daniel since he was an excellent teacher. Ludwig's mother in Berlin had a premonition that something wasn't right, although she did not dare go against Ludwig's guardian, his father's brother, uncle Count Otto Christian. Grandma had a foreboding as well, but she received a flood of letters from Daniel and even from Professor Franke explaining that Ludwig was rebellious and unruly. Ludwig continued to suffer.

Professor Francke was a very pious man. His philosophy was to bring his students to a level of a genuine,

"God centered and full of Christian wisdom" lifestyle. In his opinion, it was necessary that the natural self-willed man had to be broken. It meant the human being should not elevate his own headstrong will above the will of God. Man should become a "tool of God." Obedience next to the love for truth and diligence are the main virtues a human being should strive for.

As a student, animated, zestful, and bursting with temperament, Ludwig often became an *ärgerliches Aufsehen*, annoying attention.

Academically he progressed. He was a diligent student, could give impromptu speeches in Latin, and was an accomplished poet. When he was thirteen, he wrote a hymn that became number seventy-six in the Moravian hymnal, "You Faithful Savior, My Lovely Sweet Life."

Keeping an intimacy with his Savior was of utmost importance to him. He didn't listen to coarse jokes or indulge in worldly entertainment. Sunday sermons lifted him up and gave him solace. The witness of godly men inspired him. He received rich spiritual food in Franke's house, met missionaries from all over the world, and heard adventurous stories of Christians suffering persecution.

Ludwig grew in Christian maturity and took pleasure in drawing some friends into closer relationship with the Savior. He gathered friends for open discussion about religion and motivated them to meet in an attic for prayer. Differing opinions were accepted, and the customs and teachings of his Protestant church were not criticized. Ludwig fought vehemently not to be regarded as sectarian, a practice that continued throughout his life.

With his few friends, he formed several fraternities. Some names of these alliances were: Slaves of Virtue, Sorority of the Witnesses of Jesus Christ, and The Laudable Order of the Mustard Seed. Members of the Mustard Seed fraternity were so serious about their brotherhood that they made an

School Days

emblem depicting a mustard tree with the Latin inscription, *quod fuit ante nihil,* out of nothing, something. They had a ring crafted with a Greek engraving taken from Romans 14:7, "For we don't live for ourselves or die for ourselves."

Despite the harsh school environment, Zinzendorf excelled academically. He had a quick-witted, brilliant mind, was competent in Greek, fluent in French and Latin, and proficient in Hebrew.

When Zinzendorf was fifteen years old, the Lord helped him to overcome his pride. He wrote in his diary, "I often gave public orations in the lecture hall of the university in Latin, French, or Greek. My formal memorized discourses consisted of around three hundred words. Sometimes, a very distinguished citizen like the Marquis, a nobleman of the city of Beyreuth, was in the audience. In the middle of one of my lectures I lost my theme. It was a disgrace and I looked like a fool. Then I received a divine caution to extinguish my foolish pride, and my passion to excel. I received from above the realization that my hubris was a great sin, and I was actually a witless nonplus. From then on I earnestly decided to seek my commendation in the cross of Christ, and I was content with the mundane performance of my duties."

Professor Franke slowly realized that Ludwig was a humble, sincere young man who took his religion seriously. The professor appreciated the boy's ingenious, clear-headed mind and put him in a small group of gifted students who were preparing for university.

Zinzendorf was a natural leader and organizer. During his last years in Halle, he continued recruiting friends who desired Bible study, prayer, discussion, and fellowship. He established seven prayer groups, and the faculty used these gatherings to fan spiritual life among the students. He also enjoyed the privilege of sitting next to Professor Franke at the dinner table. A real friendship developed between them, and Zinzendorf listened attentively when the professor shared spiritual wisdom.

Spending time with missionaries was another cherished privilege. Ziegenbalg from India impressed the fifteen-year-old Ludwig so much that he talked enthusiastically with his closest friend, Baron Friedrich von Wattewille, about becoming missionaries. Before long, they realized their parents would never allow it. Aristocrats were supposed to be rulers, not shepherds, but the boys made a solemn agreement to help promote missionary outreach.

The Laudable Order of the Mustard Seed band of brothers grew. It included Friedrich von Wattewille who became a lifelong friend and was present when Zinzendorf took his last breath. The Archbishop of Canterbury, John Potter, joined this fraternity when Zinzendorf was thirty-seven years old. (Also Christian VI, King of Denmark. General Oglethorpe, Governor of Georgia. Tomochichi, Chief of the Creek Indians). The Mustard Seed had simple rules: always be faithful and obedient to the teachings of Jesus, walk in a manner reflecting the life of Jesus, and sow goodness into other people.

Zinzendorf wrote in his diary on his sixteenth birthday, "Gracious grandma gave me the first of my designed medaille of the Order of the Mustard Seed. It is a gold piece of the size of a *Taler*. On one side it shows the picture of the thorn-crowned Jesus with the engraving, *vulnera Christi*, wounds of Christ. On the other side a man with wings fallen under his heavy cross with the inscription, *nostra Medela*, our healing."

At the end of his time at Halle, Professor Franke instructed Ludwig so that he could receive the rite of confirmation and the Lord's Supper, according to the ordinance of Jesus. For some in the Lutheran church, these ceremonies were nothing more than a formality. However, Zinzendorf undoubtedly grasped the deep, spiritual meaning behind the rituals.

When Zinzendorf was sixteen, he said goodbye to the school at Halle. He had been thrown from the sheltered ambience of his grandmother's home into the lion's den at school, and he had endured. Suffering produced in him strength, wisdom, and Christ-likeness. The years of bullying at an early age taught him to forgive those who persecuted him and to let go of hurts without allowing them to become grudges. It was all good preparation for the future. To endure the hardship and misunderstandings in his later life, he would need to be as immovable as a rock.

He noted in his diary, "The various trials and frequent vexations I coped with, the conversations with 'witnesses of the Truth' who came from distant regions, the stories of visiting missionaries describing the sufferings of exiles and prisoners concerning the kingdom of Christ, the daily meetings in professor Francke's house, and the cheerfulness of that man in the work of the Lord, increased my zeal for the cause of Christ in a powerful way."

In James 1:2-4 it says, "Dear brothers and sisters, when troubles [misery, affliction, sorrow] come your way, consider it an opportunity for great joy. For you know that when your faith is tested, your endurance has a chance to grow. So let it grow, for when your endurance is fully developed, you will be perfect and complete, needing nothing."

Is it possible to have joy while suffering pain and hardship? God never punishes a disciple of Christ, but He lovingly disciplines and corrects. "No discipline is enjoyable while it is happening – it's painful! But afterwards there will be a peaceful harvest of right living for those who are trained in this way." (Hebrews 12:11). The joy in suffering is not that there is pleasure in being abused and subjected to pain, but it is knowing that in God's time we will share in His holiness and grow to be like Him.

Fruit bearing involves cross bearing. The Bible has some beautiful promises that become ours only through suffering.

The quality of gentleness, for instance, is a fruit of the Spirit that develops as we submit to God's discipline without rebellion and to men's unkindness without retaliation. Longsuffering under prolonged provocation develops the fruit of patience, which gives us grace to bear with the faults of others when they irritate and provoke us.

5

The Wittenberg Years

"I am much afraid that schools prove to be great gates of hell unless they diligently labor in explaining the Holy Scriptures, engraving them in the hearts of youth. Every institution in which men are not increasingly occupied with the Word of God must become corrupt" (Martin Luther).

From Dresden, it is easy to reach Wittenberg by train. I have visited the historic city several times, and there is much to see. I love sightseeing, especially visiting old cathedrals.

In Wittenberg, the document that ignited the Reformation, Martin Luther's Ninety-Five Theses, is displayed in bronze on the door of the cathedral where he is buried. Today, however, much has changed in Wittenberg; it is a worldly city. A brochure I picked up during my visit tells about the entertainment found there. Some of the events were titled, "Gossip in the 16th Century," "Stocks, Torture and Murder Stories," "Witches, Herbs and Bloodletting," and "Erotica at Night–A Play with Some Nudity." Luther would be appalled. Like all European countries, Germany is not a Christian nation anymore.

In the city of Minden, I saw a billboard on a large Lutheran cathedral that read, "Discover the root of your faith again, the Word of God." A course was offered about the Bible with a certain date given. However, across the billboard was a strip of paper that read, "Cancelled for lack of interest."

Wittenberg was far different in the eighteenth century. Protestantism was active and the university, prestigious. Ludwig was sent there to continue his education, but he went reluctantly. His guardian, uncle Otto Christian, insisted that he go to Wittenberg and study law. The young man would rather have studied theology to pursue his secret ambition of becoming a minister of the Gospel.

At that time, Wittenberg was a magnet for scholars as the school was preparing for the 200th anniversary of the Reformation of 1517. The university was a stronghold of the Lutheran church. Because Ludwig's uncle Otto was a traditional Lutheran and thoroughly disliked the Pietists, he was adamant that the boy study in Wittenberg. His uncle was strict about his own faith and made it clear that Ludwig ought to attend Sunday services. He also insisted that Ludwig learn dancing, fencing, and horseback riding. The boy aired his frustrations and wrote, "My uncle was obsessed to change my [Pietist] heart and put a different head on my body."

The deceptive Crisenius was still part of his life, ensuring that Ludwig complied with all his directions and arrangements. He continued reading the letters Ludwig wrote to his mother, grandmother, and friends in Halle.

From a young age, Zinzendorf was a prolific writer and an accomplished poet. Later in life, the oil lamp burned late at night as he kept up a busy correspondence. During his lifetime, he wrote over two thousand letters.

While in Wittenberg, Ludwig lived in the home of Mayor Keil. He studied jurisprudence with vigor and regularly attended church services. He knew certain people were determined to pull him away from Pietism, but he vigilantly guarded the dearest treasure of his gentle heart, his fervent relationship with Christ.

The day when his dancing lessons began, he wrote in his diary, "Today I started dancing, but I have the firm intention not ever to practice it. The only benefit I see is to learn a right posture for my body." Whether dancing, fencing, or riding, he was in communion with his Savior. How astounding it was that from his earliest youth, he practiced the presence of Christ and had an intimacy with Jesus as with a brother. He wrote, "I commune with the Friend of my heart, the ever present Savior, to give me the stamina not to be deterred by trivia, but to put the hours of the day on something solid... I am spending a whole hour, from six to seven in the morning, as well as in the evening from eight to nine, and for fifteen minutes at a quarter of ten, in **prayer.** Also, I resolve to pursue the study of civil law with all my energy, since I expect all sorts of interruptions this coming summer."

Ludwig wanted to become more like Jesus, and he knew the best way to do that was to meditate on Christ's transcendent beauty in His Word and obey it. All he needed for entertainment was the indwelling, gracious Lover. While diligently studying law, the romance of the Gospel and his private theological studies kept him busy during free hours. He was forbidden by his guardian to attend official lectures in theology. Family members expressed their convictions on this subject, "Aristocrats do not become ministers of the Gospel."

Regardless, he developed keen perception in doctrine and became quite an expert on the feuds between Pietists and traditional Protestants. Later in life, enemies accused him of being an ignoramus in theology, but Zinzendorf could rightly reply that he had studied theology more than a professional minister.

Ludwig's professors observed in him a genuine, holy passion for Christ. It is astonishing how many people visited him to engage in lively discussions about theological issues. They usually came in groups because of his aristocratic title.

Soon, Ludwig learned that not all orthodox Lutherans were quarrelsome and incorrigible, as he had often heard in Halle, but some had an ardent love for Jesus. From this time on, the Lord used him often to reconcile different views within the Christian community.

While in Wittenberg, he wanted to embark on a peace mission between Halle and Wittenberg, to reconcile the Pietists and the traditional Lutherans. When his mother found out about Zinzendorf's upcoming theological discussions, she wrote a letter, "You should not engage yourself in such important matters. It is way above your head, and I don't think you have the comprehension to grasp such weighty subjects." From Grosshennersdorf, Grandma added her opinion, "that he should not get involved in mitigating ecclesiastical disputes."

His mother even came from Berlin, bringing a letter from her husband, the Prussian Field Marshall von Natzmer. He wrote, "It is not your calling or your profession, you don't have the experience or the maturity, nor is it your Christian duty to be a negotiator in such complicated matters. Remember, you are still under your guardian and tutor and you must listen to their directions. Don't you think you still have to work on yourself? I want to remind you about the commandment to honor your father and mother."

Zinzendorf was hurt, but he obeyed. Writing to a friend he said, "The journey to Halle would have been highly beneficial, but to comply with God's commandment to obey is my duty."

While he was in Wittenberg, he showed a trace of youthful vanity. He asked his mother for extra money to furnish his room in black because some distant relative died. She wrote back, "I am surprised you request money for frivolous things like that. If you wanted to furnish your room black every time an uncle or aunt died, you would spend all our fortune." In another letter she admonished him, "You write you are content with little but you are displeased when we curtail your spending."

When his university years were completed, Ludwig's family decided he should travel. They wanted him to enlarge his mind and experience the world before settling down to practice law in Dresden. Ludwig said goodbye to his teachers, and in the spring of 1719 embarked on a year-long journey. Even at the age of nineteen, he was wise enough to be wary of worldly enticements. Hearing other young people tell of their escapades made him aware of the dangers that lurked in the world for a young man.

At last, he had a new kindhearted and helpful tutor who accompanied him on his journey. They traveled to several cities, sightseeing and visiting museums. Going up the Rhine River, they came to the city of Düsseldorf.

> If you ever get to Germany, be sure to take a regional train along the Rhine River. Along the way, you will see quaint villages, castles, and vineyards nestled on slopes, as well as tourist boats cruising down the river. The scenery between Cologne and Frankfurt is breathtaking.

Visiting a museum in Düsseldorf, young Zinzendorf had a life-changing experience. He could not take his eyes off a painting by Domenico Feti (1589-1623), depicting the suffering Savior with the crown of thorns on His head. The picture was titled, *Ecce Homo,* the words Pilate spoke after Jesus was scourged, "Behold the Man." Under the picture was another inscription, "This I suffered for you, what are you doing for Me?" Zinzendorf was mesmerized. Later he wrote, "I stood there without an answer. I implored my Savior to draw me with force into the partnership of His suffering, even if my mind struggled against it."

It was an epic event in his life. As he stood gazing, God seemed to put a fire of divine love in his heart. This experience was later expressed in his passionate preaching about the Lamb of God and the efficacious blood of the *Martermann,* or Man of Sorrows. In later years, he preached so exclusively about the *Blut und Wunden,* blood and wounds of Jesus, critics found another reason to accuse him of being simple-minded.

When my first wife and I joined the Assemblies of God Church, we were enamored of all the hymns that extolled the precious blood of the Lamb. It grieves my heart that many modern songs have so little of this wonderful theme. Hymnology should reflect theology. The title "Lamb of God" is found sixteen times in the book of Revelation alone. Christ the Lamb will be our theme, our passion, and divine entertainment in heaven, forever. How unfathomable that the sovereign Monarch of the universe died for fallen sinners! Forever we will sing, "Worthy is the Lamb who was slaughtered — to receive power and riches and wisdom and strength and honor and glory and blessing" (Revelation 5:12). Why should we be so enthralled with Him that we sing this song of the redeemed throughout eternity? Peter gives us the answer, "It was the precious blood of Christ, the sinless, spotless Lamb of God" (1 Peter 1:19).

From Düsseldorf, Zinzendorf traveled to Utrecht, Holland for three months to attend lectures on law and English. He had a natural proclivity for languages. In fact, his later letters are so interspersed with words from different languages that they can be difficult to read.

Sundays he set aside exclusively to feed his soul, diligently reading and memorizing the Word, as well as studying spiritual books.

He must have known that the quickest way to grow into the image of Christ is to "behold and be beholden." We are to behold God in and through His Word. We are beholden to do the following: continue in His Word, continue in faith, hold fast our confidence and hope, be steadfast to the end, and exert diligence in our calling and election.

Continuing his journey, Zinzendorf's road led to Amsterdam, Den Haag, Rotterdam, Antwerp, Brussels, and finally, Paris, where he stayed for six months. At that time, the French king was the nine-year-old Ludwig the XV. He was the great-grandson of Ludwig XIV, the *Sonnenkönig*. The young king was under the guardianship of his uncle Phillip II, a royal Regent from Orleans. The royal Regent's mother was a German widow, Liese-Lotte, from the royal court of Karl Ludwig of the *Pfalz* in Germany.

Ludwig moved easily in the aristocratic circles of Paris as he spoke fluent French. He was surprised that a number of aristocrats were open to the Gospel, so his stay in Paris was fruitful. He spent time in high society, with the *crème de la crème* and royalty. He wrote, "I walked among the elite. At that time I had no notion and concept of the lower stratum of society, but I preached about the grace of our Savior frequently. Some people were receptive where you would never expect it."

Zinzendorf occasionally visited the German royal duchess, Liese-Lotte. Forty years earlier, she had met Ludwig's father in Paris and had great respect for the Zinzendorf family. One evening, Ludwig was startled when the duchess greeted him in German, *"Guten Abend Herr Graf,* have you been in the Opera today?"

He replied, *"Nein,* your Highness, I would not have time for that." She commented, "I heard you can recite most of the Bible from memory."

"This would be a sweet pleasure and even more if I could comply with all the teachings," he answered, revealing once again his love for the Word.

"How sweet Your words taste to me; they are sweeter than honey," said the Psalmist in Psalm 119:103.

Zinzendorf had an aversion for the pomp and pageantry so common in Catholic services. He believed it gratified the emotions but had no benefit for the spirit. Surprisingly, he became acquainted with the Archbishop of Paris, Cardinal Louis Antoine de Noailles, a friendly, seventy-year-old Monsignore. Although the Archbishop came from a wealthy family, he had a reputation for giving alms to the poor. He took a liking to Ludwig and complimented him frequently, although his motivation may have been to convert him to Catholicism. After many disputations, he gave up and assured Zinzendorf that he still loved him as a child of God.

The Archbishop stirred up quite a controversy when he protested against a Papal Bull that condemned the book written by Johannes Arndt, *True Christianity*. (Philip Jacob Spener, who baptized baby Ludwig, was converted by the book). Of course, Zinzendorf sided with the Archbishop on this issue. When the Pope threatened the Archbishop with excommunication, he gave in.

Zinzendorf wrote the Archbishop a letter, "I can scarcely believe it. You have condemned one of the best books in the world. You yourself have emphatically recommended this book unto the flock which God has committed to your care. When a sinner stands before God to be judged, nothing will justify him but the righteousness of Jesus, and faith in His blood. Our salvation does not depend upon a Pope or works but alone on the merits of Christ. After hearing about your lamentable signature under a document, my eyes will not see you again. I thank you from my heart for all the honor and graceful words you bestowed upon me. If my candid speeches have ever aroused your disapproval, will you please forgive me a thousand times? Be assured, I love you from my heart, and I sincerely honor you. With deep sorrow I say, *adieu.*"

In the spring of 1720, Zinzendorf packed up again and left for Basel, Switzerland. He was eager to see his friend from school, Baron Friedrich von Wattewille. The *Wiedersehen*, or reunion was joyful as they caught up on their life adventures.

6

Falling in Love

"In the depth of the human heart has to be an anchor. It is a *Herzenswahrheit*, a truth of the heart of utmost importance, and only the Holy Spirit can reveal this truth: The Creator had to die for the creature to open the way to heaven. This alone opens the way to commune with the resurrected Savior" (Zinzendorf).

After a week with his friend, it was time to move on to Nürnberg, where he visited his aunt. His private mentor said *Aufwiedersehen*. His father's sister had a lovely, eighteen-year-old daughter, Countesse Theodora von Castelle. Before long, Ludwig fell in love with her. He told his aunt about the attachment and she was delighted. She promised to talk with her daughter. Silence ensued. Ludwig wasn't discouraged because Theodora had given him a portrait of herself, which he considered a green light for their relationship. He thought perhaps she was just shy, so he hurried home, thinking he would come back soon for an official engagement.

When Ludwig returned to Grosshennersdorf, a few things had changed. Grandma was quite frail, and her sister had moved into the castle to help. Aunt Henriette had taken over administrative duties. She had also started an orphanage and a home for the poor. Everyone was happy to see Ludwig again, and they approved of the pending engagement to Theodora. He longed to see her, and with a heart full of love he wanted to tell her, "I love you, I want to espouse you. Will you be my wife?"

On the way to see his beloved, the wagon broke down by the river *Elster,* and the flustered coachman didn't know how to repair the vehicle. They had just passed a castle, so they unhitched a horse and Ludwig rode off like a knight in shining armor. Much to his surprise, the castle belonged to the Reuss family whose son, Count Heinrich, the 29th, was a pal he had met in Paris.

Hearing about the wagon mishap, the family dispatched servants to repair the coach and invited Ludwig for dinner. During the meal, he learned to his dismay that his friend Heinrich was madly in love with Countesse Theodora von Castelle and planned to marry her. Ludwig was stupefied. What had gone wrong? Was Theodora really in love with his friend? Had he mistaken her indifference for shyness? As soon as he could politely leave, he escaped from the dinner table and went to his room. Sleep eluded him as he lay on his bed, asking the Lord for direction.

By morning, he had peace about the matter and revealed to Heinrich the whole story. Both men agreed to confront Theodora and ask her directly to which man she would give her allegiance. When they arrived at her home, naturally, Theodora was embarrassed and startled at seeing them together. At first, she cried as Ludwig explained the situation and then she confessed; she had been in love with Heinrich all along and was too timid to tell Ludwig. Because he had a higher rank than Heinrich, Ludwig could have forced him out of the picture. Instead, he said to both of them, "It is settled, God's benevolent will be done. I wish you two felicity and contentment." Later, he even helped with the wedding and composed a cantata for the marriage ceremony.

Falling in Love

Twenty-six years later, Countesse Theodora joined the group of widows in Herrnhut when her husband, Count Heinrich Reuss, the 29th, died. Three years later she became an Elderess and passed away in Herrnhut in 1777.

At the wedding Zinzendorf's heart was still so numb that he did not pay much attention to Heinrich's sister, a charming and intelligent young woman. Her name was Countesse Erdmuthe Dorothea, and the Lord decreed that some day she would become his wife.

From that time, Zinzendorf resolved that he would let the Lord find him a saintly wife. "O my son, give me your heart. May your eyes take delight in following my ways" (Proverbs 23:26). He wrote in his diary, "My old Adamic nature was pretty sour to let such a *holdselige,* blissful sweet cousin go for ever. But I believe the heavenly Father will take care of me, a needy person, and when it will seem good for Him, He will provide something good for me again."

After this incident of unrequited love, Ludwig focused on his secret desire to become a minister of the Gospel. The picture of *Ecce Homo* was still burning in his heart. He was determined to answer with his life the question, "And what will you do for Me?"

At this time we read an entry in his diary: "By now I have profited by an inner revelation to despise the vanity of the world. My only longing is to be more and more united with the One who governs the world. If God wants to do something significant and I could be useful in His kingdom, I am willing to put forth defiance to the world. I perceive that I will not get any gratitude from humanity. I live with the firm conviction that soon I will be used mainly as a tool to increase God's honor. Even though I will experience hatred, envy and vindictiveness, God has given me – all thankfulness to Him – an unrelenting spirit which gives me not a moment rest but to increase His fame."

Zinzendorf's wish to become a Lutheran pastor was met with insurmountable resistance from his family. They believed that being a clergyman was beneath a man of his rank. What would other aristocrats think of a Count standing in the pulpit? They reminded him of God's fifth holy commandment, "Honor your father and mother." Reluctantly, he put his desire to preach aside. He complied with his family's plan that he follow in his father's footsteps and work as a Minister of Justice. He served as a judicial councilor and lawyer in the courts of August the Strong, Prince Elector of Saxony and King of Poland.

In the eighteenth century, August the Strong ruled Saxony and Poland, the largest territory in Europe. He was a tall man, weighing 260 pounds. Today, you can see a gilded, equestrian statue of him in Dresden. To become king over Catholic Poland, he had to convert to Catholicism. He then sent his wife into exile after only four years of marriage because she refused to become a Catholic. In her absence, August spent time with his royal mistresses and on ambitious building projects. He also loved gemstones, art, fine jewelry, and porcelain, which at that time was so highly valued it was called, "white gold." A Dresden porcelain maker by the name of Böttcher made August rich and famous with his invention of fine white porcelain.

7

Life in Dresden

"A great tragedy has entered into Christendom. They talk a lot about God and very little about Christ. When they talk you would think, Christ never walked on this earth and He would not be on every page of the Scripture. Christ has become unimportant to them and they act like you could believe, live and be saved without Him" (Zinzendorf).

Zinzendorf's professional life took him to Dresden at the age of twenty. Each Sunday from 3:00 to 7:00 pm, Ludwig invited like-minded Christians who loved the Savior to come to his home for fellowship. Everyone was welcome. Some would read a chapter from the New Testament and a lively discussion would ensue.

These meetings became another reason for criticism because people disapproved of an aristocrat taking a leadership role in spiritual activities. Zinzendorf defended himself by pointing to Luther's Catechism, which stated, "Studying the Gospel gives us advice and helps against sin, and brotherly discussions promote revival." Luther made reference to Matthew 18:20, "For where two or three gather together as my followers, I am there among them."

The Superintendent of the Lutheran Church, Valentin Löscher, sided with Zinzendorf and sympathized with him because he knew of his secret ambition to be a pastor. Also, Valentin had known Zinzendorf's father, Georg Ludwig, from their university years of Wittenberg.

Zinzendorf was wise enough not to replace the Bible study sessions with open services that would compete with ordained clergymen. The Bible studies became a springboard for reaching common people with the Word. These people trusted Zinzendorf and talked to him in plain, ordinary German, a valuable preparation for his future life working among the homespun Moravians. He knew a characteristic of a true disciple is seeking fellowship with other believers. Luke observes in Acts 2:42, "All the believers devoted themselves to the apostles' teaching and to fellowship, and to sharing in meals (including the Lord's Supper) and to prayer."

Zinzendorf wrote a variety of essays while he was working in Dresden. He wrote thirty-two dissertations, under the pseudonym of Socrates, because he wanted to stimulate his readers to think deeply as Socrates had stimulated the citizens of Athens. His letters were bold, sometimes caustic, colorful, and varied in subject matter.

Having an extraordinary comprehension of the German language, he wrote eloquently about what was in his heart. Preaching was another passion, and later in life he preached up to eight sermons a day without preparation. Writing inspired poetry and sacred songs was his leisure-time activity. There is a German saying, "The heart should always be full enough for the mouth to speak out of its abundance."

He also determined not to become a friend of the world and to shy away from the sensuous royal court. Despite his tender heart, he was neither soft nor sentimental. All this is reflected in one of his poems:

Lord, as you look into my soul,
You know my inmost thoughts.
If there's one drop of blood within.
That is at all inclined to sin,
Purge it now and make me whole.

One of Zinzendorf's Socrates letters reflects this personal devotion and his views on the prevailing spiritual climate: "I am not so much a God-fearing person, but rather, a God-joyful being. It is my endeavor to make my group delight in the Lord and to be obedient to His Word. Sadly, today many Christians go to services out of tradition and not conviction. Partly, this sad fact stems from the lukewarm preachers who see their profession as a means of earning a living. Their sermons are repetitious, boring and wearisome. The critiques of the laymen are well justified. In their sermons they talk about their silly opinions and about their own human interpretations and fabrications. The teachings of Christ are divine wisdom, and if it is brought down to human, homespun folly and childishness, even Socrates would brush it off as stupidity and superstition."

Zinzendorf considered himself a thinker and student of God's Word; yet, he acknowledged the limitations of what could be discovered about divine truth through study alone. He must have known 1 Corinthians 2:10-12, "But we know these things because God has revealed them to us by His Spirit and his Spirit searches out everything and shows us even God's deep secrets. No one can know what anyone else is really thinking except that person alone and no one can know God's thoughts except God's own Spirit. And God has actually given us His Spirit (not the world's spirit) so we can know the wonderful things God has freely given us."

Zinzendorf believed that no one can partake of divine secrets except those who have the joy and honor of a close affiliation with God. He wrote, "Nothing is more reasonable than the fact that common sense comes from the One who gave us our sense, in the first place."

The "Socrates of Dresden" had an unfavorable opinion of the clergy and churches of his town, and criticized those who denied Christ with their worldly walk. Martin Luther had the same opinion. At the end of his life, Luther wrote, "The Christian is a strange bird. Some are certainly learning how to repeat words like a parrot. Their hearts, however, do not grasp the meaning, and they make no progress. They exalt the Gospel only in words. They do as they please, following their fleshly desires and becoming more sinful as before."

When the identity of the pen name Socrates was discovered, Zinzendorf certainly made enemies. Later, he wrote about this period of his life, "It is not so easy in the beginning to find the middle way. Through the guidance of the Holy Spirit and with the leniency of my Savior, I became aware of the spiritual frailty of men and I was directed to the center track." Since Zinzendorf couldn't fulfill his desire to become a minister, he decided to buy from his grandmother a sizable, old mansion in Berthelsdorf that included a large piece of countryside. His grandmother lived close by in Grosshennersdorf. A trust he'd received from his deceased father when he turned twenty-one provided the funds. His purpose was to establish a small, Christian community. Zinzendorf set to work with zest, supervising the renovation that would make the mansion fitting for a nobleman.

The mansion still exists and is currently being renovated once again.

In 2007, we watched as workers strengthened the foundation of Zinzendorf's old mansion in Berthelsdorf. They drilled holes into the granite stones of the foundation and then pumped in concrete under high pressure. As they pulled out the big, powerful drills, granite cores came out with it, and were thrown on a junk pile. As I filled a bag with those cores, one worker was curious and asked me why I would

Life in Dresden

do that. I told him that I wanted to keep them as a souvenir because they came from Zinzendorf's mansion. With a puzzled look on his face, he asked, "Who is Zinzendorf?"

Over the mansion in Berthelsdorf, the Count inscribed these words: "This is our overnight abode, and we are only guests. It is neither fancy nor forever. You are quite right, our real home is in heaven and it will look much different." Cited [not written] is Zechariah 9:12 and 2 Corinthians 5:1-2: "Come back to the place of safety, all you prisoners who still have hope! I promise this very day that I will repay two blessings for each of your troubles." "For we know that when this earthly tent we live in is taken down (that is, when we die and leave this earthly body), we will have a house in heaven, an eternal body made for us by God himself and not by human hands."

The pastor of the church at Berthelsdorf, Johann Horn, died shortly after Zinzendorf arrived, and Johann Andreas Rothe became the new shepherd. He was a Pietist, a gifted preacher, and an excellent theologian. He served many years at the university in Leipzig. He was so humble that he thought he was not worthy to lead a flock. Zinzendorf told Rothe, "Work in the vineyard of the Lord, and please consider me an equal brother and friend, not a patron." At the induction service for Chaplain Rothe, a Pietist came from Görlitz and prophetically proclaimed, "God will light a candle on this place which will illuminate the whole land." This prophecy was fulfilled when the Holy Spirit fell on the Moravians in 1727.

When he was twenty-two, Ludwig fell in love with his friend Heinrich's sister, Erdmuthe Dorothea. As you remember, Heinrich was the man whom Countesse Theodora von Castelle preferred over him. There is no record of how love eventually blossomed between Ludwig and Erdmuthe Dorothea. Ludwig might have started corresponding on his own initiative. When Zinzendorf wrote a letter in October

1727 to Erdmuthe and expressed his wishes to marry her, she wrote a crisp reply, "It is indeed very lovely that you, the Honorable, made your intentions known. But I believe you have to 'cook' your intentions in prayer. I urge you to do that and perhaps your Honor will discover other thoughts which may be for you better, more useful and happier."

Erdmuthe's mother took over the correspondence. Zinzendorf complained, "Even though I love Erdmuthe with all my heart and deep in my soul, she is too lazy to write me back." The love between Erdmuthe and Ludwig was not a "cold" love, as his grandma suspiciously said, but a genuine heart connection. Zinzendorf realized by now that he had loved his first love, Theodore, too much, and it could have been an obstacle in his total dedication to the Savior.

We get a glimpse of his heart regarding marriage in a letter to his grandmother, "I see many difficulties in my marriage. I am a poor procurement for any person. My dear Countesse Erdmuthe has to be willing to enter upon a life of self denial to assist me in gaining souls for Christ. She will have to be willing to endure contempt and persecution." The Countesse Erdmuthe Dorothea Reuss was just such a woman. After the wedding, they soon moved to Dresden where Zinzendorf was employed. To look after his estate in his absence, Zinzendorf hired a man originally from Switzerland, Johann Georg Heitz. He had Christian principles, a reformist whom Zinzendorf met while visiting relatives in Franken.

Right from the beginning, Zinzendorf wanted to use his Berthelsdorf mansion to further God's kingdom and for the spiritual growth of believers. Everyone was welcome to the evening meetings at his home. Someone would read a chapter from the Bible or from a spiritual book. Hymn singing, prayers, and discussion followed. They often talked about Pastor Rothe's sermons. Zinzendorf would add his thoughts when he was present.

Life in Dresden

The home group that gathered at Zinzendorf's mansion grew rapidly and became more spiritually alive. It included common people, servants, and aristocrats. Word quickly spread that something exciting was going on in Berthelsdorf. Soon Zinzendorf's friend from school days, Friedrich von Wattewille, also moved to Berthelsdorf.

Having spiritual bands or groups must have been popular as Zinzendorf joined with others to form the Association of the Four Brethren. They came up with two basic guidelines: The first was preaching of the crucified Jesus and proclaiming the Good News to the spiritually poor, blind, oppressed, and downtrodden (Luke 4:18). The second was seeking the lost, not only among Protestants but also among Catholics, Jews, and heathens. The means to accomplish these goals were Christian literature, correspondence, and travel. In addition to Zinzendorf, the Four Brethren included Baron Friedrich von Watteville, who was a Pietist and also a Swiss nobleman of considerable wealth and talents. The two other members were Pastor Johann Andreas Rothe, a scholarly theologian whom Zinzendorf had appointed as a pastor at Berthelsdorf, and Pastor Melchior Schäffer, a Pietist and a good friend of Zinzendorf. Pastor Melchior preached fiery sermons at nearby Trinity Church in Görlitz, and also led a *lebendige* or born again cell group. In this group was a carpenter, Christian David. Christian was born in Moravia, had a dramatic conversion, and left the Catholic Church. In one of the pietistic cell group meetings, he met the visiting Count Zinzendorf and history was in the making.

8

The Moravians in Herrnhut

"The more a person grows spiritually into the likeness of Christ, the more sin is losing the grip on him. But the realization of the immensity of his debt before God grows" (Zinzendorf).

Moravia was under the dominion and monarchy of Catholic Austria, where true Christians were continually persecuted. Christian David told Zinzendorf about the persecution of the Moravian brothers and explained that they were looking for a place of safety.

Distressed over the persecution the Moravians had endured, Zinzendorf invited Christian David and some specific families to come to Berthelsdorf. For the time being, Zinzendorf placed Christian under his protection and gave him employment as a carpenter. Christian lost no time in traveling back to Moravia and returning with the families he had mentioned earlier. This group included two brothers, Augustin and Jakob Neisser, their wives, four children, and a cousin, Michael Jäschke. They lived temporarily in an empty barn, and Zinzendorf's grandmother gave them a cow to provide milk for the children.

There was property available a mile away from Berthelsdorf, but the immigrants were disillusioned with the area at first. It looked like a swamp, and there was no fresh water. Augustin Neisser's wife said, "Where can we find bread in this desert?" alluding to the Israelites in the desert. But Christian David took an ax, gave a mighty blow into a tree and declared, "Even the sparrow finds a home there, and the swallow builds her nest and raises her young" (Psalm 84:4). It was the 17th of June, 1722. A commemorative plaque is still at this very spot in Herrnhut.

Zinzendorf received a letter in Dresden from Pastor Rothe that the Moravians were steadily coming to the vicinity of Berthelsdorf, and they were building homes. At this time, Rothe called the place Herrnhut.

Christian David had a heart for his persecuted brothers and sisters in the Lord. In his lifetime, he made ten dangerous journeys into Moravia to bring persecuted Christians back to Herrnhut. The Austrian authorities placed a price on his head and leveled homes of departed Christians as a warning to others. A letter the Moravians wrote to Zinzendorf shows the humility of those persecuted Christians who left families, familiar surroundings and homes so they could express their faith according to God's Word.

"We are very much concerned that we do not put a burden on you, erecting homes on your land. We ask you with deep humility to be gracious to accept and protect us. We are poor, simple and oppressed and seek your grace and love. We will ask the Almighty God to bless you for this in your body and soul. Being safe in the divine protection, we will be obedient until our death and forever in your debt."

Signed,
Christian David, Augustin Neisser, Jakob Neisser.

The letter shows that although they were seeking Zinzendorf's protection, their reliance was on divine protection. Even at this early date, Herrnhut inhabitants reflected the meaning of the community's name, "Under the Lord's watch." Herrnhut can also be translated, "To be on the watch for the Lord or defending the things of the Lord."

Around this time, Zinzendorf and his wife returned to Berthelsdorf to spend Christmas with his grandmother. Although it was dark as they approached the area of Herrnhut, a light was visible in the forest. Ludwig ordered the coach stopped so he could investigate. The light came from the home of Christian David. Zinzendorf entered the house, encouraged the family, and fell on his knees, praying God's blessings on them.

A year later, Zinzendorf's caretaker, Heitz wrote a letter to him reporting that eighteen more immigrants had arrived and were asking for permission to build homes. Of course, permission was granted. When another throng showed up in Herrnhut the next year, Zinzendorf became alarmed. What would royal government officials do if they thought he had enticed good craftsmen to leave their home provinces? From then on, Zinzendorf interviewed every Moravian to find out if their motives were pure. Did they leave Moravia because they were tyrannized by the Catholic Church, or did they have unrelated motives?

By 1724, so many Moravians were living in Herrnhut that a community center was built. Friedrich von Wattewille supported the idea because he wanted the center to include a school for teaching genuine Christianity to aristocratic children. The building was large enough for group activities and had rooms for classes. Also included was a library for Christian literature and a pharmacy. Zinzendorf had some reservations about the school. If other learning institutions heard about the seminary, they might become jealous.

The congregation implored the Almighty to bless and protect the community center as they laid the foundation stone, and Friedrich von Wattewille knelt down to pray. The building played an influential role in the community until a new one was built, thirty-two years later. The original idea to teach aristocratic children never took off, but the rooms were used for orphans and as classrooms for Moravian children.

As the foundation stone for the center was being laid, five men traveling from Zauchenthal in Moravia to Lissa, Poland, witnessed the consecration. They had defied an edict forbidding anyone to leave the province ruled by Catholic Austria, so they left at night. They had no intention of settling down in Herrnhut, but they were so impressed with the solemn ceremony that they felt led to stay. Three of these men had the same name, David Nitschmann. The others were Johann Töltschig and Melchior Zeisberger.

Years later, David the carpenter became the first bishop of the Moravians. David the weaver became a negotiator with various governments. Johann Töltschig established many cell groups in England. Melchior Zeisberger helped establish Moravian settlements in Germany.

These new arrivals were destined to change Herrnhut forever. They were the spiritual descendants of two well-known dissenters, Jan Hus and Jan Amos Comenius. Jan Hus was a man who lived in Bohemia three hundred years before the time of Zinzendorf. He came from a poor Bohemian family, and wanting an easy life, he became a Catholic priest. His wit and intelligence earned him a position as Rector of the University in Prague. He began to study the writings and life of John Wycliffe, the English reformer, and he had a born-again experience. He became as bold as Stephen in the book of Acts. He denounced the nobility for their vices and condemned the Catholic clergy for selfishness, laziness, and lack of concern for their own spiritual need.

King Wenceslas of Bohemia liked Hus and supported him. However, Hus provoked the ire of the Catholic Church when he wrote books criticizing indulgences, the practice of buying forgiveness for sins, subservience to the Pope, absolution through the priesthood and many other unscriptural practices. He fearlessly preached how to obtain true faith and insisted that the Holy Scripture is the only supremacy of religion and faith.

In 1415, Hus was ordered by the Emperor Sigismund to attend the Council of Constance with a promise of safe conduct. On his arrival, he was immediately arrested and excommunicated, which for a Catholic means not only being expelled from the church but also condemned to hell. He was brought before a church council and forty accusations were read against him, mostly statements intentionally perverted from his own books. When Hus gave his defense, he was laughed at and mocked. Finally, when he refused to recant, which meant he could not receive absolution from the Pope, the council condemned him to be burned at the stake.

The death of this hero is described in *Foxe's Book of Martyrs*. They sheared Hus's head and put on him a paper bishop's hat painted with pictures of demons and the words, "A Ringleader of Heretics." Hus declared, "For my sake Jesus put a crown of thorns on His head, why should I not wear this light crown." He was bound with a chain to a stake. In front of him, they burned his books and sticks were piled up to his neck. They asked him again to repent, and he replied, "No, I never preached any doctrine that was evil, and what I taught with my lips I will now seal with my blood." As the burning sticks crackled and the flames engulfed him, Hus sang a hymn, loudly and cheerfully, until the flames reached his throat and face, and then he slumped forward. "God blesses those who patiently endure testing and temptation. Afterward they will receive the crown of life that God has promised to those who love him" (James 1:12).

With continued hatred, his enemies gathered Hus' ashes and threw them into the Rhine River. But the flames of revival were blazing, and neither death, torment, fire, nor water could subdue it. Out of his death, the Hussites emerged. They were persecuted, burned, drowned, or beheaded. They had in common a relationship with the living Savior and asked people to return to the simple faith of the early disciples.

In Moravia and Bohemia, various persecuted groups, mainly Waldensians, Anabaptists [also called Mennonites], Taborites, and Adamites came together, and they named themselves in Latin, *Unitas Fratrum*, United Brethren. Persecution was intense. Fleeing to the forests, the United Brethren moved secretly by night. They prayed fervently and read the Kralitz Bible, a translation in their own language which was forbidden by Rome.

The longest, hardest conflict in recorded history is the age-old struggle of the forces of darkness against the dissemination of the Word of God. The enemy uses different tactics in certain periods of history to destroy Bibles or shut down the availability of Scripture. At times he uses demon-inspired worldly authorities, merciless pagan rulers, ruthless dictators, religious kings and queens, and the unforgiving, misguided clergy.

When the Oxford-educated scholar, John Wycliffe, translated the Bible into the vernacular of the English laity, the Archbishop Arundel wrote to the Pope in Rome, "This pestilent and wretched John Wycliffe, of cursed memory, that son of the old serpent... endeavored by every means to attack the very faith and sacred doctrine of the Holy Church, devising to fill up the measure of his malice, the expedient of a new translation of the Scripture into the mother tongue."

When Cardinal Campeggio in Rome heard that a great quantity of Tyndale's New Testament was publicly burned at St. Paul's Cross Cathedral in London, he admitted he had learned with "pleasure of the burning of the books, perverted in the vernacular tongue, and brought into the realm by perfidious followers of the abominable Lutheran sect. No holocaust could be more pleasing to Almighty God." Papal Bulls, many edicts and several Councils forbade the translation, possession and reading of Scripture in the common language.

The Dark Ages (from around 475 to 1380 AD) are a perplexing period in history because it seems there was virtually no spiritual progress during this time. I believe the puzzle is easily explained. History demonstrates again and again that when Satan is successful in destroying or suppressing the Word for the common people, the result is barbarism and the strength of the church diminishes. The vigor of the believers turns into apathy, and the divine commission to "go into all the world and preach the Good News" is neglected. Why are the evil forces so adamant to keep the spiritually poor and the captives of false teachings from reading the Holy Scripture?

The Word of God snatches people from the grip of darkness. In a true and genuine conversion are three key elements. The blood of Jesus is the means of cleansing: "It was the precious blood of Christ, the sinless, spotless Lamb of God (1 Peter 1:19). The Holy Spirit is the convicting agent: "And when He [Holy Spirit] comes, he will convict the world of its sin, and of God's [available] righteousness, and of the coming judgment" (John 16:8). And the Word of God brings people enlightenment and is the tool that reveals both their lost condition and the way out of darkness through faith in Christ. "So faith comes from hearing, that is, hearing the Good News about Christ" (Romans 10:17).

Where the Bible has been freely available, as in America, the land is free and prosperous. God's Word is a matter of spiritual survival. God has preserved His Word from the hostility of imperial monarchs, raving despots, and misguided clergy. He has saved the Scriptures through periods of apathy, misunderstandings, national calamities, local upheavals, and persecutions. The Bible has survived despite being banned, burned, branded and banished.

"But the Word of the Lord remains forever" (1 Peter 1:25). "The rain and snow come down from the heavens and stay on the ground to water the earth. They cause the grain to grow, producing seed for the farmer and bread for the hungry. It is the same with my Word. I send it out, and it always produces fruit. It will accomplish all I want it to, and it will prosper everywhere I send it" (Isaiah 55:10-11).

Dyson Hague wrote about God's Word, "Unapproachable in grandeur, solitary in splendor, mysterious in ascendancy, high above all other books as heaven above the earth, as the Son of God above the sons of men."

The more the United Brethren were persecuted, the more their true faith shone and their numbers increased. By Luther's time, the *Unitas*

Fratrum claimed more than 400 congregations and 150-200,000 members, hardly a small, succumbing, struggling church. Jesus promised that the gates of hell will not overcome His true church. The legacy of the Bohemian and Moravian brothers was deep faith, a simple transformed life, shunning wealth and power, and sincere devotion. They led disciplined lives and focused on moral character. Their lives radiated the fragrance of Christ, which attracted many followers. For over 150 years, these Brethren were the light in a world of spiritual darkness. And the light shone brightly.

Let two martyrs speak for all. Balthasar Hubmeier traveled from Switzerland to Moravia to escape persecution. He was an Anabaptist [later they were also called Mennonites or Amish]. Catholic Austria forced the Moravian government to stalk the Anabaptists. Balthasar was caught and condemned to burn at the stake. He prayed at the stake, "O my gracious God, give me endurance in my moment of great torture. O my Father, I thank You that You will take me out of this valley of sorrows today. It is with joy that I desire to die to come to You. O Lamb that takes away the sins of the world. O my God, into Your hands I commend my spirit."

Turning to the people, he said, "O dear brothers, please ask God to give me strength to go through this suffering. I want to die strong in faith. If I have injured anyone in word or in deed, may he please, for my merciful God's sake, forgive me. I also forgive all those who have caused me pain." His last shouts, out of the ocean of flames surrounding him, were, "O my heavenly Father. O my gracious God. O Jesus, Jesus!" Several days later, his wife was drowned in the Danube River. (Neff, *Mennonitische Jugendwarte*, 1926).

In 1527, Anabaptist George Wagner of Munich prayed in a loud voice before burning to death at a stake, "Father my Father. Many things in this world are precious to me, my wife, my children, my life, but more precious are You to me, my Father. Nothing can separate me from Your love. I consecrate myself totally to You in life and in death. I am ready. I know what I am doing." *(Ein seltzam wunderbarlich Geschicht,* 1527).

The end of the Brethren seemed certain during the persecution of followers of Martin Luther. These were Protestants who were throwing off the yoke of Catholicism. This persecution escalated into the Thirty Years War, a bloody conflict that raged mostly in Germany from 1618 to 1648. But so many people were also killed in Bohemia and Moravia that the population dropped from three million to one million. Germany lost more than half its population.

When the Protestant army, led by General Tilly and Prince Christian von Anhalt, lost the Battle of White Hill near Prague, the United Brethren were subjected to even more hellish wrath. Catholic King Ferdinand II showed no mercy. He ordered Prince Lichtenstein to personally behead nobles found among the Bohemian Brethren. Others were imprisoned, tortured, raped, and massacred. Dead bodies were found in every town and village. Their Bibles and books were burned and their buildings and properties were confiscated. In an attempt to wipe their memory from history, even their graves were desecrated. But a small remnant lived through all this.

The first bishop of the *Unitas Fratrum,* Jan Amos Comenius, lost his wife and one of his children. Many persecuted Christians lived in Lissa, Poland. Comenius escaped to Holland. He prayed that God would preserve a "hidden seed" that would some day grow and become a great tree again. In his book, *The Labyrinth of the World and the Paradise of the Heart,* Comenius offered the only cure for a mad world steeped in darkness and degeneration: it is faith in Christ and God's love radiating to fellow brethren.

Over the centuries, millions of Christians have been slaughtered because they believe that we are saved by faith in Christ alone. Yet, the Council of Trent declared, "If anyone says that a sinner is justified by faith alone, meaning that nothing else is required to cooperate in order to obtain justification, let him be cursed." (In the next chapter I will write my thoughts on justification).

As already mentioned above, in May 1727, five men arrived in Herrnhut, the three Nitschmanns, Töltschig, and Zeisberger. They were part of the "hidden seed" of the ancient United Brethren or *Unitas Fratrum.* They had no intention to stay in Herrnhut, since they were on their journey to Lissa in Poland to escape persecution. When they heard the prayers of Zinzendorf and Watteville as they laid the cornerstone for a large building to house an academy, a print shop and a pharmacy, they were so impressed by their devotional prayers that they decided that their search for refuge had ended. They asked Zinzendorf for permission to stay. He agreed to take them in.

They frequently talked about Comenius and the old "Order and Discipline of the United Brethren." Zinzendorf was familiar with the name Comenius, but he did not know about the principles for Christian living that Comenius had written. To find out more about this document, Zinzendorf traveled to nearby Zittau, and in a library found a book of Comenius and his conviction that the "hidden seed" would some day come to fruition again. He realized now that these five men were not just a secluded, persecuted cell group, but part of a denomination. The book also contained the "Order and Discipline," which Zinzendorf translated from Latin into German.

Zinzendorf believed that the "hidden seed" for which Comenius prayed was germinating among the people of Herrnhut. He also remembered and took to heart what one of the settlers, Jakob Neisser, told him: "Even though we have gone through trials, we are sure it is God's will for us to be here. As he was dying, my grandfather saw an angel who said, 'It may seem that the end of the Brethren has come, but you will see a great deliverance. The remnant will be saved. An exodus will take place and you will find a spot to serve the Lord without fear. You, my grandson, will be among the first to leave.'"

In the meantime, Christian David again traveled to Moravia, urging other brothers to come and find refuge that the Lord provided under Zinzendorf's protection. Soon, eighteen more pilgrims set out during the night with nothing but a few loaves of bread for provisions. The Catholic priest in their town was so enraged that he enticed a mob to burn down Christian David's house.

Another David with the last name of Nitschmann (a brother of Anna Nitschmann, Zinzendorf's second wife) also urged brothers to come. On one journey to fetch his father from Kremsir, Moravia, he was caught, and without trial put in a dungeon. Zinzendorf journeyed to Kremsir to meet with the Catholic Cardinal and reminded him of the Peace Treaty of Westphalia that guaranteed religious freedom.

In 1648, dozens of delegates from several countries had met in the city of Münster, the main city in Westphalia, to sign this treaty that ended the Thirty Years War.

Nevertheless, the Cardinal firmly rejected Zinzendorf's plea and wouldn't even allow Ludwig to visit David Nitschmann. Zinzendorf returned home, brokenhearted. Three years later, the message came that David died without seeing the sun again. Zinzendorf wrote in his diary, "Half of my heart died with him." Later, Ludwig learned that the Cardinal had sent a militia of soldiers to arrest him, but the brevity of his visit saved him.

Many of the Moravians and Bohemians told stories of imprisonment and death and swapped stories of amazing escapes. Some of them experienced miraculous rescues similar to Peter being freed from prison by an angel. A rope would mysteriously appear, allowing prisoners to climb out of a tower. A metal latch to a dungeon door would open or prisoners would walk by guards as if invisible. True followers of Christ always experience persecution and miracles as the disciples did in the book of Acts.

When I was a boy of ten, we moved the short distance from Telgte to Münster, where the Peace Treaty of Westphalia was signed, ending the Thirty Years War. The large ornate chamber where royal dignitaries from several countries signed the treaty in 1648 is still intact. After WWII, the damaged building was rebuilt and today, tourists can visit the Rathaus, City Hall on the Prinzipal Markt, and view the table where the treaty was signed.

In this period of growth, we read in Zinzendorf's journal, "Homes were built small and low. Nobody was ashamed to do manual labor. Everybody was lending a hand to haul sand, stones, lime and other material on wheel barrels. No mansions were built. Only wooden door handles were used. Nobody worried about thieves. Partly there was nothing desirable to steal, partly there were always groups of people who were up all night, praying and singing with 'warm and alive hearts,' and partly the angels were protecting us."

We also read in Zinzendorf's rulebook #23 about work ethics: "Nobody in Herrnhut should borrow or lend money without knowledge of the Elders. Avoid going into debt. Everything should be done out of love. The focus of our brotherly community is the winning of souls. Work is holy and necessary, because we live and need to sustain ourselves. But remember, bread comes from the Sustainer of the whole world and we actually work for Him. Buying and selling is not to become rich but for the service of your fellow brothers and sisters, and if you cannot fully satisfy a customer with your product, then forget about the transaction even if you think it is important for you."

9

Thoughts on Justification

"Before you comprehend that the Word of God is the infallible Holy Ghost inspired Word you have to believe that justification is by faith alone. Then Scripture becomes an internal *Zugkraft,* a powerful force to draw you to Christ" (Zinzendorf).

Down through the centuries, the evil one has worked relentlessly to eradicate God's people. His most cunning device is disguising himself as an angel of light. He also uses people who call themselves Christians to persecute the remnant. True followers of Christ believe God's Word regarding justification by faith and not by works. Those who are self-righteous and rely on works or grace plus works will not enter the kingdom of heaven. "Idolatry is not only the adoration of images...but also trust in one's own righteousness, works, and merits" (Martin Luther).

Grace is a central doctrine of true Christianity, and the enemy fights vehemently against it. Paul wrote, "For God made Christ, who never sinned, to be the offering for our sin, so that we could be made right with God through Christ" (2 Corinthians 5:21). The word *justification,* or "just-as-if-I-never-sinned," means that any sinner who believes, trusts, and rests in the saving merits of Christ's righteousness has the **positional** standing of being a saint in Christ Jesus. Charles Hodge, in his book, *Systematic Theology*, devotes ninety-eight pages to this important doctrine.

From the church's inception, the prince of darkness has tried to undermine the doctrine of justification by faith. The souls of men are at stake when the gospel is perverted. Paul repeatedly warns against legalism in the epistles and sharply rebukes this dangerous heresy. He called the legalists "dogs," and would not listen to their arguments, not for a minute. When Peter was confused about this issue, Paul openly called him a hypocrite. When the Galatians were tinkering with the idea of adding circumcision [effort] to justification, Paul asked them, "Who has put an evil spell on you?" Paul was so beside himself when he heard about the foolish, vacillating Galatians, he wrote them a letter and came right to the point:

"I am shocked that you are turning away so soon from God, who called you to himself through the loving mercy of Christ. You are following a different way that pretends to be Good News but is not the Good News at all. You are being fooled by those who deliberately twist the truth concerning Christ" (Galatians 1:6-7).

Paul had a loving, pastoral heart, and with tears he wrote letters to young churches and pastors. He prayed day and night for those who had come to Christ, but was distraught and said, "Let God's curse fall on anyone" who preached any other Gospel (Galatians 1:8-9). He warned believers not to listen to such a message, even if it came from himself or an angel from heaven.

Unfortunately, by the third century, legalism had crept into the church. Sacraments and sacerdotalism (relying on priests as mediators between God and man) became essential parts of salvation. Water baptism and the Eucharist acquired magical power to remove sins and to impart eternal life. Priests became powerful, as they were the only ones with the right to administer the sacraments. Actually, the word sacrament is never mentioned in the Bible.

A new, false doctrine was proclaimed: apart from the church, there is no salvation. If water baptism is the means of forgiveness for sins and regeneration, the Apostle Paul did not know it because he wrote that Christ did not send him to baptize (1 Corinthians 1:17). Faith in the atonement of Christ always precedes water baptism because baptism is merely an outer sign of an inner identification with Christ.

By the fourth century, the Eucharist became an act of atonement. Slowly, the Catholic Mass developed and the unscriptural dogma of transubstantiation became part of church doctrine. To sum it all up, the claim that an institution can save is nothing less than blasphemy, but that is Rome's doctrine. To prove its point of view, Rome fought viciously against all contrary scriptural evidence, and the result was that millions who dared to dissent were slaughtered.

Finally, in 1517, Martin Luther took a hammer and nailed his Ninety-Five Theses to the door of a Roman Catholic Church, and Europe started to awaken. Martin Luther also wrote very clearly about justification by faith: "I greatly longed to understand Paul's Epistles to the Romans. Even though I tried to be an impeccable monk, I stood before God as a sinner in my conscience, and I had no peace that my merits would assuage God. I did not love a just and angry God and I had a great yearning to know what Paul meant by, the just shall live by faith. Then the light came into my soul. God justifies us through grace and mercy and by faith in Him. I felt reborn and walked through an open door into paradise. The justice of God filled me with hate and trepidation before but now it became to me inexpressively sweet in greater love. The passage of Paul became a gate to heaven for me" (Quoted in, *The Holiness of God,* R. C. Sproul, p. 125).

The doors of paradise opened for me when I came to Christ in 1978. What bliss to read Romans 5:9, "And since we have been made right in God's sight by the blood of Christ, he will certainly save us from God's condemnation." Since then, I have never doubted my salvation. I enjoy the most wonderful privilege of calling God my Father. I am His child because His Son redeemed me. I was bought with a price and it was paid for with Christ's precious blood. Think of it, I am loved by the Father with the same love He has for His Son, Jesus (John 17:23). My sins have been wiped away once-and-for-all. Theologians call this **judicial** forgiveness (Romans 3:24; 8:1).

The experience of basking in the finished work of Christ at Calvary, expressed by the Greek word Jesus cried out to His Father and to all the world with His last breath, "Tetelestai," which means paid in full, is the most exquisite and rapturous joy a human soul can know. Of course, I fall short every day and slip, but because of Christ, the Father forgives me when I confess my sin. It is His **parental** forgiveness (Luke 15:8-10).

In view of my own personal history and the centuries of European conflict over justification by faith, I'm concerned that ecumenism has become so popular. In the name of ecumenism, denominations are willing to cast aside doctrinal truth.

Not long ago, a group of influential evangelicals hammered out a document called, "Evangelicals and Catholics Together." Notable evangelicals and representatives of the Catholic Church signed it. The Protestants were not theologians but leaders of para-church ministries. The document stressed agreement to a mutual creed and cooperation on social and cultural issues, such as abortion and homosexuality. They also agreed to refrain from evangelizing, which they consider "sheep stealing." Because of my personal experience in the Catholic Church, this distressed me. I prayed a creed for many years, but I was not saved. A creed is merely a litany of facts, and for years I gave mental assent to those facts. However, that creed never mentioned the atoning power of the blood, or God's longing to have a personal relationship with each person.

In response to the ecumenical creed, another document was written and signed by 129 Christian leaders. Among them were John Walvoord, David Jeremiah, John MacArthur, Jerry Fallwell, Charles Stanley, Tim LaHaye, J. I. Packer, Pat Robertson, and others. Roman Catholic bishops and cardinals were noticeably absent. If they had signed such a document, the Pope could have excommunicated them by referring to the Council of Trent, which states, "Eternal life is said to be merited by the good works that are performed by the person in the state of grace. Any deviation from this dogma, the person is accursed."

Here is the second document devoted to the biblical doctrines of justification:

"God's justification of those who trust Him according to the gospel, is a decisive transition, here and now, from a state of condemnation and wrath because of our sins to one of acceptance and favor by virtue of Jesus' flawless obedience culminating in his voluntary sin-bearing death. God justifies the wicked and ungodly, (Romans 4:5) by imputing (reckoning, crediting, counting, accounting) righteousness to them and ceasing to count their sins against them (Romans 4:1-8). Sinners receive through faith in Christ alone, the gift of righteousness, (Romans 1:17; 5:17; Philippians 3:9) thus becoming 'the righteousness of God' in Him who was made sin for them (2 Corinthians 5:21). As our sins were reckoned to Christ, so Christ's righteousness is reckoned to us. This is justification by the imputation of Christ's righteousness. All we bring to the transaction is our need for it. Faith links us to Jesus, but inasmuch as it involves an acknowledgement that we have no merit of our own; it is confessedly not a meritorious work" *(Christianity Today,* June 14, 1999).

The last sentence means that merely possessing faith does not save us. Having faith in faith is not enough. The Pharisees had faith and looked straight at the Light of the World for three years, but not one flicker of sight reached their inner being. The Gospel is light, but the Holy Spirit gives sight. Faith must have an object, a person worthy of trust, our Savior Jesus Christ, "Nothing in my hands I bring, simply to Thy cross I cling." All of His righteousness, dazzling in brilliance and glorious in its perfection, is charged to our account because we receive Him, Christ, as our Messiah-Redeemer as a substitute for our sins, a death penalty.

When I was in Germany in 2007, the newspapers wrote articles about the tenth anniversary of the death of Mother Teresa. In no way do I want to judge Mother Teresa's lifelong sacrificial service among the poor in India.

The German newspaper included some excerpts from Mother Teresa's writings to her confessor, "Deep in my innermost being there is only emptiness and darkness. In the last few decades I feel alone and abandoned by God. I have no faith left. I do not dare to express in words and thoughts the indescribable torment I experience. The darkness and agony I have can only be compared as being in hell. I am close to losing faith in the existence of God."

I sincerely hope and pray that for the dear, selfless Mother Teresa, the doors of paradise also opened at last as for Martin Luther when he read in Romans 1:17, "The just shall live by faith alone." How sad that she did not have the joy of her salvation. Did her mind and soul stay in bondage to the Catholic teaching? Again reiterated by Pope John Paul II in his book, *Crossing the Threshold of Hope*, pg. 194, quoting, "A good life is the condition of salvation." How can we know just how good a good life has to be? Catholicism is a religion of human merits. True biblical Christianity is based upon divine accomplishments.

The older I get, the more abiding joy I have in my life. The reason is simply this. Through the power of the Holy Spirit [called the Sanctifier in Romans 15:16], I am more and more detached from sin, the lures of the world, and from my biggest enemy, "the fallen nature." I am also joyfully anticipating getting a new glorified body, seeing Jesus as He really is, and receiving my priceless inheritance (1 Peter 1:4). As an old man, Peter also wrote these encouraging words, "You love him even though you have never seen him. Though you do not see him now, you trust him; and you rejoice with a glorious, inexpressible joy" (1 Peter 1:8).

I, for one, can say without any pretense that I experience daily what Isaiah wrote in 12:3 and 61:10. "With joy you will drink deeply from the fountain of salvation." "I am overwhelmed with joy in the Lord my God! For he has dressed me with the clothing of salvation and draped me in a robe of righteousness. I am like a bridegroom in his wedding suit or a bride with her jewels."

10

The Great Sifting

"Only a passionate Father can have a genuine pain for the lostness of a human race. The God of the Trinity experienced an immense drama, the death of His Son on the cross. A God untouched and unperturbed by human fateful destiny would be a *metaphysical,* an abstract God, and would not be appealing and would be irrelevant to us" (Zinzendorf).

Christian harmony can be a fragile thing. As more settlers came to Herrnhut, Zinzendorf received a letter from his caretaker, Heiz. The news wasn't good. The congregation was bickering, and the spirit of unity was falling apart. There were different ideas about communion, ceremonies, and customs between the Moravians and Bohemians. Some had traditions of Calvinism and Hussites, others of reformed and traditional Lutheranism. Former Catholics and Anabaptists had also moved to Herrnhut, and by 1726 the population swelled to 300.

A man named Johannes Sigismund Krüger showed up, who proved to be a wolf in sheep's clothing. Although he was eloquent and had a certain charisma, he spoke vociferously against the Lutheran Church and called it the "Whore of Babylon." He had the audacity to call Zinzendorf "the Beast out of the Abyss," and Pastor Rothe "the False Prophet." Some people were won over, including the first settler, Christian David. The antagonism of Christian David, the Moravian Moses, was so strong that he defected from the community, built a cottage next to Herrnhut, dug his own well and waited for judgment to fall. He and Johannes Rothe were not speaking to each other anymore. Reverend Rothe forbade his congregation from visiting those "fanatics" up on the hill in Herrnhut. Krüger's ravings were wild and demented. He was later so maniacal that he spent his life in an asylum in Berlin. Zinzendorf's enemies used this disunity to criticize him, reminding him that it was his magnanimous idea to take in the troublesome refugees.

Zinzendorf was devastated. Although he had the authority as the aristocratic owner to order the settlers off his land, his loving heart dictated that he go after the confused sheep. The independent Moravians were not easy to handle. Zinzendorf immediately took a leave of absence from his judicial appointment in Dresden. Before hurriedly leaving for Herrnhut, he recorded his thoughts and prayer, "The old wise Comenius was lamenting that the little remnant of the United Brethren has almost come to an end and the door is being shut. I remember his melancholic prayer, 'Bring us home again and renew our days as it was in the past.' Therefore I, as far as I can, want to be used to bring a revival. Even though if I have to sacrifice my earthly possessions, my honor, and my life. As long as I live I will do my utmost to see to it that the little company of the Lord's disciples shall be preserved for Him until He comes."

Zinzendorf was quite serious in this. Some time later, he resigned his position in Dresden to devote his life fully to the Moravians.

On his arrival, no welcoming bell was sounded as in previous visits. He did not sleep in his Berthelsdorf mansion, but moved into the manor house in Herrnhut. His wife came with him and was in fervent prayer. (She was a remarkable woman, who I'll later profile).

As Zinzendorf worked through this conflict, the humility of this great saint was clearly evident. He showed the fruit of the Holy Spirit through his kindness and meekness as he visited each family for three days and nights in a row. He paused for only a few hours sleep at night. His main theme was the doctrine that would have a unifying effect for all sinners: "Look! The Lamb of God who takes away the sin of the world" (John 1:29).

Some time later, on Sunday the 12th of May, 1727, around 300 residents were present. Zinzendorf spoke for three hours about the disunity and their mutual obligation as Christ's followers to Christian behavior. The sermon was compelling and eloquent. He reminded his audience of Comenius and the written document of the "Order and Disciplines." Zinzendorf had already translated Comenius' original document, and he added some additional principles. The ears of the Bohemians perked up when they heard about the Order and Discipline, and the Moravians came to the conclusion that their own ideals were quite close to those of the writer Comenius. Zinzendorf demanded that the people agree to these basic principles. At the end of the meeting, everyone shook hands and sealed the Order and Discipline of Comenius with a symbolic handclasp.

Some time afterwards, Zinzendorf drafted his own document, the *Notariats Instrument,* a signed document of "Brotherly Agreements." He gave the Brethren time to think about it and gave them the freedom to move to Berthelsdorf if they did not agree. He asked the congregation to seal it this time with a signature.

Slowly, the mood in Herrnhut changed. The Brethren met in the evening for prayer and singing. Spiritual fervor returned. In just a few months, Pastor Rothe witnessed positive changes, which he had not been able to achieve with all his preaching. Zinzendorf was more convinced than ever that the "hidden seed" indeed had been entrusted to him by the hands of God. He also forgave Christian David. He told his wife, "Although our dear Christian David was calling me the Beast and Pastor Rothe, the False Prophet, I see an honest heart. Give a decent man who has temporarily failed a new obligation and he will learn from experience and not from lecturing."

Once again, the congregation was in harmony through much prayer and forgiveness, and the Lord's blessing became evident. Among the thirty-four homes and almost 300 souls, everyone was eager to be faithful to Comenius' simple but profound principles for Christian living. Here are some highlights of the Order and Discipline:

* All brethren should seek harmony and love with other Christians, even if they have different or divergent views.
* Never condemn a fellowman but hold steadfast to your personal convictions and faith.
* All human endeavors are excluded in justification by faith.
* The process of personal sanctification should be a serious, solemn matter.
* With the children of the world and the unsaved have friendly conversations, treat them honestly, and talk with them, but never become angry or have a *Lehrsucht,* a know-it-all attitude (Romans 12:16).
* If persecution comes, consider it a wholesome, healing test, carry it with courage, and give respect and honor to the perpetrator.
* To prevent any splits by harboring hard feelings within the community, brothers who make caustic or untrue remarks will be called before the Elders and required to confess openly and withdraw these remarks.

* In caring for the sick, brothers who are called to this service should do it with love. If a doctor is available, go to him. Be aware of ignorant quacks who claim to know cures.
* Witchcraft and superstition are atrocities.
* No brother should take advantage of another brother's professional position.
* No trade is lower or higher than another trade.
* No marriage should be proposed without knowledge of the Elders, and an engagement is valid only when permission is granted.
* Among single people, males and females, there should be trust, faith, and confidence. If they walk with lustful eyes or careless frivolity, the Elders have the right to reprove and stop the folly.
* No Elder should use his authority to lord over a brother but stand firm with him according to 2 Corinthians 1:24, "But that does not mean we want to dominate you by telling you how to put your faith into practice. We want to work together with you so you will be full of joy, for it is by your own faith that you stand firm."

With this document in place, twelve men were elected as Elders. Christian David was among them and it moved him to tears. Zinzendorf did not want any Elder with a noble title. He wanted plain, humble men, skilled as carpenters, weavers, cutlers, potters, cobblers, blacksmiths, iron-workers and tanners. This was an excellent decision, since most of the Elders became missionaries, and they were able to support themselves. Zinzendorf received the title of *Ordinarius Fratrum*, overseer of the Brethren. He and the Elders met regularly to discuss congregational affairs.

Here is the *Notariats Instrument,* better known as the *"Brotherly Agreement"* drafted by Zinzendorf and signed by eighty-three men from forty-seven families in Herrnhut.

Preamble: Be mindful forever, this town of Herrnhut was built by the grace of God. It is His work for the establishment of the United Brethren. The inhabitants must remain in an abiding bond of love with all God's children. Never dispute or judge your Brethren. Maintain a true evangelical doctrine. Make every effort to live together plainly and saintly.

(*Webster's Dictionary*'s definition of Evangelicalism: Agreement with the Christian Gospel. Salvation by faith in the atoning death of Jesus through personal conversion. Authority of Scripture and the importance of preaching as contrasted with rituals).

* The true church of Christ is only where the Word of God is preached in incorruptibility and simplicity and members live accordingly.
* Do not separate from anyone who believes in Jesus as his Lord and in the power of the Holy Spirit even though such a person may through ignorance or misguidance misinterpret some part of Scripture.
* Lack of discipline among awakened people is a great defect. The congregation is not to be blamed when a person does not allow himself to be disciplined. The blame lies upon the individual himself.
* Do not stress the titles Moravian and Bohemian to the point that it could be considered sectarian.
* Do not rest upon the goodness and faith of your fathers, but seek to be spiritually alive yourself.
* Do not love your life above eternal things. It is better to lose your life here than to deny spiritual truths.
* Every Saturday there should be a meeting of the Elders. If somebody misses two gatherings, Count Zinzendorf has the power to remove that person.

Zinzendorf was a man of prayer, and his habit of prayer undoubtedly played a large role in the reconciliation at Herrnhut. The first sentence in Psalm 133 reads, "How wonderful it is, how pleasant when brothers live together in harmony!" And the last sentence of the Psalm is, "And the Lord has pronounced his blessing, even life forever more." On the heels of reconciliation, a great blessing was coming to the United Brethren. An English poet, James Montgomery, wrote a poem about this period of disunity and strife in Herrnhut. He describes the subsequent Christ-like harmony that occurred when the Holy Spirit came upon them and brought them together.

They walked with God in peace and love
But failed with one another;
While sternly for the faith they strove
Brother fell out with brother.
But He in whom they put their trust,
Who knew their frames that they were dust,
Pitied and healed their weakness.
He found them in His house of prayer
With one accord assembled,
And so revealed His presence there
They wept for joy and trembled.
One cup they drank, one bread they brake,
One Baptism shared, one language spake,
Forgiving and forgiven.
Then forth they went, with tongues of flame
In one blessed theme delighting;
The love of Jesus, and His Name,
God's children all uniting.
That love our theme and watchword still;
That law of love may we fulfill
And love as we are loved.

11

Fire From Above

"For I will pour out water to quench your thirst and to irrigate your parched fields. And I will pour out my Spirit on your descendants, and my blessing on your children" (Isaiah 44:3).

On August the 13th of 1727, a dramatic event occurred among the Moravians. Just as Jesus talked about rivers of living water, the Holy Spirit gushed down upon the community. Several days before, Zinzendorf and fourteen of the Brethren spent the whole night in spiritual conversation and prayer. At midnight, a large group assembled on the Hutberg [a hill by Herrnhut with a breathtaking view of the nearby scenery] for an all-night prayer meeting. The dawn was greeted with the song, "He is the Son of righteousness which rises with resplendent grace." The Sunday before this miraculous event, Pastor Rothe talked about the significance of the Holy Spirit. In the afternoon service, Pastor Rothe was so overcome by the nearness of God that he sank down into the dust. The congregation also became convicted of their sins of disunity and they asked their Savior for forgiveness. Many tears and earnest pleas were heard to dwell together from now on in love and unity. God's forgiveness and the forgiveness of each other were healing the *Unitas Fratrum*, and there was an intense bond of brotherly love.

The coming Sunday was the first Communion celebration of the reconciled community. Zinzendorf went from house to house, urging the Brethren in a friendly and familiar manner to come to the communion service that was planned in Berthelsdorf. The night before, all the folks gathered together in the evening and all were deeply moved as two young girls, Katharina Heintschel and Anna Friedler, answered the forty-six questions Zinzendorf had prepared for their confirmation. The two young girls confessed the Lord Jesus Christ as their Savior and spent the rest of the night in prayer and meditation.

The unforgettable day dawned. Early in the morning, Pastor Rothe expounded on the meaning of the Lord's Supper in Herrnhut. The congregation then walked the mile to the little church in Berthelsdorf. Small groups of people walked together in interactive conversations and in bonding love. They had been convicted of their sins of disunity, the grace to think lowly of themselves, and to be compassionate and tenderhearted to one another. As they approached the little church, they sensed already a deep stirring in their hearts that caused them to wonder.

The church was crowded for this service. The two girls, Katharina and Anna, were to be confirmed. Zinzendorf led the kneeling worshippers in fervent prayer and made a penitential confession in the name of the congregation. After a time of lamenting about their sins, Pastor Johannes Süss of Hennersdorf said a prayer, asking God for absolution and offered Holy Communion. Pastor Rothe pronounced an apostolic blessing and confirmed the two youthful girls. The congregation sang several songs. "Deliver me, O God, from all my fetters," and "My soul before Thee prostrate lies, To Thee, its source, my spirit flies."

Then they started singing a hymn written by Zinzendorf, beseeching God. The book printed in 1860 records the lyrics:

Now establish by Your grace Your building again.
It is under Your strong watch.
Our walls are crooked, but make them straight.
The pillars need to be touched by Your blood.
Only the wounds of Jesus can heal us,
And the wounds have conquered our hearts again.
For Your healing we come together.

While they were singing this hymn, a powerful wave of emotion swept over the congregation. The awareness of the holiness of God was like a purging fire, leading them to a deeper repentance. People began to weep so profusely that their loud cries drowned out the singing. Some began to pray fervently with intense voices. New vigor and passion to worship filled their hearts as the power and the glory of the Holy Spirit descended upon the assembly. The presence of the Lord was so overwhelming, some reeled, and some sank down to the dust before God. As time went on, the sweetness and joy of tasting the Lord's presence was so intoxicating, they did not want to leave the church grounds. People gathered in small groups, embracing each other and asking for forgiveness. Others were praying, weeping, talking, and singing. They had already been one body as a religious community, but now they were bonding their hearts in one spirit and warmth.

As the afternoon wore on, the united brotherhood was not ready to go home. Ludwig sent some people to Herrnhut to bring back food, and they had a love feast right next to the church. As in the second chapter of Acts, they shared their meals with great joy and generosity, all the while praising God and enjoying the good will of all the people.

"Oh, lover and beloved, eat and drink! Yes, drink deeply of your love!" (Song of Songs 5:1). "Is anyone thirsty? Come and drink – even if you have no money! Come take your choice of wine or milk – it's all free!" (Isaiah 55:1).

In his writing, Zinzendorf repeatedly referred to this event as "that glorious summer," or the "Herrnhuter Pentecost." This day, August the 13th, is regarded by the Moravians as the spiritual birthday of the renewed Moravian church, and the revival of the "hidden seed," for which Comenius had prayed.

Christian David wrote later, "It is truly a miracle of God that out of so many backgrounds including Lutherans, Reformed, Separatists, and Calvinists, we melted into one." Spangenberg wrote, "There we were baptized by the Holy Spirit Himself in one love." Zinzendorf wrote, "We saw the hand of God and His wonders, and we were all under the cloud of our fathers, baptized with the Spirit. The Holy Ghost came upon us, and in those days great signs and wonders took place in our midst. From that time, scarcely a day passed but that we beheld His almighty workings among us." David Nitschmann wrote in his diary, "From the day of our encounter in Berthelsdorf we became a vibrant, lively congregation of Jesus Christ. We thank our Savior that He led us to Count Zinzendorf in Herrnhut and not to Lissa in Poland."

One of the old books recounts, "Those who formerly could not forbear, fell on one another's neck in the graveyard before the church and pledged themselves together most sincerely, and so the whole congregation came back to Herrnhut as new-born children. There was nothing to be seen and heard but joy and gladness. Herrnhut represented truly a tabernacle of God among men." We find another entry in one of the Brethren's diary, "From this time on Herrnhut became a fervent congregation of Jesus Christ. The unity of the brethren was rejuvenated and promises were spoken by all to be faithful to their Savior regardless where and how He would lead."

John Wesley visited Herrnhut eleven years later in 1738, and wrote in his diary, "The inhabitants of Herrnhut are a living proof of the power of faith. The love of God resides in their hearts. They have no doubt or fear, and the abiding witness of the Holy Ghost has been given unto them."

The outpouring of the Spirit was not localized to only Berthelsdorf. When two Brethren returned from far away Hungary, they asked, "What happened at ten o'clock in the morning on August 13th?" They had also been touched by the Spirit.

In Zinzendorf's writing, we discover his thoughts about the Holy Spirit: "He is continually working in those souls which He found, captured and sealed. He *verklärt*, beatifies (or as a blissful appearance) the wounds of Jesus and teaches us to be pure and blameless in our daily behavior with sisters and brothers. He also teaches us, that we are under the Lord's watch and we see His hand in all our toils. The primary work of the Holy Spirit is the maintenance of our faith. We are sitting on the Holy Spirit's lap and He tutors us through all the school classes. Even when we are in the casket, the Holy Spirit will not leave us in the dust. He is the life-giving Spirit and He will wake up our *Körperchens,* puny bodies, for resurrection. The Holy Spirit is the source of all our comprehension of God. He uses the Scripture for this purpose. His main striving in us is to magnify Christ in our lives. He relentlessly pursues us to make us *gottähnlich,* Christlike. Just as we learned as a child to listen to the cautionary reminders of our earthly parents, we believers have to become sensitive to the admonitions of the Holy Spirit. He also prepares us, the Bride of Christ, for the wedding. He is making us *jungfräulich,* virgin-like and adorns us inside and outside. The bejeweling of His Bride will not end until we are with Jesus."

After this filling of the Holy Spirit, life among the Bohemians and Moravians was never the same. Fruits of the baptism with the Holy Spirit were evident by action. Prayer groups called *Banden,* or bands were formed. They consisted of five to seven people who came together frequently during the week for prayer and singing.

In the Moravian annals we read, "The thought struck some of the Brethren that it might be well to set apart certain hours in fervent, persevering prayer to pour out their hearts before the Lord to receive all the promises of the Lord wrestled through prayer."

An Elder was always present. Leaders had no vestments or special attire, all dressed the same. Singing was their favorite pastime, and early on they learned hymns by heart. They lived together like the early Christians. Each person had a trade and supported their family by the sweat of their brow. Because no one owned land, very few tilled the ground as farmers, most worked as craftsmen. The Brethren put in long days. Ten to twelve hours a day working in their craft was expected. Early in the morning, a watchman walked around the town, singing in a loud voice, "The clock is at five. Five virgins will be lost and five will be at the wedding." After one hour of singing and praying, the watchman cried, "The clock is at six, from the watch you free, now your own watchman be."

Books about the Holy Spirit could fill innumerable libraries. Most biblical scholars and theologians agree that a believer must be filled with the Holy Spirit. The Holy Spirit is mentioned over 200 times in the New Testament. These verses teach that the Holy Spirit fills and controls us (Ephesians 5:18), gives us boundless love for our Father (Romans 5:5), and helps us to pray (Romans 8:26). The Holy Spirit also tells us we are God's children (Romans 8:16), reveals to us God's deepest secrets (1 Corinthians 2:10), helps us to become more like Jesus (2 Corinthians 3:18), produces fruit in our lives (Galatians 5:22), makes us holy (2

Thessalonians 2:13), helps us to obey and teaches us intimacy with Jesus (1 John 3:24), and gives us a share in God's divine nature (2 Peter 1:4). He also gives us boldness, imparts power to witness, and does so much more.

There is minor tension between Evangelicals and Pentecostals on this subject. Evangelicals believe that baptism or indwelling of the Holy Spirit occurs at the moment of conversion and is automatically and unconsciously given. One verse supporting this view is 1 Corinthians 12:13, "Some of us are Jews, some are Gentiles, some are slaves, and some are free. But we have all been baptized into one body by one Spirit, and we all share the same Spirit."

The Pentecostals believe that baptism with the Holy Spirit is distinct from and subsequent to conversion. It is an addition to Christ's regenerating work. A text used in support of this perspective is Acts 8:14-17, "When the apostles in Jerusalem heard that the people of Samaria had accepted God's message, [they believed the Gospel or Good News that Jesus died for their sins and that they were saved and would go to heaven] they sent Peter and John there. As soon as they arrived, they prayed for these new believers to receive the Holy Spirit. The Holy Spirit had not yet come upon any of them, [notice not yet] for they had only been baptized in the name of the Lord Jesus. [Water baptism] Then Peter and John laid their hands upon these believers, and they received the Holy Spirit."

My personal belief, based on my own experience in 1978, is that the baptism with the Holy Spirit is a definite event and a person will know whether or not he has received it. The baptism with the Holy Spirit can happen at the same time a person is regenerated and receives new life, or it can be a subsequent or additional experience to that of being born again. The issue regarding the baptism with the Holy Spirit is not whether a person is saved without this baptism. In every true conversion, the Holy Spirit comes and dwells within a believer and he is born of the Spirit and the person is saved. The issue is not whether the person speaks in tongues, is slain in the Spirit, or has a mountaintop, emotional experience. The issue is this: Do we allow the Holy Spirit to occupy, guide and control every area of our lives? Was there a significant, life-changing encounter with Jesus Christ? Is there confident and joyful anticipation of God's glory? (Romans 5:2). Does the Holy Spirit give assurance of God's acceptance? (Acts 15:8) Is there a hunger to read the Word and be sanctified? (John 10:28) Is there a deep and true sorrow when you sin? (2 Corinthians 7:10)

Gifts (prophecy, healing, teaching, tongues etc.) and a willingness for service and power for evangelism, the Holy Spirit surely desires to impart, but holiness and spiritual worship is paramount and must come first.

William MacDonald, a conservative theologian, calls the baptism with the Holy Spirit a "crisis" experience. *Webster's Dictionary* defines crisis as, "an emotional event which radically changes a person's life."

Charles Finney, John Wesley, D. L. Moody, Oswald Chambers, Hannah Whitall Smith and many others call it either an enduing with power from on high, or a second blessing, or fire from above, or a higher Christian life or entire sanctification.

This is exactly what happened to me in 1978. I was illiterate about spiritual things when I came to Christ. My life changed radically. It was not a slight change of attitude. It was the beginning of the demolition of my old nature and a creation of a new heart. I had a craving for the Word of God and yearned for fellowship. Even though I had never heard the word rapture, I looked up to heaven for His coming. I was set free from a false religion and had joy in my heart. In the "Jesus movement" vernacular that was popular at the time, I was also "groovy on Jesus."

12

The Losung, Watchword for the Day

"Our God is called the 'Father of Love' and it is proven by His willingness to sacrifice His Son. Jesus Christ is the example of obedience, and we are called to emulate Him. The Holy Spirit has *Treue und Geduld*, faithfulness and patience to tutor believers in their daily lives" (Zinzendorf).

Two weeks after the glorious "Moravian Pentecost," the community was urged by the Holy Spirit to pray more, and twenty-four men and twenty-four women entered into a commitment to pray around the clock. Before long, they had many names on their list of people for whom they were praying. They prayed for brothers and sisters in prison, those who were ill, people struggling with repentance, and later, the many needs of those on the mission field. Many miraculous cures and miracles were reported. Even more intercessors joined as they kept on praying through lonely nights, in spite of the pressures of work and family. They took the admonition of Isaiah 62:6 seriously, "O Jerusalem, I have posted watchmen on your walls; they will pray day and night, continually. Take no rest, all you who pray to the Lord." This twenty-four-hour prayer watch continued for over 100 years. The Moravians posted this notice, "Our church is young, the devil is alive, we cannot rest, and we all need intercessory prayer warriors."

The Moravians' heartbeat for prayer and singing started at the beginning of each day with a devotional called morning blessing. In the evening, they met at the community hall for worship, prayer and Bible reading. Adoration of the Lamb was their passion. Zinzendorf's hymns were especially loved, and they were sung with devotion to the Lord. Often in between hymns, the Brethren broke out in spontaneous worship with personal verses of praise.

On Saturdays and Sundays, the Brethren spent most of the day in church. Long before daybreak, all Brethren came together for the "sing-along" hour. From six o'clock on, ten different *Chöre*, or groups of adults and children, came together in different places for prayer and singing. The regular morning service started around 10 o'clock in Berthelsdorf, a mile away. Early in the afternoon there was a repeat of the morning service in Herrnhut. An Elder or Zinzendorf would repeat the sermon. It was for all those who could not attend the morning service. Later in the afternoon, the congregation walked again to Berthelsdorf for the official afternoon service. And finally, at the end of the day the last service was held in Herrnhut. Every day at nine o'clock in the evening, young men marched through the streets, singing hymns to close the day.

Zinzendorf, a skilled organizer and initiator, launched another idea that he called *Losung,* or watchword. He gave to the Brethren Bible verses or words from a hymn, and urged them to contemplate these. Each morning, an Elder visited the homes, bringing them the Losung for that day. He would occasionally ask wife and husband whether there was a Christian environment and an aura of harmony in their home. It is unbelievable how seriously they regarded sanctification of family and personal life. Paul's writing

The Losung, Watchword for the Day

confirms this emphasis. The fact that we are members of God's household should certainly be reflected in our lives.

I have in my library a new edition of the Moravian Daily Texts. This book is the modern version of Zinzendorf's Losung. For almost 280 years, this book has been published, and currently has a circulation of over 1.5 million. There are one million copies printed in the German language alone. It is one of the more widely read devotional guides in the world. Biblical texts from Zinzendorf's compilations are chosen in Herrnhut three years before publication and are sent around the world to be printed. The English edition includes a prayer for each day. The Moravian Daily Texts are used as a guide for family worship as well as for personal devotions.

The community in Herrnhut often shared meals together, giving different events unique names, such as congregation day, or love feast. They had preparatory hours for Holy Communion, sing-along hours, and meetings of *Chöre*, group gatherings of same gender and age. At their love feasts, everyone would bring a simple meal, often only water and bread. Because heartwarming joy was the prevailing attitude, these meetings were their recreation.

The book written in 1900 gives a heartwarming glimpse of the community. The hearts of the Brethren were laughing for joy when they sang the old Bohemian hymns. It reminded them of their homeland where they endured persecutions and could only sing in hiding places. Now they could sing loud and unrestrained, "O God, we want to adore You, You gave us noble gifts" (No. 692). "How lovely are all Your mansions for us" (No. 693).

The Moravians and Bohemians were a joyous community, but they also worked hard and were excellent craftsmen. Neighboring cities such as Zittau, Löbau, Görlitz and many villages enjoyed articles these craftsmen made.

Some days, Zinzendorf preached sermons, sang hymns, and read from the Word from morning to evening. He did not show any weariness and would preach with anointing. He also introduced foot washing, admonishing that members in a "full of life" congregation who read the thirteenth chapter of John should recognize the importance of this ceremony. Zinzendorf wrote, "Those who wash the feet and those who let their feet be washed should meet three conditions. They should know in their hearts they are truly a child of God, they should love each other with genuine affection, and they should have an honest trust to one another."

The highest celebration was observance of the Last Supper. Pastor Rothe in Berthelsdorf conducted this solemn ceremony once a month. The day before celebrating the Lord's Supper, the congregation came together for "preparation hour." During this time, the Elders reviewed with the community the essential biblical tenets of communion. However, Zinzendorf forbade any public discussion about personal interpretations of this ordinance, knowing it would only generate heated arguments and division.

Concerning the bread and wine of communion, Luther taught consubstantiation. This means the body and blood of Christ are present in, under, and through the elements of bread and wine. This was a cosmic leap from the Catholic teaching of transubstantiation, which means actually eating the body and drinking the blood of Christ. Calvin denied the physical presence of Christ at the Lord's Supper, but affirmed the spiritual presence of Christ. Zwingli taught what he considered the biblical perspective, which he called "the memorial view of the Lord's Supper." Most Evangelicals share Zwingli's view, summarized in Christ's command, "Do this in remembrance of Me." When Jesus said, "This is My body and this is My blood," He was using figurative language similar to His words, "I am the Good Shepherd, I am the Door, or I am the Vine."

When I left the Catholic Church, the bizarre teaching of transubstantiation was the most difficult thing for me to overcome. In speaking to Catholics about this issue, it is important to show love and pray that the Holy Spirit will open their eyes. Share with them that drinking blood in the Old Testament was forbidden (Leviticus 3:17). Also, when Christ said at the Last Supper that the bread and wine were His body and blood, He had not yet died and was physically present with the disciples.

The Moravians became a spiritually alive congregation reflecting the fruit of the Holy Spirit. Their lives focused on brotherly love and sympathy. One Elder, Martin Linner, slept on a wooden bed during the summer and winter because he wanted to be equal to his younger companions. When a Moravian baker saw his competition, who was also a baker, struggling financially, he voluntarily gave up his trade and became a weaver.

By 1732, there were 600 settlers in Herrnhut. The Elders established various prayer groups consisting of mature Christians, boys and girls, single men, single women, married couples or widows. Zinzendorf gave all these groups, called *Chöre* or choirs, biblical examples to live by. For the young people it was Jesus at twelve years old, for the tradesmen it was Jesus the carpenter, for the missionaries it was Jesus as an itinerant preacher, and for couples it was Paul's instruction about marriage found in Ephesians 5:23-33. Zinzendorf also put a great deal of effort into children. He wrote, "We have to be diligent that children have good examples. It is a grave sin if we neglect them. These are young souls we have dedicated to God. They are little majesties, the baptism is their anointing, and we should treat them like little kings."

The *Unitas Fratrum* established a cemetery near Herrnhut, which they called *Gottesacker,* God's Acre. The first departed brother was laid to rest in 1730. The oldest grave remaining today is that of an unnamed baby marked with a small square stone. Rather than crudely referring to the end of life as death, they described it as "taking down a tent." This phrase is from 2 Corinthians 5:1, "For we know that when this earthly tent we live in is taken down (that is, when we die and leave this earthly body), we will have a house in heaven, an eternal body made for us by God himself and not by human hands." This sentiment was expressed in a letter by a simple tailor who lost his son, "In this hour of grief I praise the Lord even more so. I have seen with my own eyes how the earthly body of my dear son was committed to the holy ground. When he is raised again, both he and I shall be forever with the Lord."

It was a joy for Zinzendorf to take visitors to the *Gottesacker* and tell them about the history of departed saints. For Zinzendorf, the *Gottesacker* was a reverent place because of the departed saints, and as he said, "Jesus also was in a grave."

Every Easter morning since 1733, the entire congregation walks to God's Acre. The chaplain calls out, "The Lord has risen," and the congregation replies, "He is risen indeed."

> My wife and I were privileged to participate in this moving liturgy. The Moravians instituted another tradition that takes place at midnight on Christmas Eve and has been practiced from 1733 to the present. The congregation gathers in the big white Moravian church, and each person holds a lighted candle that illuminates the darkness.

Zinzendorf enjoyed correspondence. Deep into the night, the oil lamp burned on his desk. In so many ways, his life and work reflected Jesus' words that a city on a hill cannot be hidden, and a light should not be put under a bushel basket but on a lamp stand. Perhaps that is why Herrnhut became known all over Saxony and as far as Poland and Denmark.

Zinzendorf received a letter from Bishop Daniel Ernst Jablonsky in Poland, grandson of the well-known Bishop Comenius. Reverend Jablonsky wrote a very encouraging letter to Zinzendorf, "With immeasurable joy and heartfelt rapture I have heard that the all-gracious God has revived a small group of Bohemian Brethren. The *Unitas Fratrum* is so despised in the world, but the morning sun of reformation has risen again. I cannot thank you enough that God has chosen you, most honorable Count, and that you are willing to protect these poor refugees living in exile.

"My parents were born in the Brethren Church in Poland. I was born there as well and raised with the love of that church from the time I was drinking my mother's milk. When I heard the news about Herrnhut, I knew that the ancient, apostolic lifestyle and truth of the early Christians that was written in our Bohemian Disciplines had come to life again. What also gave me a jubilant heart was to hear that the Lutherans and Brethren live in brotherly harmony. Actually, this has always been the character of the Bohemian Brethren, to practice the righteous nature of Christ and not to fight over trivial theological matters. The Bohemian Brethren wanted not to be named the Hussites or Lutherans, but simply, United Brethren. Nevertheless, they honored Luther and believed that he was a tool in God's hand. God has planted a noble vine branch under your care, and we implore Him in heaven to keep an eye on it.

"I have observed with great sorrow from printed circulars that the harmless *Unitas Fratrum*, which the Christian world ought to regard as a shining light, are vilified and despised by an evil and perverse generation. Yet, it cannot be otherwise. Since they are not of the world, the world hates them. You must not lose courage; it cannot be easier for Christ's servants than it was for Christ himself."

13

Salt of the Earth

"The reason we have *Banden,* cell groups, is to disclose the condition of our hearts. We begin to trust one another, and we dare to disclose openly and honestly, like little children, from our inner being. With childlike trust we talk about our lives. We encourage each other and we remind ourselves to give the nursing of our lives to our Savior. *Mutuum colloquium et consolatio fratrum.* Brotherly mutual admonition and consolation" (Zinzendorf).

(In 1732 there were seventy-seven Banden. In 1734, one hundred).

Four years after the Holy Spirit fell on the little band of brothers, God seemed to be telling the congregation that He was preparing them to be the salt of the earth by going out as missionaries. The Herrnhut community reflected John Wesley's words, "Who among you is so alive to Christ as to carry fire wherever you go?"

In 1731, Zinzendorf traveled with a few young Moravians to Copenhagen, where King Christian VI had been crowned with pomp and pageantry. The Count had an excellent relationship with the Danish court, which he hoped would help him establish a revived church in Denmark. He was so admired that King Christian awarded him the highest Danish honor, "Cross of the Order of the Knights of Danegrog." However, the Danes did not approve when Zinzendorf became a clergyman, so he was not able to establish a congregation in Denmark. Because of this controversial issue, relations with the royal court became strained and he returned the award. Years later, after his exile from Saxony, there was a reconciliation and he was able to establish a congregation.

A much more momentous event occurred while Zinzendorf was in Copenhagen. He met a former slave from the Danish-owned island of St. Thomas in the Caribbean. His name was Antonius Ulrich, he was a Christian, spoke Danish, and with a sparkle in his eyes he said to the Count, "If only a missionary could go to my island and tell my sister and brother about Jesus, they would believe just as I do." When Zinzendorf returned to Herrnhut, all of the Brethren were excited. His wife and some town folks greeted him already some miles outside Herrnhut. He told them all about the crowning celebration and about the freed slave with the name Antonius. Eight days later, July 29th, Antonius arrived in Herrnhut. He told the breathless Brethren the spine-tingling news that the slaves in the Caribbean had to work hard all day, and the white managers treated them harshly. To preach to the slaves, it might be necessary for the missionaries to become slaves themselves. Two Moravians were so stirred and fired up they wanted to set out immediately. After one year of prayer and preparation, Leonard Dober, a potter, and David Nitschmann, a carpenter, were ready to leave for the Caribbean.

When Leonard Dober was asked to write a letter why he wanted to be a missionary, he wrote, "At this time in my life I had no intention to travel, but only to ground myself more steadfastly in my Savior. However, when the gracious Count came back from his trip to Denmark and told us about the slaves, it gripped me so hard that I could not get free of it. I vowed to myself that if one other brother would go with me, I would become a slave and would tell him so. This I have experienced of my Savior, that the lowliness of His cross shows a special strength to a soul. Even if my commitment is not helpful to any one, I still want to give witness in obedience to my Savior. I leave it to the good judgment of the congregation and I have no other reason than this, on the island there are souls who cannot believe because they have not heard."

The congregation had an evening song service to bid the two young pioneers farewell. For several hours they sang sacred hymns. Singing and music were part of their adoration of the Lamb, as was preaching or communion or obedience to Christ's Great Commission. After so many years of oppression in Moravia and Bohemia, the gift of song was theirs. With good reason it has been said, "The Moravian church gave to hymn singing a prominence in worship not to be ever paralleled within traditions of other denominations."

The United Brethren had already in 1457 a collection of eighty-nine hymns. Several hundred years later, God saw fit to give the Moravians a man gifted in poetry, and a lover of songs. It was Zinzendorf. He wrote hymns all his life, at night and at daybreak, on the sea or even in the midst of a service. Hundreds of Zinzendorf's rhyming hymns were added to the songbook. The congregation, which possessed an unusual command of all the sacred songs, would fall in with the leader before he reached the end of the first line of each stanza, singing by heart. No number was given on many occasions, as none was needed. Zinzendorf was of the conviction that a hymn must be memorized to express the feeling of the heart.

All night long before they left, Zinzendorf prayed and talked with these young pioneers, and before the sun was up all three of them left Herrnhut in Zinzendorf's coach. They traveled together to Bautzen, a little over twenty miles northwest of Herrnhut. When the carriage stopped, they knelt down, and Zinzendorf laid hands on them and prayed.

The young men traveled across Germany by foot, occasionally catching a ride. Their only provisions were six *Talers*, (root word for dollar), which they saved for an emergency, and one *Ducat* [a gold coin] that Zinzendorf had given to each of them. They also received from him a few last minute instructions. He said, "In all things and in all your ways, let the Spirit of Christ guide you."

These two young men were not highly talented, not intensively trained and not widely experienced, but they were endued with the power of the Holy Spirit, a holy boldness for preaching the gospel, which is an indispensable endowment for Christian witnessing.

After Zinzendorf sent the first two Moravians on their way to the Caribbean, he pondered what instructions he should give to young missionaries. Later, when he had more experience in missions, he gave this simple but incredibly profound advice to messengers of the Good News: "Do not start with theological explanations of the existence of God. Heathens know by intuition and through nature that there is a God. Discuss creation and the fall of man later. Do not start preaching the need to exercise godly virtues, but preach about the God they know also has a Son. That He became the Lamb of God and that He poured out his blood to reconcile them to God. Do not hesitate to preach the crucified Christ. When they believe in the Son, in His crucifixion, and in His wounds and blood, then tell them that this Son, Jesus, has a loving Father. Virtues will develop in response to the love for Christ in them. Then they will soon find out that it is a joy to be thankful to their Savior through their obedience to Him. Live humbly among the heathens. Never lord over them. Work diligently with your hands for your own support."

As an example, we read in a letter from Surinam, "Brother Kamm is picking coffee. Brother Wenzel is mending shoes. Brother Schmidt is making a dress for a customer.

Zinzendorf continuous, "Live with them as peers in a *vita communis,* life-partnership, and in such a godly manner before them that they become curious and ask, 'Who is this God that makes such virtuous people?' Do not have great ambitions to convert whole nations, but look for hungry souls seeking after the truth as the Ethiopian eunuch did in Acts 8:31."

The wisdom of this approach was corroborated by the testimony of a Native American named Job, "Brothers, I was a heathen and I lived among heathens. I should know how it works to be converted. One clergyman came and wanted to prove to us the existence of God. We asked him, 'Do you think we don't know about that? Go home!' Another preacher came and told us, 'You should not steal and you should not drink and lie.' We said, 'You are a fool to think we don't know these things. Why don't you go back and tell that to your own people. We see them stealing, drinking, and lying.' Then another fellow came to my wigwam, Christian Heinrich Rauch. He sat down and told me something I hadn't heard, 'I come in the name of the Lord of heaven and earth. He wants to bring you to heaven and pull you out of your miserable, sinful condition. He became a man for this purpose; he gave his life for all mankind and shed his blood for you.'

"The man laid down in my hut, tired from his long journey. I thought to myself, 'Who is this young man who sleeps so peacefully without a worry? I could kill him and throw his body into the woods and nobody would know.' His words about the blood shed for me stayed with me. I thought, 'This is a different message,' and I told my people about it. This is how the revival started. That is why I tell you, brothers, preach Christ and His blood if you want to see God's blessings among heathens."

Perhaps one reason the Moravians and Bohemians so readily went out as missionaries was because they had already left their homes once before because of their faith. Being accustomed to uncertainty, they were detached from worldly possessions and were willing to put everything they had into the kingdom of God. For twenty years, they were unsure whether they could stay on Zinzendorf's land. Of course, he wanted them to stay, but the royal authorities in Dresden could chase them away at any time. They had the power to exile Zinzendorf from Saxony for ten years, which they eventually did. They could even confiscate his land. If someone was branded a heretic, their life, family, and land were in jeopardy. Zinzendorf was aware of this and subsequently, he transferred all his holdings over to his wife.

For example, the Schwenkfelders, another group of born again believers who were persecuted because of a charge Jesuits brought against them, came to Zinzendorf in 1726, and Zinzendorf allowed them to settle on a different part of his estate. However, by a royal decree from Dresden they were forced to leave a few years later, and 280 Schwenkfelders sailed to America. Today the Schwenkfelder church has five congregations with about 2,500 members in southeastern Pennsylvania. Their former Schwenkfelder meeting house in Berthelsdorf is being renovated as of 2010.

Their founder, aristocrat Caspar von Schwenkfeld (1489-1561), preached that regeneration is an inward, spiritual action by the life-giving power of the Holy Spirit. His favorite maxim was, "The knowledge of Christ is the utmost wisdom we need." Several outstanding theologians, such as the probable founder of the Quakers, Georg Fox, and the Pietist Friedrich Breckling agreed with Schwenkfeld in several points:

* God reveals himself to a human soul through the pursuit of the Holy Spirit.
* True inner light comes through the true [whispering] revelations of the Holy Spirit.

* Without the grace of God you cannot become a true servant of the gospel.
* All acceptable worship is in the heart and comes through the inspiration of the Holy Spirit.
* Regeneration does not come through external rituals and rites such as communion and baptism.

The Schwenkfelders were known as the serene people of the land. Tranquility, unruffled composure, and steadiness in all trials were their noticeable virtues. There are some differences between Luther and Schwenkfeld. Luther pressed home the finished work of Christ as the center of his sermons. Schwenkfeld focused on the indwelling of Christ in a person. Luther emphasized preaching, Bible reading, sacraments, and belonging to a church as the main means of sanctification. Schwenkfeld strongly advocated baptism with the Holy Spirit (he called it an inner *Verschmelzung*, a coalescence or an intermingling of the Spirit of God with the soul of man), and the result would be the fruit of the Holy Spirit exhibited in the person's life. Luther believed in parishes and large organized dioceses. Schwenkfeld stressed house churches and the communion of saints striving for holiness. Luther believed in organized, ordained clergymen. Schwenkfeld believed in the priesthood of all believers. Some theologians called Schwenkfeld's insights, the completion of the reformation.

Caspar von Schwenkfeld and his friend, Hans Magnus von Axleben, tried to convince the Bishop of Salza to reform the Catholic Church, but to no avail. Schwenkfeld was often misunderstood, and he endured exiles and persecutions. He did not become bitter and saw all tribulations as the suffering of saints who are closely united with Christ.

Whoever has Christ Jesus in his heart,
Is resting gently from morning to evening.
He is consoled in all his anguish,
Even though he may be lodged in dung,
And may become the scorn of the world,
He will not ever separate from his God
Who protects him from hell and death,
And feeds him from His 'Heaven's Bread'

(Poem of Caspar von Schwenkfeld).

14

Exile

Ambassadors of Christ,
Do you know your way?
It leads into the jaws of death,
It is sprinkled with thorns of affliction
(Hymn of Zinzendorf).

"My call from the Lord is to spread the word of the blood and cross of Jesus to the world. I am not concerned what happens to me as a result. This call was on my life before I knew the Moravian and Bohemian Brethren. I have been and will always be affiliated with the Brethren. In the meantime I will not restrict myself as a witness to one fraternity, for the whole wide world belongs to the Lord and all souls belong to Him. I have an obligation to all" (Zinzendorf).

As the Band of Brothers in Herrnhut became well-known throughout Germany, the evil one was working in the hearts of worldly people. Articles of slander were published against Zinzendorf. Aristocrats in Dresden's courts were staunchly against the idea of a Count devoting his life to renegade commoners. But a kindhearted new friend wrote to Ludwig, sharing his perspective, "I am satisfied that what you preach resembles the truth because I personally know you now and I have listened to you. But I must be honest; before I met you some of the things I heard were unbelievable and dubious. You'll have to forgive your enemies. While I have observed in Herrnhut many wonderful things about your life and community, if you were personally to tell others these things they would think you were boasting."

Zinzendorf was well aware of his weaknesses. He once wrote, "I know that I have an astute mind, and I have to watch that I do not fall into the temptation and fascination of extravagancies." A hymn he wrote reflected these thoughts:

Around the throne of the Lamb
With all the souls sings Abraham.
But the sordid history of each case
Shows they're sinners saved by grace.

Zinzendorf wrote many letters defending himself against the slander, but to no avail. Twice, commissioners came from Dresden to examine the unusual conditions at Herrnhut to come to some decision about censuring Zinzendorf. The ruling took so long that August the Strong died, and August II took the throne. The new Prince Elector was opposed to Zinzendorf, and once in power his decision was not long in coming. Zinzendorf was to be exiled from Herrnhut and Saxony. However, an official permit allowed the Moravians to remain as long as they adhered to Luther's catechism and the Augsburg Confession. Enemies hoped that Herrnhut would disintegrate under this harsh judgment. An official letter arrived from Dresden with a request that Zinzendorf sign a statement agreeing with all the allegations against him. He refused. He believed the indictments were untrue and frivolous. Zinzendorf steadfastly contended with forceful speeches and writings that he was not the founder of a new sect. He loved his Protestant faith and considered himself a true child of the Lutheran reformation. The exile was intended to be permanent, but the Lord had a different plan. After ten years, the banishment was lifted, and one of his fiercest opponents sought Zinzendorf's forgiveness. This was granted immediately, just another admirable example of Zinzendorf's generous heart.

There were other concerns as he went into exile. He loved upper Lusatia, the land of his youth. He loved his Band of Brothers. What brought him much pain was the thought that his life's work among the Moravians might come to an end. He had been instrumental in bringing peace and harmony to Herrnhut, and now he was branded as an outcast and outlaw, and called, *ein Schwärmer,* a sentimental dreamer.

> The godless famous German poet, Heinrich Heine, wrote mockingly about him, *"Ein süsslich vermuffter Betgraf."* A sweet musty smelling praying Count.
>
> Catherine Booth, co-founder of the Salvation Army, poignantly describes what often happens to a true saint who has a burning zeal for the Lord: "True saints are mighty, and their heat will make more impression on the hearts of sinners and stir more opposition from hell than all the intellect and learning of a whole generation of lukewarm professors. True saints ensure opposition from the Pharisees, the casual, weekend religious professors who are not true possessors. They look with contempt on true saints; call them fanatics, extreme, and troublers of the church, division makers, cultish, and occasions of reproach to the respectable part of the church. True saints are hated by the world because they look with contempt on its pleasure, set at naught its maxims and customs, trample on its ambitions, disregard its applause, ignore its rewards and live all together above its level. The world can tolerate a lukewarm religionist, who appreciates this world as well as the next and can see how to make the best of both, but these hot, mad fools, who are always at everybody about their souls, who are always talking about God, death, judgment, heaven, and hell — away with them!"

Zinzendorf was tested and walked through the dark valley of death, but he never lost his faith in God's providence. He wrote in his diary, "I will pray daily for my superiors and persecutors. They may think I want to die in my nest, but if I did it could become a hindrance in my life and a stumbling stone for what my Savior wants to do through me. It would make me a slave to my headstrong self-will. In the place where I can do the most for my Redeemer, I will consider that my homeland. I have to say goodbye to Herrnhut because I need to tell the world about the Son of God."

Everywhere he traveled there were those who considered him a heretic. It is humbling to read how he pleaded with people for an opportunity to defend himself as a true son of the Lutheran church. Zinzendorf must have felt like Paul when he wrote to the Corinthians, "We are pressed on every side by troubles, but we are not crushed. We are perplexed, but not driven to despair" (2 Corinthians 4:8). Reflecting about this time, Zinzendorf wrote later in his diary, "The hatred against us was in such a cruel way that they were determined to trample down and exterminate the United Brethren. They were looking for any nastiness, one way or another, to destroy their prized treasure of the 'Moravian Church Discipline and Foundation.' Even though their forefathers gave their lives for this cause to bring us true life which comes from Christ."

Zinzendorf also endured sharp criticism from some Pietists in Halle, where Zinzendorf attended the academy. They started a malicious rumor that Zinzendorf was not genuinely saved. [Covetous jealousy may have played a role]. Their reasoning was that they never detected in Zinzendorf's life a "dramatic break" from his past life. They pointed to the striking conversion of the Apostle Paul when he was on his horse to Damascus and was delivered from a Saul to a Paul. Zinzendorf defended himself and he wrote, "I am convinced that some people grow gradually deeper and deeper into the union with Christ as the Apostle John. These souls benefit from the upbringing and blessings of their pious and god-fearing parents who infused the grace of faith into their children from the earliest youth. I had such a blessing. Nevertheless, I went a hundred times through *Not, Flehen und Tränen,* anguish, beseeching, and tears about my sins. I would not even require that from any sinner. My heart always told me that my salvation is as secure as my existence. Of course, I knew the necessity of the atoning death of Jesus on the cross for my sins and the deep mystery of the word, ransom."

While exiled from the state of Saxony, he traveled to Stralsund in Sweden where two theology professors, Langemack and Sibeth, examined him for three days. Finally, they gave him a certificate stating that in all points of the Lutheran faith his teachings agreed with church doctrine.

Zinzendorf wrote, "I told them with my lips, in writing, and in five sermons what I believed and taught, both in theory and practice, including all the mistakes I ever had made, but they retained their favorable opinion of me."

Zinzendorf also asked for an opportunity to defend himself before the King of Prussia, Friedrich Wilhelm I. Surprisingly, the king granted his request. He met the king at his hunting castle, Wusterhausen. Field Marshall General Von Natzmer, Zinzendorf's step-father, warned him that the Prussian *Soldatenkönig,* soldier-king, was unpredictable and peculiar and the king had heard many false accusations about him. Zinzendorf realized that immediately as he was greeted by a court jester to accompany him to the king. Zinzendorf acted in his rank as a Princely Count and refused to go on the ground that he was not a fool. This daring disobedience must have made the king curious. He sent a court servant for an audience. Zinzendorf wrote in his diary, "I knew the king considered me a simpleton, and the reception was so appalling that I don't want to describe it to any person.

His intention was to get me to lose my composure, but that tactic did not work. Then he discredited my character and opinions. But that course of action did not work either. His inquiries were cold, abrupt and thorough. But soon he must have noted that I was not what he expected. The second day he was open, more trusting, and even granted me a third day. In the end he showed me genuine love and deep respect. At the conclusion of the third day we had the following conversation:

The king: 'My land is open to you and your congregation.'
I replied: 'Maybe as long as until somebody discredits me.'
The king: 'No human being can change my mind.'
I replied: 'No great lord might be able to promise that.'
The king: 'But I can.'
Zinzendorf finished later his entry, "And he kept his word."

The king admitted that he had been *belogen und betrogen*, lied to and deceived by malicious gossip. He declared before the queen and the entire royal court that the Count was a man of faithfulness and honesty. He could find no fault except for the unusual circumstance of the Count being an aristocrat who devoted his life to God. The king assured Zinzendorf of his trust and promised his help.

Zinzendorf humbly requested to be examined by theologians in Berlin for any evidence of aberrations in his teachings compared to Lutheran doctrine and convictions. The king immediately granted his request. He wrote a letter to the Deans and to the Bishop of the *Unitas Fratrum*, Jablonsky,

"I have seen and spoken with Count Zinzendorf myself, and found him to be an honest and intelligent man. His only intentions are to promote true and real religion and the doctrine of the Word of God. It is my will that you speak with him in Berlin. Please discuss those points which he has to propose with regard to examination of his orthodox and religious sentiment. I have given instruction regarding this matter to the two Deans of Berlin. If their testimony, as I hope, should prove favorable, you can ordain him at his desire. I myself have the opinion that the Count's profession of faith is worthy of all honor and degrades no one."

Your affectionate King,
Friedrich Wilhelm

Friedrich Wilhelm kept his word to be Zinzendorf's friend, and supported him throughout his life. The two maintained a lively correspondence, and Zinzendorf became the king's spiritual mentor. In his letters, the king often inquired about Ludwig's well-being. When the king received malicious letters about Zinzendorf, he forwarded them to Ludwig and asked him to write to the accuser and clear up any misconceptions. Sadly, the king's son, Friedrich the Great, did not keep up the communication or the friendship.

The ardent wish to become a clergyman remained in Ludwig's heart. "Take delight in the Lord, and He will give you your heart's desire" (Psalm 37:4). His desire was soon fulfilled. As a bishop, overseer, pastor, presbyter, doors would open for him to preach in any Protestant church. He could ordain missionaries for work in other parts of the world and conduct the ordinances given by Jesus, baptism and communion. (I use the word *ordinances* because the word *sacrament* is not in the Word of God. As a former Catholic, the word *sacrament* has a connotation of some mystical power).

The court in Denmark declined to assist him in becoming a clergyman, so Zinzendorf traveled to England. There he met the Archbishop of Canterbury, Professor John Potter, who agreed to help Zinzendorf. John Potter and Zinzendorf became good friends, and after examining Zinzendorf the Archbishop wrote, "The Brethren Church is an Apostolic and

Episcopal [governed by Bishops] church. The Herrnhuter Brethren are not a new sect but the renewal of the ancient church, and they adhere to all the Protestant Articles of Faith." John Potter and General Oglethorpe, Governor of Georgia, also helped Zinzendorf in that the British Parliament had exempted the Moravian Brethren from military service.

Some time before, General Oglethorpe became a friend of Zinzendorf. The General was in prison in London. He had been court-martialed for somehow failing to capture the Scottish rebels who were called Jacobites. Zinzendorf visited him in jail and Oglethorpe told him, "I have received so many drawings from the grace of God and I have been so many times disobedient to Him that I will not murmur if I get executed." Oglethorpe was completely exonerated and was reinstated in all his offices. He never forgot that Zinzendorf visited him in jail.

Nothing stood in the way of Zinzendorf's ordination. Zinzendorf received support from the professors in Berlin and Stralsund, and he had the backing from King Friedrich Wilhelm I in Berlin. He was also examined by the official theological faculty in Tübingen, and was given their approval. Zinzendorf and the Moravians were well known in Tübingen. Christian David, [the unwavering Moravian who cut the first tree in Herrnhut] had some bold debates with the scholarly theologians, Oetinger and Steinhofer.

This was Zinzendorf's last discourse before the examining professors: "I was but ten years old when I began to direct my companions to Jesus, as their Redeemer. My deficiency in knowledge was compensated by sincerity. Now I am thirty-four, and my mind has undergone no change. My zeal has not cooled. My conscience agrees with my internal call to the ministry. Yet, I am not a free thinker. I love and honor the established church, and shall frequently seek her counsels. I will continue to win souls for my precious Savior, to gather His sheep, welcome guests, and hire servants for

Him. I shall continue, if the Lord pleases, to devote myself to the service of that congregation whose servant I became in 1727. Agreeable to her [Lutheran church] orders and decrees, under her protection, enjoying her care, and influenced by her spirit, I shall go to distant nations, who are ignorant of Jesus and of the redemption in His blood. I shall strive to imitate the labors of my Brethren, who have the honor of being the first messengers to the heathens. I will verify all things by the only criterion of evangelical doctrine, the Holy Scriptures. Among the Brethren of Herrnhut and elsewhere I shall uphold their ancient church discipline. The love of Christ shall compel me, and His cross refreshes me. I will cheerfully be subject to the higher powers, and I will be a sincere friend to my enemies. I am imperfect and needy, yet the Lord is thinking about me, as He shall deliver the poor and destitute."

After hearing Zinzendorf's speech, the faculty was unanimous in giving him the title, "Minister of the Lutheran Church." This was their official statement, "We admit this is unprecedented. We are surprised that an elite Count of such a high rank and gallantry wants to become a minister of the Protestant church. It is contrary to the assumption of the world and to the aristocratic milieu for a person like him to endeavor to preach the Gospel and to build up the Church of Christ. The Count shows an unusual reverence and zeal for the Lord and he adheres to all the teachings of the Lutheran faith. Because of his position, we cannot deny the candidacy and we have no reservation to declare him qualified."

Zinzendorf was ordained as a Lutheran pastor. Now he enjoyed the "delight of his heart" and preached two anointed sermons, one in the main Tübinger Cathedral and another in the St. Thomas church. About his sermons, Zinzendorf wrote once, "My preparation is the wretchedness and poverty that I feel in the hour before the sermon. When I begin to preach I feel the coals from the altar, and I lose myself and

I hardly know where I am. The Spirit makes me sensitive to the varying moods of my hearers. They often shed tears, even hardened soldiers are among them, and I pray that my Savior may give permanence to their emotions."

For years, Zinzendorf's main theme was the pardon of every sin by the merits of the sacrificial Lamb of God and the power of the cross to lead a sanctified life. "For God's will was for us to be made holy by the sacrifice of the body of Jesus Christ once for all time" (Hebrews 10:10).

Some time later Bishop Jablonsky, the son-in-law of Comenius, the court preacher for the royal family in Berlin and the man who thanked Zinzendorf for protecting and reviving the *Unitas Fratrum,* was more than happy to also ordain Zinzendorf as a bishop of the United Brethren. The Brethren wove a victory banner with this inscription:

Vicit agnus noster, eum sequamur.
Our Lamb has conquered, let us follow Him.

Armed with these two ecclesiastical titles and the Prussian king's endorsement, Zinzendorf was now better able to defend himself against spiteful attacks. He insisted that his ordination and title were mainly for the Moravian and Bohemian Band of Brothers. His status was the same as any Lutheran clergymen. The congregation in Herrnhut was overjoyed by their leader's ordination. They realized the very important fact that Zinzendorf could now ordain Brethren. If they were ever evicted from Zinzendorf's land by a royal decree, they could pack up their few belongings and go to America like the Schwenkfelders, and the *Unitas Fratrum* would continue. Another important fact was also realized. Zinzendorf could now ordain as preachers some of the United Brethren who were willing to spend their lives as missionaries. Then they could baptize new believers. Brethren Nitschmann, Seidel, Zeissberger, Neisser, David, and Töltschig, all received ordination before they left on missionary journeys. By the year 1757, over 200 Brethren had gone out from Herrnhut as missionaries.

The Moravians' unshakable sense of belonging gave them strength. Their relationships went much deeper than a casual, "How are you?" A strong sense of community also played a key role in their ability to send out and wholeheartedly support young men and women on the mission field. Once a week, letters from overseas were read to the whole congregation. Missionaries knew that prayers were offered up for their safety and success.

The spirit of belonging to each other demonstrated by the United Brethren was a revelation to me and confirmed my own experience. When my wife and I were saved in 1978, we immediately felt an urge to join a church. I experienced what Paul wrote in Romans 8:15-16, "So you have not received a spirit that makes you fearful slaves. Instead, you received God's Spirit when he adopted you as his own children. Now we call him, 'Abba, Father.' For his Spirit joins with our spirit to affirm that we are God's children."

In the New Testament, those who accepted Jesus are referred to as the "holy ones," or "saints." Sixty-one times the word "hagioi" or "holy ones" is used, referring to all believers. The meaning is clear: God is holy, and because we belong to Him, we are holy. Holiness includes an overwhelming sense of belonging. In Christ Jesus, the wonderful reality of our new, holy identity compels us to progressively be transformed into His likeness. Jesus gives His holy ones the grace to live holy lives. "You must be holy because I, the Lord, am holy. I have set you apart from all other people to be my very own" (Leviticus 20:26).

To be His own is the very essence of what it means to be a disciple of Christ: "For we don't live for ourselves or die for ourselves. If we live, it's to honor the **Lord**. And if we die, it's to honor the **Lord**. So whether we live or die, we belong to the **Lord**. Christ died and rose again for this very purpose – to be **Lord** both of the living and of the dead" (Romans 14: 7-9). [Emphasis mine]

15

Moravians Overseas

"The Savior, our dear Evangelist and Teacher preached to the whole world. There is no man, no nation, no religion, and no worldly evil that can resist His fire. We are to carry the sparks into all the earth and many will catch them" (Zinzendorf).

Before setting out on their missionary journey, the two young Moravians, Leonard Dober and David Nitschmann, visited the Danish court. News of their arrival and the nature of their mission created a stir of curiosity and questioning. People discouraged the two young men from going to the Caribbean, predicting dire conditions, how they might die of malaria or be chased away by slave owners. The royal court was also curious about these young missionaries. Zinzendorf had been given Denmark's highest award the previous year, which no doubt paved the way for the good will and benevolence shown by King Christian VI. The royal family had pietistic leanings and even the king belonged to the Order of the Mustard Seed. Princess Charlotte Amelia gave the two missionaries money, the queen gave them encouragement, the pharmacist medicine, and the cupbearer arranged passage on a Dutch ship. When the ship left the harbor, both young men fell on their knees and prayed, "May the Lord that was slain receive the due reward of His suffering."

The two men were not ministers but lay missionaries, and the first ones to be sent by a congregation rather than a government organization. They lacked credentials but were filled with power from heaven (Luke 24:49). With the filling of the Holy Spirit come two primary activities: the gift of service and supernatural boldness in preaching with anointed words.

It might be interesting to read a chapter from a book written in 1777 by a German with the name of Christian Georg Andreas Oldendorp. It gives a rare insight into the early days of modern missions. The writer describes part of the overall picture. I will translate the chronicle in the same way as I read it in German at that time: "In Copenhagen, where they arrived on the 15th September, Frau Countesse von Stollberg in Wernigerode strengthened the Brethren in their intention and cheered them up for the Savior to dare, who is, as she said, worthy to meet death for. It was for the Brethren, since it came out of the mouth of this honorable Countesse, pleasant and encouraging, since, except from Count Zinzendorf, so far nobody spoke in this reassuring tone. Only discouragements were spoken to them. Nobody was getting a convincing light in their minds to help. That became a great difficulty to fight against. They introduced these obstacles: First, no ship would take them along, and then, if they would ever arrive there, they could not survive. Second, the possibility to the residing slaves to preach would be utterly doubtful. Third, about their intention themselves to become slaves, so to preach to this pitiful race of mankind, the 'Way to the Everlasting Life,' was for those who knew the condition of the Caribbean islands, the prevailing climate, and the oppressive labor of the slaves, a good reason not to constrain themselves of laughter. On the other hand they gave the Brethren for their faithful conviction to expand the 'Kingdom of Jesus Christ' deep respect. The chief servant, Von Pless, to them made it clear that their intentions, slaves to become, were *ganz und gar*, never

ever possible, since no *Blanker*, a white person, would ever be needed as a slave."

After sailing for ten weeks, the two Moravians arrived in St. Thomas. Lush green hills and palm trees greeted them. A man by the name of Lorenzen gave them lodging. David, the carpenter, quickly found work, but Leonard could not find suitable clay to make pottery. They located the sister and brother of Antonius and gave them his letter. The slaves were curious about these two missionaries, and soon a crowd gathered to hear them speak about God. There was no immediate sign of fruit in terms of slaves accepting Christ, but a big awakening was on the way.

> These Moravians knew the mandate from Romans 10:14-15. "But how can they call on him to save them unless they believe in him? And how can they believe in him if they have never heard about him? And how can they hear about him unless someone tells them? And how will anyone go and tell them without being sent? This is why the Scriptures say, 'How beautiful are the feet of messengers who bring good news!'"

After four months, David Nitschmann went back to Herrnhut, as previously planned, and gave a detailed account of their ventures. Soon, eighteen more Moravians, including women, arrived to work on the Caribbean islands such as St. Croix. A year later, eleven more missionaries sailed for the islands. Sadly, within a short time twenty died of yellow fever or malaria. Think about it. Twenty young people lost their lives from the small village of Herrnhut. Was the seed of these martyrs a waste? Read on about the ensuing revival and the end of bloody uprisings against plantation owners. Many years later, William Wilberforce used this as a trump card in his arguments before the British Parliament against the despicable slave trade. He described how slaves lived peacefully after their conversion. The opponents' contention that slaves were savages and freeing them would be disastrous was refuted.

There was no stopping these ambassadors of the Good News from telling others that Jesus died for their sins. By the end of the century, seventy years after that "glorious summer," over one thousand Moravians had gone into the world to places like Greenland, Newfoundland, South Africa, the Far East, Russia, and even to the Arab world.

John Wesley gives a glimpse into the soul of the Moravians. Encountering twenty-four Moravians during a storm on board the ship *Simmonds,* he wrote in his journal, "At seven I went to the Germans [Moravians]. I had long before observed the great seriousness of their behavior. Of their humility they had given a continual proof by serving other passengers, which none of the English would undertake. When they were offered pay for their servile tasks, they refused, replying, 'Their loving Savior had done more for them, and it was good for their proud hearts.' Every day had given them occasion of showing meekness. If they were pushed, struck, or thrown down, they rose again. They would not strike back or even take offense. They walked away, and no complaint was found in their mouth.

"Many perceived these German missionaries as cowards until a great storm broke over the ship. Now an opportunity arose to show that they were delivered from the spirit of fear. Their service began and in the midst of a Psalm, the wind started to roar and whistle. The ship began to rock violently to and fro. You could not stand without holding on. Some waves came as a great shock and you would think the planks would be broken in pieces. The mainsail mast broke in fragments, debris everywhere, terrible screaming among the English. The Moravians kept on calmly singing hymns. I asked them afterwards, 'You were not afraid?' and they answered, 'Thank God, no, we are not afraid to die.'

"Then I went to their crying neighbors, and I pointed out to them the difference in the hour of trial, between him that feareth God, and him that feareth not. At twelve the wind fell. This was the most glorious day which I have hitherto seen."

While Wesley was in Georgia, he had a conversation with Zinzendorf's close friend, August Gottlieb Spangenberg. August inquired of Wesley, "My brother, I must first ask you one or two questions. Do you have the Spirit of God witnessing in you that you are a child of God? Do you know Jesus Christ?"

"I do," replied Wesley, "He is the Savior of the world." Spangenberg persisted, "Do you know He saved you?"

Wesley wrote in his journal, "I fear my reply was vain and trifling."

Some time later, Wesley attended a Moravian Bible study held in London. In his diary of Wednesday, May 24, 1738, he wrote, "In the evening I went unwillingly to a Moravian society in Aldersgate Street, where one was reading Luther's preface of the Epistle to the Romans. About a quarter before nine, while he was describing the change which God works in the heart through faith in Christ, I felt my heart strangely warmed. I felt I did trust in Christ, Christ alone for salvation. An assurance was given to me, that He had taken away my sins, even mine, and saved me from the law of sin and death."

Four days before his conversion, Wesley received a letter from the Moravian Bishop Böhler. Wesley wrote, "I was sorrowful and very heavy in my spirit when I received a letter from Peter Böhler which refreshed me. Böhler wrote, 'I love you greatly and think much of you in my journey, wishing and praying that the tender mercies of Jesus Christ the Crucified, whose bowels were moved toward you, may be manifested to your soul. That you may taste and then see, how exceedingly the Son of God has loved you, and loves you still; and that you may continually trust in Him, and feel His life in yourself. Beware of the sin of unbelief; and if you have not conquered it yet, see that you conquer it this very day, through the blood of Jesus Christ. Delay not; I beseech you, to believe in Jesus Christ. But so put Him in your mind of His promises to poor sinners that He may not be able to refrain from doing for you, what He has done for so many others. O how great, how inexpressible, how unexhausted is His love! Surely He is now ready to help, and nothing can offend Him but unbelief. The Lord bless you! Abide in faith, love, the teachings, the communion of saints, and in all which we have in the New Testament. I am your unworthy Brother," Peter Böhler.

Peter Böhler (1712-1775) studied law in Jena, Switzerland. He had a profound conversion when he met young Moravians on campus. He studied theology and spoke seven languages. He worked many years in England to prepare missionaries to sail to Georgia. Between February and May 1738, he was in constant communion with the Wesley. He was the first Moravian Zinzendorf ordained as a bishop. He worked for several years together with the famous evangelist, George Whitfield, in Pennsylvania. When Zinzendorf visited America for a full year, Böhler assisted him in his work for several months in Bethlehem.

After his conversion, Wesley was curious about Herrnhut and eager to know how the Band of Brothers lived as a community. He traveled there with friends in 1738 and was astonished at the Moravian lifestyle. In a letter, he told his brother Charles, "The spirit of the Brethren is above our highest expectations, young and old; they breathe nothing but faith and love at all times and in all places. This is a happy place; I would gladly have spent my life here. O, when shall this Christianity cover the earth, as the waters cover the sea? I was constrained to take my leave of this happy place, but my master is calling me to labor in another part of his vineyard."

In the third century, St. Cyprian wrote to a friend named Donatus, "This seems a cheerful world, Donatus, when I view it from this fair garden. But if I climbed some great mountain and looked out, you know very well what I would see; brigands on the high road, pirates on the seas, in the amphitheaters men murdered to please the applauding crowds. Yet in the midst of it I have found a quiet and holy people. They are despised and persecuted, but they care not. They have overcome the world. These people, Donatus, are called Christians."

At a 1739 New Year's Eve all-night prayer meeting on Fetter Lane, John Wesley, his brother Charles, evangelist George Whitefield, and some Methodist brothers joined sixty Moravians. Wesley wrote in his diary, "At about three in the morning, as we were continuing instant in prayer, the power of God came mightily upon us, inasmuch that many cried out for exceeding joy, and many fell to the ground. As soon as we recovered a little bit from that awe and amazement at the presence of His Majesty, we broke out with one voice, 'We praise Thee, O God, we acknowledge Thee to be the Lord!'"

Scripture says, "You will show me the way of life, granting me the joy of your presence and the pleasures of living with you forever" (Psalm 16:11).

16

Zinzendorf's Work in Exile

"The truthfulness of Scripture can be validated by everyone who applies its maxims to his life. The Word and reader should come so close together, that the reader himself becomes a living Bible. In their lives you should be able to validate the truthfulness of what is written in the Gospel. In the congregation of the living God everybody is continually joyful as a disciple of Jesus Christ. It is the 'breathing' proof that there are many living 'Handbooks of God.' Where there is a true congregation of Jesus Christ, it cannot be otherwise, that every verse of the Bible becomes alive again and again for them. It manifests in their hearts ever new again, as it was written 1700 years ago. You don't need irrefutable proofs of the veracity of Scripture, you feel it in your own soul, it is so" (Zinzendorf).

The book printed in 1900 describes extensively Zinzendorf's journeys and sermons while he was exiled from Saxony. Some stories are almost unbelievable. In 1738, while he was in Berlin, Zinzendorf preached over sixty sermons in five months. One evening, forty-two horse-drawn carriages were parked in front of his apartment. Clergymen in Berlin had unanimously forbidden Zinzendorf to preach in their churches. Could jealousy be the reason, or did the chaplains think he was not properly trained as a bishop? Paul wrote, "Let us not become conceited, or provoke one another or be jealous of one another" (Gal 5:26).

Michael Langmuth faithfully recorded Zinzendorf's sermons. He did this directly after each sermon, while it was still fresh in his mind. Later, they were printed, far and wide in demand, and even translated into English. Michael Langmuth was adopted by Zinzendorf's friend, Friedrich von Watteville. His new name was Johannes von Watteville, and he married Zinzendorf's daughter, Henriette Justine Benigna. Zinzendorf suggested the match.

There was such a great revival in Berlin that commoners and aristocrats begged Zinzendorf to stay and establish a community. He encouraged them to attend private Bible studies and to stay in their respective parishes. A few years later, a *Unitas Fratrum* was started in Berlin, as many had moved there from Bohemia.

While living in exile, Zinzendorf also moved to Amsterdam. His wife, Erdmuthe Dorothea and his daughter, Henriette Benigna and twelve Moravians accompanied him. Zinzendorf rented a house big enough for the entourage. He was well liked in Holland. A Dutch scholar, Isaak Le Long, wrote a well-received book about Herrnhut and the Moravians with the title, "God's Miraculous Church." Zinzendorf was an attraction. Visitors from far away came to see him. Heathens came to be saved, and saints came to be encouraged and sanctified by the Word. "Make them holy by Your truth; teach them Your word, which is truth" (John 17:17). Commoners and aristocrats came to join in hymn singing, participate in Bible studies, and to hear Zinzendorf preach about his favorite subjects, the Lamb of God and the cross. He knew much of Scripture by heart and shared Paul's decision in 1 Corinthians 2:2: "For I decided that while I was with you I would forget everything except Jesus Christ, the one who was crucified." Because of this single-minded perspective in his preaching, he was often accused of being a simpleton, but he did not change his focus.

Zinzendorf wrote at this time, "I was determined to preach more and more concerning the atoning sacrifice of Jesus. Before this I tried very often to use apologetics to explain the life of Christ to skeptics. But after some wrestling, I found peace, and I resolved to preach about the mystery and the depth of the atonement and about the cost the crucified Jesus paid to ransom us. Since 1734, the teaching of *Erlösung,* redemption of a sinner, and the *Versöhnung,* reconciliation of a sinner to God the Father through his Son, the Lamb of God, was my main theme. This theme helped a great deal against all evil and false teachings and cleansed sinful lives. Even when my mockers accused me of not knowing anything else, I lifted up the wounds of Jesus again and again. I told them if I would again let this teaching go so as not to offend the wise people of this world, they would not be worthy anyway to comprehend the secrets of the cross of Christ and all the grace radiating from it."

Paul wrote, "The message of the cross is foolish to those who are headed for destruction! But we who are being saved know it is the very power of God. As the Scripture say, 'I will destroy the wisdom of the wise and discard the intelligence of the intelligent'" (1 Corinthians 1:18, 19).

Zinzendorf also spent time in Frankfurt, where Philip Jacob Spener had previously lived and had done marvelous work. (He was the man who laid hands on Ludwig when he was four years old with a prayer that God would use him to further the kingdom of God.) But some sheep in Frankfurt had no shepherd, and they became embroiled in wrong theology. Once again, Zinzendorf preached from his heart, "Listen now, my dear hearts, you have to believe three things as your foundation. First, you do not have one spark of goodness in you to mix with grace. The most honest and pious citizen in Frankfurt cannot save himself more than a street robber who is put upon the torture wheel. Second, do not give yourself a false consolation that you do not need to do anything for God. In this matter you should remember that God is a taskmaster, and a childlike fear will not harm you. Third, you will never become joyful until you tell lost sinners how to be saved. In doing that we demonstrate the love we should have for our wayward brothers."

As his popularity spread, the opposition became venomous. As he was leaving Frankfurt in his coach, the mob threw stones at him. Zinzendorf sang his own hymn,

"My calling is to imitate Christ, as He endured the treatment of disgrace, through crushing from the outside, and through breaking in the inside, I will win the empty spaces [hearts] which have gates, but Jesus broke."

For a time Zinzendorf lived with his family in the dilapidated Castle Ronneburg. Christian David warned him he could not possibly live there. His daughter said, "It was a residence only fit for owls and bats." Nevertheless, Zinzendorf started working among fifty families of Jews, gypsies, and riffraff. He felt he could save some. On the first Sunday, he preached about the Lost Sheep. Soon he had prayer meetings, sing-alongs, and Bible studies. His young son played with the poor children, and his daughter, Henriette Benigna, ate with the girls who lived in the Ronneburger castle. The Count forbade the peasants from begging food in the village; instead, he fed them and gave them clothes. The newspapers had a heyday. They accused Zinzendorf of exposing his family to riffraff.

One very interesting event occurred at this castle. Zinzendorf met Rabbi Abraham, who confided to Ludwig, "My heart longs for the dawn, I am sick with longing, and I don't know why. I am seeking for something. It feels I am chased, yet, I don't see an enemy except the one within me, my old evil heart." Zinzendorf shared the gospel and told the Rabbi about Jeshua. On the hill nearby was a small church with a cross. Ludwig pointed to the cross and told him that at the cross there was blood shed for all of us. He urged Abraham to find his salvation in Christ. The Rabbi responded, "So be it, blessed be the Lord who has mercy on me," and for the first time, he prayed in Jeshua's name. *Baruch Hashem Adonai.* Blessed be the name of the Lord.

This feeling about Christ is common among God's chosen nation, the Jewish people. Ben Gurion was a statesman in 1948 when Israel was recognized as a nation. He once wrote in his diary, "That man [Jesus] pursued me all my life." We don't know whether he became a Christian. The late mayor of Jerusalem, Teddy Kollek, said once, "When the Messiah comes we will ask, 'Sir, is this your first time here or your second?'"

Zinzendorf once wrote a letter to a Jewish community. He closed the letter with these words: "You have to change your attitude and point of view. You have to forsake your self-righteousness. You have to believe that you are lost sinners. You need somebody who has pity on you. Because of the slaughtered Lamb, I love you exceedingly in my inner being. With tears of joy and tears of love I want to tell you about the One which I cannot live without. With this One I would rather be in hell than without Him in heaven. I am certain you know which One I mean."

After a few months at Ronneburg, Zinzendorf and his family moved back to Frankfurt. He traveled to England in 1737 to negotiate with the government about establishing missions in America and obtaining real estate grants. In London, he was busy again, preaching among Methodists, Quakers, Protestants, and members of the Anglican Church. His lifelong desire was to reconcile denominations and to teach misguided souls how to become true disciples of Christ. He was more than willing to listen to heretics as well, and he admonished them with fatherly love. Zinzendorf had a spiritual clarity on how to maintain unity and harmony among the different cell groups and communities.

By now there were seven communities like Herrnhut in Germany. There were also such communities in other countries and hundreds of cell groups. He knew that people joined from different backgrounds and upbringings. Through Zinzendorf's anointed preaching, the sheep learned how to have a *Herzensreligion*, a personal relationship with their Lord and Savior. But Zinzendorf allowed for total freedom in regard to the mode of worship. They could keep their customs, style of worship, and all non-essentials. He called this perspective the *tropus* principle from the Greek *tropoi paideias*, meaning method or background of training. He realized that the *tropus* of Lutherans, Reformed, Pietists, or Moravian United Brethren make a unique contribution to Christianity. This was a trail-blazing, visionary concept, far ahead of the existing attitude of most denominations. It had the potential to heal all the harmful divisions within the church.

It is noteworthy that Zinzendorf tried for years to establish a *tropus* of Messianic or saved Jews in Holland and even Herrnhut, but to his great dismay only a small number of Jews converted.

During the ten years of exile from his beloved Saxony, Zinzendorf traveled tirelessly. He preached and taught what he called "heart religion," and many cell groups of born again Brethren were established.

Members of the cell groups that Zinzendorf organized understood that a personal and intimate knowledge of Jesus Christ as Savior and Friend was the only way to heaven. External declarations, affiliation with a denomination, or observances of religious rituals would not save anyone. Zinzendorf believed that everywhere an invisible body of believers is scattered among visible denominations. This conviction gave him impetus to preach among all visible, organized denominations, seeking the invisible *Unitas Fratrum*. Zinzendorf believed the essence of being a follower of Jesus is to stay in the will of the Father, "This is my dearly loved Son, who brings me great joy. Listen to him" (Matthew 17:5).

Zinzendorf visited Holland, England, the Caribbean, America, Silesia, Switzerland, the Baltic States, and a dozen other areas. He traveled in heavy coaches or in the faster mail carriages. As was his custom, he often got out of the coach to walk and pray. In one incident, a coachman heard him talking intimately with Jesus. The man became convicted and gave his heart to the Lord. We also find a note in his diary about his excursions: "For days I could talk to my Savior without interruptions on my lonesome, long journey on foot." He also never traveled without the New Testament.

Prayer sustained this pious giant. For days he pulled out of the limelight to pray in seclusion. Through prayer he matured to such an intimacy and familiarity with his Savior that he could foretell when a storm at sea would stop. He said that Jesus always told him the reason for every illness he had except for the last one that called him home. In his travels he was frequently protected in supernatural ways. One time in Amsterdam, he slept in the same room with his friend David Nitschmann. In the middle of the night, he felt as if someone was shaking his arm. He jumped up and saw that the nightstand, his clothes, and the bedcovers were smoldering. He doused the area, and in the morning he saw how close he had come to dying in his sleep.

Another time he stayed overnight in a castle of a Count Gersdorf. At midnight, as he was praying on his knees, he felt an urge to leave immediately and continue his trip. Shortly after he left, the ceiling in the room where he would have been sleeping came crashing down.

One evening, he knocked at a farmer's door, asking for bread and water. Sneering laughter was the answer as the farmer slammed the door shut. In his diary he wrote, "I did not feel any resentment against the *Bäuerlein*, simple farmer, as it was dark and my attire was dirty."

In the city of Halle, he was completely penniless, and he had no travel fare left. He asked a farmer for a horse, a carriage, and some money, and his request was granted. Soon after, one of his servants brought back the horse, carriage, as well as the borrowed twelve *Gulden*, and the interest of six *Kreuzer*, plus a friendly note, "Now, I wish nothing more to my companion in life, that my good Savior will fill your heart with His love." Zinzendorf was extraordinarily generous, and because he could never turn down a beggar, he rarely ever had money in his pocket.

Zinzendorf was never embarrassed or self-conscious in talking about his Savior. He once wrote, "Carriages are a good mission field. I always ask fellow passengers, 'Would you like to hear about the grace given to me?'"

In Marienborn, located in central Germany, he saw a little girl standing by a creek holding a suitcase. She was unable to get across the water. The Count helped the girl to jump over the creek and together they traveled on. Zinzendorf walked a few steps behind the small traveler, and with tears prayed for her out loud. A year later he brought this child to his wife, and she became a dear servant. His prayer and tears for the soul of this little girl paid off. She was the lovely fruit of Zinzendorf's supplication.

One more incident reveals Zinzendorf's character. When he traveled back from the West Indies, a poor Jew, Nunnez Dacosta, asked with tears in his eyes for Zinzendorf to pay for his boat ticket. Zinzendorf had already paid the fare for a Dane and a Negro. He had also paid for the slave's freedom. He was easily persuaded to pay for Nunnez and his wife. Because the living quarters were all occupied, Zinzendorf gave up his private room for the Dacostas. He shared a cabin with a fellow traveler, even though he was weak and had ulcers on his body. He wrote to his wife, Erdmuthe, "In my heart, I was full of joy." In Romans 8:29, Paul writes that God knew His people in advance and He chose them to become like His Son. Zinzendorf's life exhibited God's power and grace to work in a believer to become progressively sanctified.

Despite their leader's absence, the congregation in Herrnhut flourished. After all, Herrnhut means, "under the Lord's watch." The Moravians and Bohemians became well known all over Germany and beyond. *Die Herrnhuter,* or people of Herrnhut, became a household word. Many wanted to know, "What happened in 1727?" Letters arrived from God-seeking people, requesting Moravian emissaries to come and teach them how to have revival and how to establish cell groups. These curious seekers were also interested in the community's disciplines and daily living practices.

The Moravians had *wanderlust* in their hearts and were more than happy to fulfill these requests. They shared with all the God-seekers about the short history of Herrnhut, how the "hidden seed" had germinated, and what the Lord had done for them. They took their message to the royal court in Denmark, German universities, and to the Baltic Sea area. The English were also curious about the harbingers of the Moravian Pentecost. Two Brethren traveled from Herrnhut to England and returned with a letter from the English royal court. A German-born lady, a chief cabinet administrator of the high British royal court, Countess Schaumburg-Lippe, gave the Brethren a letter that read, "We assure you that those burning coals have had their desired effect."

These simple craftsmen stirred others with profound words about the Holy Spirit's power to change lives. They were instrumental in spreading the fire of Pentecost. A few Brethren were treated roughly, and Zinzendorf cautioned them not to preach sermons in churches, since they were not ordained clergymen.

People from all over Germany and Europe also visited Herrnhut. Many visitors stayed at the guest house there. They left Herrnhut with a fiery spark in their hearts, and most started cell groups for Bible study, fellowship, and prayer.

The number of communities connected to the Moravian movement grew phenomenally, considering the small size of the itinerant wandering Band of Brothers. By 1748, there were 540 large cell groups. In the Baltic Sea area alone, an estimated 45,000 people were connected to these circles.

Groups were formed by the Moravian missionaries in Ireland, Holland, Sweden, Denmark, South France, Switzerland, and also in England, where there were twenty congregations. Two communities like Herrnhut were established in Lusatia (Nisky and Klein-Welke), three were founded in Silesia (Gnadenberg, Gnadenfrei and Neusalz), and five set up in other parts of Germany (Ebersdorf, Neudietendorf, Neuwied, Pilgerruh and Marienborn). Cell groups were also brought into existence as far away as Russia, East India, Surinam, Guinea, Algiers and South Africa. Paul and Silas were accused of turning the world upside down in Acts 17:6. The Moravians were doing the same.

Zinzendorf's antagonists continued to brand him as the founder of a sect. That is why he encouraged the revived or born again believers to stay in established, recognized churches in their own regions. As today, in almost every denomination, there are movers and shakers who are Spirit-filled Christians. The filling of the Holy Spirit imparts power to serve and witness as the Apostles did on the day of Pentecost. Despite all the criticism, Zinzendorf loved his Lutheran church and saw no need for a radical, new denomination. He was happy to revive the ancient *Unitas Fratrum* that began in 1415 with Jan Hus's spiritual descendants. He also understood Paul's question, "Can Christ be divided into factions?" (1 Corinthians 1:13).

17

Missionary Journeys

"The pressure to become *gleichgesinnt*, like-minded in every form of devotion or liturgy with threats of ostracizing sheep is, at best, foolish. Human pressure will only bring human counter-pressure. The unity of children is already manifested when we all believe in the reconciliation of us all to God through the death Christ suffered on the cross" (Zinzendorf).

Opponents criticized the Count, saying that he sent young missionaries overseas, sometimes to their death, while he lived in comfort at home. It distressed him to hear that plantation owners in the Caribbean gave the missionaries a hard time. After much prayer, he decided to visit the Moravians in St. Thomas and St. Croix. Before the voyage, he became sick and wrote in his diary, "I talked to my Savior and told Him it would not be convenient to be sick on the ship, so He healed me before we sailed."

After waiting for some violent storms to end, the boat left Holland with Zinzendorf and three Moravians, including a husband and wife team. As they approached the Caribbean Islands, Zinzendorf asked his traveling companion, Valentin Lohans, "What happens when we don't find anybody there?"

Lohans replied, "The Lord would not let that happen."

Then Georg Weber piped in, "Well, but we are here anyway."

"What a stout-hearted race are the Moravians!" Zinzendorf said.

After their landing, a black slave informed Zinzendorf that the missionaries had been in jail for over three months. Zinzendorf was incredulous and asked, "What is happening to the slaves?"

"Well," he answered, "they grow in doing good and a big revival is among us. You see, Mister Martin is preaching nightly through the prison bars and large crowds gather every night to hear him."

Ludwig wrote to his wife, "I stormed into the governor's office like a lightning." The governor was caught off guard, and he released the Moravians within twenty-four hours.

When the governor brought the released Brethren, Friedrich Martin, Matthias Freundlich, and his wife, Rebecca, Zinzendorf bowed down before them and openly kissed the Brethren and Rebecca in the presence of the bureaucrat, showing his esteem for the Moravians who suffered for Christ.

The reason for their imprisonment was as follows: Matthias Freundlich dared to marry a mulatto, Rebecca. She was a former slave-girl and one of the first converts. The wedding was considered a scandal by the plantation owners. Friederich Martin married the couple. A Dutch pastor, Borm, discovered that the signature of the King of Denmark was missing on Friederich's ordination papers. Consequently, the pastor declared that the couple was living out of wedlock. The Danish law decreed for such an offense lifelong forced labor, and for the time being they had been thrown into jail. Paul had a similar problem and humbly wrote ..."I have faced danger from men who claimed to be believers but are not" (2 Corinthians 11:26).

Friedrich Martin had replaced the first missionary, Leonard Dober, as agreed. Friedrich would walk in his spare time [during the day Moravians missionaries toiled with their hands for their own support] through towns and plantations and made individual contacts with every black slave. Moved by his personal interest and care, 700 slaves had been converted in the first year to faith in Christ. They would meet in a church building, on a plantation property, bought with Moravian funds. When Martin died in 1750 in St. Croix, he was forty-six years old. Shortly after his death, the Moravian church reported that 1,600 slaves had been baptized and 3,600 souls were under the care of the mission.

On Saturday nights, the slaves came together from fifty different plantations. They spent most of the night singing, praying, and listening to Zinzendorf's preaching. For a while the freed Moravians were too weak to participate. Some slave owners tried to prevent the slaves from attending these meetings, and some poor souls endured beatings and curses. But the harsh treatment could not prevent them from listening to the sweet Gospel. We find an entry in Zinzendorf's diary, "The many tears they shed in their meetings, the faithfulness they show despite their oppressive misery, the steadfast devotion of the apostolic workers out of their midst, causes me to love and treasure them very much."

Soon, Ludwig received permission from the governor to allow the ordained Moravian, Friedrich Martin, to baptize slaves. After three weeks, Zinzendorf visited two more islands, St. John and Santa Cruz. He also paid his respects at the graves of Moravians who had given their young lives as a seed to expand God's kingdom.

After six months in the Caribbean, Ludwig sailed home. Sundays on the boat he preached to the sailors and wayfarers. When two sailors pulled knives in a fight, he jumped between them, took their weapons and placed them under his pillow until the voyage was over. To pass the time on board, he indulged in his hobby of writing hymns and sermons. Many of his devotional songs are in the Moravian *Book of Worship*. Hymn number 279 was composed as he sailed back:

My Savior's blood and righteousness
That beauty is my glorious dress.
Thus well arrayed, I need not fear
When in His presence I appear.
His incarnation, wounds, and death
I will declare while I have breath;
Until I see Him face to face,
Adorned with His holiness.

Zinzendorf returned home very sick. He wrote to his friend, King Friedrich Wilhelm, who was always interested in Zinzendorf's undertaking, "I have been gravely ill. I had high hopes the Lord would call me home to be with Him and deliver me from my labors. But at the present I feel better and my hopes have disappeared." When he returned, he gave thrilling reports about his visit. He said, "St. Thomas is a bigger miracle than Herrnhut." The Brethren listened attentively, but they were appalled by his malaria-ravished countenance and ulcer-covered body.

Meanwhile, members of the *Unitas Fratrum* sailed all over the world as missionaries to North and South America, India, Egypt, and Ethiopia. Many never came back. There is a memorial on God's acre in Herrnhut for a Bohemian who died on the way to Africa when the ship capsized in a violent storm.

Zinzendorf had a deep love for the Jewish people and frequently reminded his congregation to pray for God's chosen people. He composed a beautiful poem for them. Here is a prose translation: (I can't make German poems rhyme).

"When, my admired Jew, will your hour come?
When will your people see the wounds of Christ?
Is it not time to save yourself with His blood?
Which your forefathers caused to flow
When you braided a crown?
How I wish your chosen hour would come
And the scales would be taken from your eyes!
Then we would all see you
You—who are our firstborn brothers,
In our beloved Father's house.
What a hallelujah would that be,
An anthem to the Lamb throughout eternity!"

Zinzendorf sent a Messiah-believing Jewish brother, Samuel Lieberkühn, to the Jewish community in Amsterdam. Samuel lamented once that the time for the ancient people to become cognizant of their Messiah may not have arrived. However, one Jewish lady, Esther Grünbeck, was gloriously saved. The Jews respected Lieberkühn and called him Rabbi Samuel. He also worked among the Jews in Zeist. Large Jewish crowds came to hear him. They loved Samuel and were drawn to him by his affection for God's chosen people. Zinzendorf wrote once, "The more you fall in love with the crucified Savior the more tenderly you love the Jews." It was always his deep desire to bring the Jews to their crucified Savior.

In 1741, Zinzendorf sailed to the Americas with several purposes in mind. He wanted to work among the Indians and visit some Moravian Brethren who settled in Pennsylvania. Some sixty years earlier, the British Quaker, William Penn, bought large areas of forest land southwest of New York. He established the city of *Philadelphia,* brotherly love, and called the area *Pennsylvania,* Penn's forest land. He gave them a constitution guaranteeing them freedom of religion. Many other denominations, splinter groups and sects settled in this Land of Promise. The Schwenkfelders, who had been forced from Zinzendorf's land, were also living in Pennsylvania. Ludwig's lovely sixteen-year-old daughter, Countesse Henriette Benigna Justine, accompanied him. (Ancient names in German sound nice).

The travelers landed in New York and journeyed on to Philadelphia. Near the Delaware River, Zinzendorf found the group of the astonished Moravian Brethren from Herrnhut. The *Wiedersehen*, reunion, was heartwarming and jubilant. Bishop David Nitschmann [he was among the first five settlers in Herrnhut from Bohemia], Anna Nitschmann (nineteen years later she would become Zinzendorf's second wife), and her father were among the rejoicing group. It was the 24th of December, 1741 and they celebrated Christmas Eve together in a log cabin. They fittingly named the place Bethlehem, which today is the steel city in Pennsylvania. Zinzendorf fervently preached from the Word and it was a memorable celebration. For this event, Zinzendorf also composed the hymn; "Never Was A Night So Blissful."

Ponder this. In a city-park in Bethlehem is a metal statue of a man dedicated to the Moravian iron workers. Two hundred years later, "Bethlehem Steel" had a major part in the war effort to defeat the evil, sinister regime of Nazi Germany. In the beginning of Deuteronomy, the Lord promised many future blessings to those who **obey** Him. "The Lord will conquer your enemies when they attack you. They will attack you from one direction, but they will scatter from you in **seven.** Then all the nations of the world will see that you are a people **claimed** by the Lord, and they will stand in **awe** of you" (Deuteronomy 28:7, 10). [Emphasis mine.] God was on our side in the Second World War to help us scatter the enemy in **seven** directions. Out of Russia, Japan, Italy, France, Holland, Norway and Germany. The Bible says, "I watch over my Word and it will perform."

Was this nation **claimed** by the Lord? On November 11, 1620, (156 years before the Declaration of Independence) forty-one male adults signed a document on the Mayflower before they stepped ashore, to ensure order. The document is called the Mayflower Compact. Here are a few quotations. The very first sentence is, "In ye name of God Amen. We whose names are underwritten ...by ye grace of God ... for ye glory of God, and advancement of ye Christian faith."

Almost three centuries later, it was confirmed again that this nation is a Christian nation. In the U.S. Supreme Court decision in 1892, titled Holy Trinity vs. U.S. we read, "It is the opinion of the court after so many examples of Christianity's indelible imprint on the soul of America, adding a volume of unofficial declarations to the mass of organic utterances that this is a Christian nation."

Generally speaking, this nation always obeyed God and acknowledged His Son as our Savior. We honor God in public prayers, in our constitution, and even on our money. "What joy for the nation whose God is the Lord, whose people He has chosen as his inheritance" (Psalm 33:12).

General George S. Patton sent a letter on December 14th, 1944, to all the chaplains of the 3rd Army, underscoring **prayer.** Here are some excerpts, "Our glorious march from the Normandy Beach across France to where we stand, before and beyond the Siegfried Line, with the wreckage of the German Army behind us, should convince the most skeptical soldier that God has ridden with our banner. Pestilence and famine has not touched us. But we must urge, instruct, and indoctrinate every fighting man to **pray** as well as fight. Urge all of your men to **pray**, not alone in church, but everywhere. **Pray** when driving. **Pray** when fighting. **Pray** alone. **Pray** with others. **Pray** by night and **pray** by day. We must march together, **all out for God.** Now is not the time to follow God from 'afar off.' This Army needs the assurance and faith that God is with us. With **prayer** we cannot fail." [Emphasis mine.]

Are the nations still standing in **awe** of us? I believe so. We have privately spent more money than any other nation to help alleviate poverty and misery in this world. We hardly hear about our record giving to the Tsunami survivors. We are number one in sending out and supporting missionaries, also in printing and distributing the Word of God.

Even our language is loved and used all over the world, and millions are learning our language to communicate with other nations. Young students in Germany learn English, and speaking it is a sign of higher education. When my school friend, Klaus, and his wife, Elisabeth, visited us a few years ago, she said, "In our generation many still say I wish I could visit America at least once in my lifetime."

Will you pray with me the prayer in Joel 2:12-13, that God will not take His blessings away from us? "

"That is why the Lord says, 'Turn to me now, while there is time. Give me your hearts. Come with fasting, weeping, and mourning. Don't tear your clothing in your grief, but tear your hearts instead.' Return to the Lord your God, for He is merciful and compassionate, slow to get angry and filled with unfailing love. He is eager to relent and not punish." (For our sins of abortions, homosexuality, and apathy).

At that time, around 120,000 Germans lived in Pennsylvania, mostly farmers scattered all over the state. There were Lutherans, Reformed, and Quakers, and some who belonged to splinter groups such as Dunkers, New Lights, Inspired, and Schwenkfelders. The condition of the Lutheran church was deplorable. There were no Lutheran ministers, and many lived godless lives. There was a saying at that time about people with no church affiliation, "They have the Pennsylvania Religion." Many written requests had been made by the Lutherans to congregations in Germany, requesting a pastor, but to no avail.

Zinzendorf was happy to help. In a barn in Philadelphia, he preached anointed sermons. On Palm Sunday, the listeners were so deeply moved that they asked him to celebrate Holy Communion with them. They established a congregation and asked Zinzendorf to be their pastor. He accepted, but told them it would not be permanent. Later, he appointed a godly man, Johannes Christoph Pyrläus, who would lead them when he was absent.

Zinzendorf also had a heart for all the different sects and splinter groups. A letter was sent out all over Pennsylvania to have a conference at a place called Germantown, near Philadelphia. Some traveled great distances. Many had left Germany to break away from organized state religion. Most attendees distrusted Zinzendorf until he started preaching. When they observed his sincerity, his godly wisdom, and his profound knowledge of the Word, their misgivings eased. At the second meeting they already asked him to be their chairman. For seven months, they came together each month for three days to listen to Zinzendorf's anointed preaching. Zinzendorf's unifying theme was: Jesus is the Creator, Sustainer, Redeemer and Sanctifier of the whole world. All other focal points and theses should be in the background. Many became born again and Spirit-filled. Zinzendorf did not call them Brethren, but "Band of God in the Spirit." They lived according to the Apostle Paul's instruction for Christian harmony. "Love each other with genuine affection, and take delight in honoring each other. Live in harmony with each other. Don't be too proud to enjoy the company of ordinary people. And don't think you know it all! Do all you can to live in peace with everyone" (Romans 12:10, 16, 18). These true disciples were described by Zinzendorf as having, *ein Herz und eine Seele*, one heart and one soul. They knew that the great joy in life is to live with Christians and all people in harmony and in love. Paul wrote in Romans 5:5 ..."For we know how dearly God loves us, because He has given us the Holy Spirit to fill our hearts with His love."

The Lutheran theologian, Rupert Maldenius, who lived at the same time as Comenius, coined an axiom of true Christianity: "In essentials, unity; in non-essentials, liberty; in all things, love." Zinzendorf heard this phrase from the Pietist Philip Jakob Spener and adopted it as the motto for the Moravian Brethren.

But God's arch-enemy, the adversary, was also at work in the meetings at Germantown. Animosity and ill will were being sown into the hearts of confused children. Malicious rumors were spread that Zinzendorf was a spurious charlatan who was expelled from Germany because of drunkenness and sexual improprieties. When they observed the tender and loving relationship with his daughter, Henriette Benigna, they accused him that his daughter was actually his secret mistress. The newspapers joined this alliance against him and went so far as to use pictures out of Revelation, depicting him as a brute. Some Christians believed these lies.

One Sunday, when Zinzendorf was absent, Christoph Pyrläus preached the Word of God in Philadelphia. A group of Reformists, including a bunch of rowdy hooligans, burst in, pulled Christoph from the pulpit, and kicked him with their feet. Christoph did not fight back. That was the end of the ecumenical meetings. The flock still loyal to Zinzendorf and the Lutheran faith decided to build their own chapel. He had the great satisfaction of dedicating it to the Lord before he left for Germany. The Reformists and the unruly mishmash of different persuasions chose a pastor, Heinrich Mühlenberg, a hard-working, intelligent man who was influenced by the gossip against Zinzendorf and chose not to work with him.

It is perplexing that believers have such a difficult time laboring together and loving each other. Two underdeveloped virtues, humility and a forgiving heart, are often neglected and are crucial for Christians to live and work in harmony. We have brothers in our lives whom we may not like, but the love of Christ constrains us to forgive them, pray for them, and wish them well. Paul addressed this problem beautifully in Colossians 3:12-14, "Since God chose you to be the holy people he loves, you must clothe yourselves with tenderhearted mercy, kindness, humility, gentleness, and patience. Make allowance for each others' faults and forgive anyone who offends you. Remember, the Lord forgave you, so you must forgive others. Above all, clothe yourselves with love, which binds us all together in perfect harmony. And let the peace that comes from Christ rule in your hearts. For as members of one body you are called to live in peace. And always be thankful."

Notice that the verb *clothe* is mentioned twice. Let's get practical. I can attest that when I have something against a brother, my heart doesn't listen to my will, telling my heart to love that brother and forgive him. But when I put on the cloak of Christ's kindness, admit my own sin, and reach out to hug my brother in forgiveness, then I put on the clothes of God's love. The heart may revolt, but I have an expectant faith that Christ will genuinely transform my heart. When I do my part and obey Paul's divine admonition to be clothed in love and forgiveness, then God does His part and gives me the grace in time to supernaturally love and forgive my brother. I shared this with a group and they jokingly asked me, "Is that why you hug us so much?"

Before we judge Zinzendorf's critics and the hooligans who broke up the meetings, we have to remember how carnal the New Testament Corinthians were. They quarreled, broke into factions, boasted about their worldly wisdom, tolerated immorality, sued fellow Christians, lacked unity in using their spiritual gifts, questioned Paul's apostolic authority, and had misgivings about his integrity concerning money. And yet, he addressed them as saints in Christ. The word "saint" describes our position in Christ, which is unchangeable, versus our practice or condition, which should always change for the better. As we grow through sanctification, our **practice** will increasingly reflect our **position** in Christ. We become more conformed to His image. Many Bible verses support this crucial doctrine, but let me mention two of them:

"For by that one offering he forever made perfect those who are being made holy" (Hebrew 10:14). "Therefore I, a prisoner for serving the Lord, beg you to lead a life worthy of your calling, for you have been called by God" (Ephesians 4:1).

In essence, Scripture admonishes over and over, "You are a saint in Christ, now walk in the power of the Holy Spirit and act like one."

Leaving Germantown, Zinzendorf put his energy mainly into the Moravians in Bethlehem. He helped the Brethren to establish a healthy assembly patterned after Herrnhut. Zinzendorf invited all who lived close by to come. He did not request a change in their *tropoi* (ways) as long as they were willing to be taught the *Erkenntnis der Wahrheit*, the realization of the truth, according to 2 Timothy 2:25, "Gently instruct those who oppose the truth. Perhaps God will change those people's hearts, and they will learn the truth." The community must have been successful. As of 2012, there are six Moravian churches in Bethlehem.

In the second half of the year 1742, Zinzendorf, his daughter, and a translator, Konrad Weisser, embarked on three dangerous and arduous journeys to reach native Indians. Konrad Weisser had grown up among the Indians and had their trust. He introduced Zinzendorf in a meeting of Tulpehoken with several chiefs of different tribes. Konrad made the following declaration, "This man comes in peace. God sent this man over to us. He came over the large water to proclaim to the white and red men a great truth, the famous declaration of the plan of salvation. He is begging you to give him permission."

Konrad gave the Indians a valuable gift from Zinzendorf. The chiefs then had a Pow-wow and came back with a response, "Brother, you came from far away over the big water to preach to the white people and to us. You did not know us or our hunting grounds. We also never heard about your name. This must have come about from the 'Great Hand' in the sky. Come to us, you and your brothers. We grant you our welcome."

An Iroquois chief gave Zinzendorf a *Wampom*, a string of seashells. Several years later, Zinzendorf gave the seashells, the sign of friendship, to the Moravian David Zeisberger and he worked mightily among the Iroquois and converted many. Ludwig, Henriette Benigna and Konrad stayed with the Iroquois for a time. Then the trio set out for a journey beyond the Blue Mountain. It was the land of the Mohawks. Christian Heinrich Rauch was the first Moravian working among them. It was a small settlement, called Shekomeko. When Zinzendorf arrived, they built a hut for him in a hurry. It was made out of bark. He wrote to his wife, "It was the loveliest dwelling I ever lived in. In our inner being we had a few afflictions. Outside we had relentless rain, but the heathens gave us blue skies in our hearts. Every day we made new friends, I enjoy our most beloved Indians." He also observed the Pow-wows and wrote in his journal, "The meetings were conducted with such solemnity and decorum, it caused me great astonishment."

On his third missionary trip to the Shawanoes, he almost lost his life. Konrad Weisser had to urgently go on a journey for three weeks and left Zinzendorf alone. Since he could not communicate with the Indians, he spent most of the time in his tent to pray and to study the Word. He closed the entrance of his tent for hours with a big needle. Somehow this annoyed the Shawanoes, who were already suspicious of all Europeans. They decided to slay Zinzendorf. Just in the nick of time, Konrad showed up to rescue Zinzendorf. Konrad told him, "I had an unexplainable uneasiness and I was compelled by worries to come back sooner as planned."

Zinzendorf's work in America had some success and some disappointments. As mentioned, his work in Bethlehem had lasting fruits. His three missionary tours into Indian territory resulted in a few converts. About Philadelphia he wrote, "I encountered a great deal of mistrust and suspicion. The lukewarm attitude of many countrymen depressed me. But I kept silent and beseeched the Lord for help. I traveled and prayed, and wept and bore witness, and sought for peace, and seek it still." The free spirit of the new immigrant generation was still suspicious of anything that might hamper its newfound individualism.

Zinzendorf tried to hide his aristocratic name, traveled in ordinary clothes, and renounced his title in a meeting with a declaration made before Governor Thomas of Pennsylvania, Benjamin Franklin, and other leading citizens. Benjamin Franklin was Zinzendorf's printer, and published a collection of Zinzendorf's hymns under the title *Hirtenlieder*, Pastoral Hymns. Even though Zinzendorf insisted on being addressed as Brother Ludwig, his aristocratic title remained a major obstacle. Lutherans remembered the aristocrats in the old country as controlling, and they had an aversion to nobility.

Zinzendorf was able to celebrate his second Christmas among his Brethren in Bethlehem. One third of the Brethren were always away on missionary trips. The rest stayed in Bethlehem and Nazareth and toiled hard to finance all the outreaches, since no financial help came from the Brethren in Herrnhut. Zinzendorf realized that the Brethren needed help. Two years later, he sent them the talented organizer and his close friend, August Gottlieb Spangenberg.

Bethlehem was modeled after the early Jerusalem church. For twenty years, all of the facilities were used by all members. All meals were cooked and served in the community kitchen. Husband, wife and children lived in small log cabins. All sacrifices and inconveniences were joyfully endured for missionary outreaches and for the resulting expansion of God's kingdom. Some time after Zinzendorf's death, the Moravian Elders in Herrnhut felt that the pioneering days were over and they asked the Brethren in Bethlehem to become a more conventional community.

After a year and a half, the pair of globetrotters returned to Europe, landing in England and traveling to Holland. While sailing the Atlantic, they encountered a great storm at the southwest coast of England. The waves were so high that Captain Nicholas Garrison prepared for shipwreck as the boat drifted near the rocky beach. After praying to his Savior, Zinzendorf informed the captain that the storm would subside in two hours. The captain recorded in his log, "After two hours, I went on deck to check the weather. Scarcely had I been there when the storm diminished and the wind changed; we were soon out of all danger." Captain Nicholas was curious about how Zinzendorf received the prophetic word, and he asked him how he could so accurately forecast the storm's end. Zinzendorf replied, "All my life I had a trusting relationship with my Savior. In any predicament I first ask myself, am I to blame? If I find sin in my life I fall at His feet to ask for forgiveness. My Savior forgives me, and He lets me know how my trying situation will end. If He keeps silent I conclude it is better for me not to know. However, this time He assured me that the storm will end in two hours." Captain Garrison became a life-long good friend of Zinzendorf. He later joined the Moravians and became their captain again when the Brethren owned their own ship, Irene.

By this time in his life, Zinzendorf had accomplished so much. He had started the day and night prayer vigil, revived the ancient *Unitas Fratrum*, established the Order and Discipline by Comenius, and sent missionaries into all the world to preach the Gospel. The fire from on high was bestowed on the Moravian community, allowing them to have a victorious lifestyle as true disciples of Christ.

Because these victories damaged the kingdom of darkness, the adversary set traps for Zinzendorf. The first trap initially seemed like a great honor and opportunity. The godly, royal family of Denmark offered him a highly esteemed position in the royal court. However, this would surely have taken him away from his spiritual calling. He declined, having the wisdom to say no to worldly accolades and ingratiating praise.

Zinzendorf wrote a poem about the attractions of the world:

"Let my name and honor fly into the wind.
Including all my earthly possessions and temporal gain.
I have only one petition to my Lord.
Let me die while I win souls for the Lamb."

The second trap (in my opinion) was the edict that came from Dresden, declaring he was banished, supposedly forever, from his beloved Herrnhut brothers and his homeland of Saxony. For a time, he was tempted to despair. Beelzebub gave him a lemon, but Ludwig made lemonade.

During the exile, he traveled all over Europe and America, preaching, exhorting, and working to further the Kingdom of God.

The third potential pitfall occurred at the newly established community in Herrnhaag by Frankfurt. But first, a review of the history of that time will be helpful.

18

The Rise and Fall of Herrnhaag

"Jesus, my sweet desire!
Out of my love-filled breast it flows.
Take me into Your stillness.
From Your fullness let me taste a morsel of Your delight.
It will give me a higher bliss
Than an ocean of worldly pleasure" (Poem of Zinzendorf).

Count Ernst Casimir von Ysenburg allowed Zinzendorf and a handful of Moravians to build a congregation on his land in Herrnhaag. It wasn't long before the community was attacked with venomous articles in newspapers, defamatory sermons in churches, and slanderous lectures in universities. But the effect was just the opposite of what was intended. High and low, clergymen and lay people, scholars and workers, and it seemed, the whole world came to Herrnhaag out of curiosity. Many stayed and became true believers. The growth rate was so phenomenal that houses could not be built fast enough.

Zinzendorf was so concerned about the rapid growth that he began advising people who had been saved to return home and become witnesses for Christ in their own villages and churches. His advice fell on deaf ears; people wanted to stay. Zinzendorf's response was to thank the Lord for the growth.

His son, Christian Renatus, came to Herrnhaag and brought his tutor, Johann Nitschmann, and a friend, Baron von Schrautenbach. These men founded two schools, a seminary to equip "servants of the congregation," and a kindergarten. The kindergarten became so crowded that a newspaper notice was put up informing the public that there was no more room. The miraculous rise and growth of the Moravian communities gave the born again brothers the joyous conviction that God was on their side, and He was.

Joy is such an integral part of knowing Christ. The words *joy*, *joyous*, and *joyful* are used over 160 times in the New Testament. The Bible is a book filled with joy. Joy should continually spring from the inner life of a believer. Heart jubilation is essential for both strength and sanctification. Nothing in our lives should ever diminish that joy. It is commanded that believers be full of joy in the Lord (Philippians 4:4). The apostle Peter expressed the greatest motivation and reason for gladness and jubilation in 1 Peter 1:4, 6, "And we have a priceless inheritance – an inheritance that is kept in heaven for you, pure and undefiled, beyond the reach of change and decay...So be truly glad! There is wonderful joy ahead, even though you have to endure many trials for a little while."

Jesus mentions joy eight times in His high priestly prayer in John 17. James writes in 1:2, we are to "count it all joy" when we go through trials. Jude 24 says that Jesus will bring us into the presence of His Father with great joy. The Psalms are saturated with joy. In a sermon, John MacArthur gives a poignant definition of Christian joy, "The emotion [excitement] springing from the deep down confidence of a true Christian that God is in complete and perfect control of everything, and He will bring forth from it our good in time and our glory in eternity; a feeling on top of a fact, not a feeling on top of a fleeting emotion."

For the Christian, happiness is not the ultimate goal. God never promises happiness, but He guarantees joy. Joy is a fruit of the Spirit of God and is not affected by external circumstances. It is present no matter the depth of grief in our hearts. In the presence of a thousand tears, joy can still be there because joy is the presence of God, always by your side. You are never alone.

C.S. Lewis once said, "If we find ourselves with a desire that nothing in this world can satisfy, the most probable explanation is that we were made for another world."

A joyful Christian thinks more of the Lord than about his life and his difficulties. A joyful Christian thinks more of his riches in Christ than his poverty or possessions on earth. A joyful Christian thinks more of his glorious eternal future than his present weariness and pain. The overarching consolation in all the travails and vicissitudes of life is knowing that all things work together for good for those who love Jesus and are called according to His purpose (Romans 8:28). And His purpose is to make a joyful saint out of you who glorify Him and delight in Him now and forever.

In the Beatitudes (Matthew 5:3-10), Jesus gives us wonderful guidelines for how to become a joyful Christian experiencing the "Kingdom of God" in our hearts. The word "blessed," in the context of the Beatitudes, means "fulfilled with inner joy."

We are fulfilled with inner joy when we realize we are impoverished sinners, lament about our helpless estate, and recognize that our condition is destitute and we need a Savior (poor in spirit).

We are fulfilled with inner joy when we bewail the appalling condition of the world, as they reject or do not know Christ as their Savior. When we repent of our conceited self-sufficiency and we begin to trust and obey Jesus (mourning).

We are fulfilled with inner joy when we relinquish all worldly pleasures, surrender our lives to Him, and we solemnly vow obedience to the promptings and wooing of the Holy Spirit to make us Christ-like (meekness).

We are fulfilled with inner joy when we have a passion for holiness, honesty and integrity. When we are love-sick for His presence and yearn for more of Him (hunger and thirst).

A thirst no earthly stream can satisfy,
a hunger that must feed on Christ or die.

We are fulfilled with inner joy when we actively help those who cannot help themselves. When we are able to fully forgive and make allowances for the frailty in brethren (merciful).

We are fulfilled with inner joy when we allow the Holy Spirit the total demolition of our old nature. Our thoughts become pure, our conscience clean. When we change our frame of mind and attitude and only behold what is true, honorable, right, pure, lovely, and admirable (pure in heart).

We are fulfilled with inner joy when we are actively involved in creating peace, even if we are subjected to harsh language, mistreated and abused (peacemakers).

We are fulfilled with inner joy when we suffer hostility because the world hates followers of Christ who display to the world righteous living. It exposes their unrighteousness and infuriates them (persecuted).

In Herrnhaag, jubilant, joyful parties and celebrations were held regularly. Every birthday, every Christian festival, every holiday gave reason to engage in festivities. They justified their activities by describing themselves as the felicitous Bride of the Lamb who adorns herself for the wedding feast.

The Brethren in Herrnhaag were of a different fabric from the Moravians in Herrnhut. They came from all over Europe, Switzerland, Holland, England, and France. Many were better educated and came from a higher stratum of society. They loved art, poetry, and elaborate liturgy. Many oil paintings have come out of Herrnhaag, and some still remain in the Herrnhut archives.

The Moravians in Herrnhut were more somber, hard working, and disciplined. Some had been in jails before coming to Herrnhut, and all had forsaken homes and land to live in peace as Christians. Their suffering had matured them.

As Zinzendorf memorized more and more of the New Testament, his language and sermons became filled with figurative biblical words and concepts. He was convinced that spirituality is an intimate heart language. His style at times was excessively elevated, and he painted extreme word pictures. He defended his methods by saying, "I have to bring the passion of Christ down to an earthly level, since the Lamb of God on the cross is an incomprehensible mystery." At this time he wrote a number of poems. Here is one example:

"A little birdy in the air,
Flying to the cross,
It is afflicted with pangs of love,
Longing to be in the side wound of Jesus."

Zinzendorf based this mystical love language on some verses of the Song of Songs, such as 5:8: "Make this promise, O women of Jerusalem–If you find my lover, tell him I am weak with love." In one word picture, he depicted Christ's side wound as a dwelling chamber for sinners. |We sing today, "Rock of Ages, cleft for me, let me hide myself in Thee; let the water and the blood, from Thy wounded side which flowed, be of sin the double cure, save from wrath and make me pure"|. The Lamb of God became the dear little Lamby. He called the Holy Spirit the Mother. Zinzendorf used Luther's words to back up this concept that the Holy Spirit is our counselor as only a mother can be. "I will comfort you there in Jerusalem as a mother comforts her only child" (Isaiah 66:13). Members in the congregation were dubbed the "order of little fools," based on Jesus' words, "unless you become as little children." In one sermon he told the congregation they should visualize themselves as "little splinters in the cross and little worms bathing in the blood." Through these word pictures, Zinzendorf was trying to instill in the congregation the *Herzensgenuss*, heart relish he enjoyed with his Savior.

Herzensgenuss, pleasure, fondness, or relish of the heart, and *Herzensfreund*, friend of my heart. These lovely sounding German words were frequently used in his sermons. He knew the Word and what it said about the friend of our heart, Jesus,

"He was supreme in the beginning and leading the resurrection parade He is supreme in the end. From beginning to end He's there, towering far above everything, everyone. So spacious is He, so roomy, that everything of God finds its proper place in Him without crowding. Not only that, but all the broken and dislocated pieces of the universe–people and things, animals and atoms–get properly fixed and fit together in vibrant harmonies, all because of His death, His blood that poured down from the cross" (Colossians 1:15-20, The Message).

The growth of Herrnhaag, the love they had for one another, the passionate sermons, and the joyous festivities gave community members a lighthearted, carefree and chipper exuberance. There was little talk of the more serious side of Christianity. Taking up the cross and denying the narcissistic, egocentric self was given little attention. Some thought that enjoyment of Christianity represented a more mature level than the spiritually militant, suffering church. Their beliefs were similar to the current, false prosperity preaching. In every age there are Christians who are content to let Christ do all the dying while they do all the extravagant living.

Simplicity, thriftiness, and austerity were gone at Herrnhaag. But festivities and celebrations cost money, and the Count supported many brethren. He wrote, "What an honor and grace for my house to feed with culinary delights all those pilgrims who endured sufferings and anguish." The expenses became higher than his income. Some Brethren still went out into the world as missionaries, but that number dwindled. The Herrnhaag community lacked the balance between joys and suffering that is so essential to Christian living. Without that balance, the church becomes weak and powerless.

The words of Jesus to His disciples in every age cannot be dismissed as symbolic. "Then Jesus said to his disciples, 'If any of you wants to be my follower, you must turn from your selfish ways, take up your cross, and follow me'" (Matthew 16:24). The cross means a slow, agonizing death to our inherited fallen nature of Adam. The cross means a lifetime of dying to our self-sufficiency and is part of the lifelong process of sanctification.

It is true that no redeemed sinner can boast that he achieved salvation by his intellect, but a fool for Christ means that you pursue Him with all your might.

Troubles certainly came to the "little fools" as disunity and strife came into the Herrnhaag camp. The more serious, sober friends warned Zinzendorf about the frivolous members. For a while, he refused to listen. He told them he did not want to become like Uzziah and invoke God's wrath by attempting to steady the Ark of God (2 Samuel 6:6-7).

But God was looking out for the community. Carl von Peistel, a retired soldier, an aristocrat, and a fervent believer journeyed from Herrnhut and accosted Ludwig with his misgivings. Zinzendorf, the man of God, was still teachable, and he repented before the whole congregation. Humbly, he admitted that he was the cause of the unrelenting media attacks, the financial distress, and the dissension in the congregation. God blessed his repentance and the Brethren reconciled.

Meanwhile, Ernst Casimir, the old count who owned the Herrnhaag land, passed away in 1749. His son Gustav Friedrich was unhappy that his property had become a show place for accusations and conflict. He issued an edict that the Brethren leave his property within three years. In those three years, almost 1,000 Brethren left Herrnhaag. In one day, ninety single Brethren left for Pennsylvania. In 1750, Zinzendorf traveled to Neuwied, Germany, and begged Count Johann Friedrich Alexander to allow some of the Brethren to settle on his land. The count granted Zinzendorf his wish and Neuwied became a fruitful community.

In 1753, Herrnhaag's demise was complete. Zinzendorf paid many bills for relocating settlers to America, Neuwied, and other Moravian settlements. He paid for others to go as missionaries into different parts of the world.

Zinzendorf asked a young man in Hernhaag, "What about you? I heard you want to go to Greenland."

"Yes," the young single lad replied, "if I could have a pair of shoes." The very same day, Ludwig bought him a pair. The chap left shortly and afterward returned in 1793, having worked for forty-six years as a missionary in Greenland.

The time in Herrnhaag became known as the "sifting time." It was a sad landmark in the otherwise successful and fruitful history of this great movement. Herrnhaag proved that even Christians can be vacillating. One moment they cause outsiders to cringe at their behavior, and the next moment they take off for foreign lands, giving their lives sacrificially to expand God's Kingdom.

Martin Luther coined the phrase in Latin, *"Simul justus et peccator,"* simultaneously a saint and a sinner. Herrnhaag proved that even godly movements can fall into heresy or fanaticism, and yet God's grace and mercy can restore hearts fallen into error. The experience at Herrnhaag demonstrated that God always has a plan when His people find themselves in difficult circumstances. Jesus continually intercedes for us as He interceded for Peter. "Simon, Simon, Satan has asked to sift each of you like wheat. But I have pleaded in prayer for you, Simon, that your faith should not fail. So when you have repented and turned to me again, strengthen your brothers" (Luke 22:31-32). Being sifted like wheat suggests that trials, though undesirable and painful, have a necessary refining effect.

In the year of Hernhaag's demise, 1753, Zinzendorf visited London. The Brethren showed him many unpaid bills and entreated him to help. He wrote to all the creditors that he would take over the payments. He expected the remittance of a promissory note of one thousand pounds Sterling from Holland, but the payment did not come. Zinzendorf's predicament was so serious that he prepared to go to the *Schuldgefängnis,* jail for debtors. Just in the nick of time the money came in, only because the mail was ahead of schedule. His heart was full of gratitude.

Zinzendorf accepted these trials as lessons to pull him out of frivolity. He deeply appreciated the help and consolation of His Savior during this ordeal. However, it took the rest of his life and beyond to pay off the debts he acquired.

The Moravian Brethren appointed a godly man, a lawyer and accountant, Johann Friedrich Köber, to manage the financial affairs of the Brethren and they faithfully paid off the remainder of all his obligations, even after his death.

Herrnhaag was the third of the three major pitfalls in Ludwig's life. By God's grace, he overcame the evil one's strategy to neutralize him. God is faithful to the humble. Zinzendorf wrote in his diary, "In the last year the heat of the sun burned on me quite a bit. However, in my heart there were no tempest ocean waves. My heart was serene and even. I was humiliated and the music was subdued, but I can honestly say I felt good. This time of distress was from the viewpoint of my Savior a glorious time. He put me and the Brethren into the schoolroom to teach us besides loving Him, we also needed to learn about His providence."

19

New Horizons

"An essential prerequisite for a revival is to exercise humiliating self-reproach and a cry for forgiveness and mercy. A renewal is not possible when a congregation perceives itself alive but it is actually dead" (Zinzendorf).

While living in Herrnhaag, Zinzendorf traveled to England and through Germany to meet with solid, mature Christians leaders. He loved these conferences and looked forward to seeing old friends again. He called these frequent meetings, *Synods,* assemblies. In the beginning of every discussion, Zinzendorf had established these guideposts: First, let us ponder and review the relationship with our Savior. Second, survey the interrelationship or bonding with your neighbor. Third, what can we do together different with our Brethren and in our temporal civil matters? They also discussed congregational affairs and the possibility of establishing new settlements. With a shepherd's heart, he preached to them, encouraged them, and helped them develop new strategies for their congregations.

Paul displayed a similar attitude about fellowship. "Therefore, my dear brothers and sisters, stay true to the Lord. I love you and long to see you, dear friends, for you are my joy and the crown I receive for my work." (Philippians 4:1). Meetings where Christians come together are refreshing. Paul wrote to his good friend, Philemon, "Your love has given me much joy and comfort, my brother, for your kindness has often refreshed the hearts of God's people" (Philemon 7). Next to having Christ in your heart, there is nothing more precious than to fellowship with true saints. Christ loved the church and gave Himself for her. We follow His example through loving, glad service and by sacrificially devoting ourselves so that the *ekklesia* or the "called-out company of saints" may progress, prosper, and triumph. This was Zinzendorf's life's work; he devoted his talents to increase the United Brethren by building new congregations. "And the church is His body; it is made full and complete by Christ, who fills all things everywhere with himself" (Ephesians 1:23).

The Brethren in Herrnhut were not idle while the Count was in Herrnhaag. As mentioned before, Moravians transported the igniting fire of the Holy Spirit to the Baltic Sea area and other parts of Germany and Europe. New life was infused into these spiritual battlefields. Two new communities modeled after Herrnhut came into existence in Silesia. Count Ernst Julius von Seydlitz was one trailblazer there. He was a fervent disciple of Christ and a good friend of Zinzendorf. Because of his faith, he was jailed for eighteen months in the city of Javer. Another congregation was established on the estate of a German aristocrat and cavalry officer, Von Falkenhayn.

When Zinzendorf heard that the official Protestant church wanted nothing to do with the revived Brethren, Zinzendorf was once again disillusioned. He wrote in his journal, "If my dear Savior would ever in His unfathomable ways allow my expulsion from the Lutheran denomination, I would have no choice but to acquiesce to His divine will. But I would still preach the Lutheran faith, because I don't preach for Lutheran theologians. I preach the truth of God."

These new spiritual camps that were springing up in Silesia were called *Gnadenhill*, hill of grace and *Gnadenfrei*, free by grace. The words reflect Isaiah 61:1 "...to announce that captives will be released and prisoners will be free."

While Zinzendorf was in Silesia, his intention was to travel to St. Petersburg in Russia via Königsberg and Riga. He wanted to be examined before a commission of theologians about his faith, hoping to send more Moravians to do some missionary work there. Some months before, he had sent a Russian-speaking Moravian, Arvid Gradin, to St. Petersburg to pave the way. Arvid was promptly arrested and thrown in jail. He remained there for four years. Three other Brethren, Conrad Lange, Zacharias Hirschel, and Michael Kind had already been in custody for a year. Their crime was applying for a passport to further the Kingdom of God among the people in Siberia. Zinzendorf also wanted to visit Russia in response to an edict of her Majesty Katharina to ban all Brethren from entering or working in Russia. Around seven thousand Brethren were already in active fellowship on Russian soil. Zinzendorf got no further than Riga when he, his son Renatus, and Anna Nitschmann were arrested by Governor General Laski. The governor confiscated all Zinzendorf's papers and transported the group to the city's citadel. He declared he had to wait for further instructions from her Majesty, Empress Katharina. After three weeks, an order came from the Empress, "Her Majesty does not see any compelling reason for a theological examination, rather Count Zinzendorf must bid her country farewell as swiftly as possible." This was her edict, "It has been brought to the attention of her Royal Majesty that a new sect called the Herrnhuter has arisen in Livonia and other parts of the country whose founder is a certain Count Zinzendorf. This sect has so multiplied that already large buildings have been erected, for the gathering of those followers. Meetings are held in secret and among them are nobility, pastors, and especially peasants. Therefore, be it ordered that these Livonians, be who they may, be forbidden to continue to adhere to the teachings of the Herrnhuters, that their buildings immediately be closed, and all members forbidden to communicate with their leaders in buildings or elsewhere."

Some fifty German Diaspora workers were ordered to leave. Yet the Russian Diaspora continued to prosper, so firmly had it taken root among the people. The ban was in effect for four years, until the German-born Empress, Katharina the Great, reversed it.

Zinzendorf had learned by now that incessant persecutions were to be expected, and he was not dispirited. He wrote, "It is better to strive a hundred times for the honor and truth of the Lord, even if it is in vain, than to have a slumbering life and not to risk any ventures."

In 1747, while participating in a two-week Synod in England, Ludwig was reminded once again that Jesus is the Head of His church. Jesus said ..."I will build my church, and all the power of hell will not conquer it" (Matthew 16:18). This lesson was learned when Leonard Dober, First Elder, decided that he was unable to carry the responsibilities of his congregation. After much debate, the Brethren were unable to find a suitable replacement. They put the matter at the feet of Jesus and were given a solution from Isaiah. ..."Do you question what I do for my children? Do you give me orders about the work of my hands?" (Isaiah 45:11). Based on this Scripture, they unanimously voted that the title of First or Upper Elder be abolished. The Moravians still recognize this day of "spiritual clarity" on the 13th of November, celebrating that Jesus is their First Elder that no human being is.

Zinzendorf once explained the condition of the Moravians and Bohemians as *Erweckte*, or born again ones (John 3:3), and *wahre Anbeter*, or true worshippers (John 4:23).

"Do not assume that I think that every member of the *Unitas Fratrum* is a true child of God, nor do I think that outside our Brethren nobody is saved. The Kingdom of Jesus is not only in the hearts of the Bohemians or the Moravians, which would be contrary to my Savior's prayer in John 17. There are other throngs of believers who are as close or even closer to the heart of Jesus. Every believer who has the *Martermann*, Man of Sorrows, in his heart is as wise as we are. The true ekklesia of Jesus is not visible and it is spread all over the world. However, a soul must have a *Spezialbund,* special bond with Jesus and an *Anbindung*, a close tie to his Savior."

Zinzendorf's critics once asked him why people joined his centers of the United Brethren. He answered, "When I ask people, 'Why don't you want to stay in the city of your fathers, cobbling and tailoring there?' these Brethren tell me that it is the love of Christ exhibited in the community that makes them stay. Can I not give them the right to remain and give them the title, 'People of the Savior'?"

Thirty years later, August Gottlieb Spangenberg wrote about Zinzendorf's character and the way he confronted his critics, "Zinzendorf was the most honorable man I ever knew. There was never a question that Jesus was the Shepherd and the Bishop of our souls. In our hearts we knew we had a *Spezialbund* with our Savior, but we also had an affinity with Count Zinzendorf, our *Ordinarius Fratrum,* overseer of the Brethren."

It would be helpful to share a perspective on the true church, which is foundational and elementary knowledge. However, during Zinzendorf's time, few people had access to sound biblical teaching, few owned a Bible, and there were hardly libraries full of Christian books. We are now rich in bedrock, orthodox Christian teachings if we choose to read the books available or listen to anointed, born again preachers.

We know there are churchgoers with an outer appearance of Christianity but without an inner reality of Christ as their Savior and His indwelling presence. They have never tasted the transforming power of becoming a child of God. But in most churches there are also regenerated, Spirit-filled Christians who hold Christ in their heart as their only hope of glory. They know and have experienced the words of Jesus in Matthew 7:13-14, "You can enter God's kingdom only through the narrow gate. The highway to hell is broad, and its gate is wide for the many that choose that way. But the gateway to life is very narrow and the road is difficult, and only a few ever find it." The narrow gate is only through faith in Christ. It is narrow and small because only few choose that path, which calls for recognition of the truth, repentance, and full surrender to Christ as Lord and Savior. Relying on self-righteousness and human effort to gain divine favor for an entrance into heaven is futile.

Of course, the apostle Paul knew the difference between a true follower and a false pretender. When he wrote to the Philippians, he must have been brokenhearted when he saw the downfall of some teachers, both Jewish and Gentile. Most men do not cry easily, but Paul wrote, "For I have told you often before, and I say it again with tears in my eyes, that there are many whose conduct shows they are really enemies of the cross of Christ" (Philippians 3:18). They may not have openly opposed Christ and they may have had a mental understanding of the cross, but they did not exhibit true regeneration as new people in Christ. Paul explains the reason: ... "Their god is their appetite, they brag about shameful things and they think only about this life here on earth" (Philippians 3:19).

God's Word characterizes the true congregation as a flock of sheep under the tender care of the Good Shepherd, who hear His voice and follow Him (John 10:16). The flock shares Christ's life and are all linked together in living union by the Holy Spirit. It is a communion of saints, not an organization but a living organism without institutional character.

There are many word pictures in Scripture that describe the church. It is described as a garden plot, and His purpose is to raise fruit for His glory (Galatians 5:22-23). The church is referred to as a building, and we are the living stones He is adding. When we devote our lives to this construction project, it gives Him glory (1 Corinthians 3:9.) In the same chapter, believers are called a temple of God, and worship takes place only in those temples, the hearts of those who belong to His true church. In Ephesians 1:2-3, we are called the body of Christ, which is the specific means the Lord chooses to express Himself to the world. Realizing that we are His body provides a wonderful impetus for living our lives so others will see Him reflected in us. The early disciples were recognized as Christians because of their love.

Another beautiful truth is that we are His dwelling. God resides in His church rather than in a material tabernacle or in a physical temple. Paul describes this mystery of Christ living in a believer, and this is our assurance that we will share His glory (Colossians 1:26-27).

The most amazing declaration found in Scripture about the believer's unique identity is that we are the Bride of Christ. In Him we are washed by His blood and by the water of the Word, we are glorious and delightful, we have no spot or wrinkle, no blemish, and we are a pure Bride. Jesus loves His Bride so passionately that He gave Himself for her. Shouldn't we be filled with bridal affection for Him?

Paul tells Timothy that we are the household of God, a pillar and support of the truth. A household implies order and discipline. At one time, pillars were used for posting public notices and proclamations, so it means making Him known to the world. A bulwark provides support for a building and is a symbol of supporting and defending His truth (1 Timothy 3:15).

Christ's church is a royal priesthood of all believers (1 Peter 2:9). We don't need to be from the Old Testament tribe of Levi or from the family of Aaron. We are united with a royal priest, Jesus Christ, who ever lives to make intercession for us before God's throne.

Christians are royalty because we belong to the King. With the privileges of that title, we also have responsibilities. We are in the construction process, adding living stones each time a soul is saved. We don't need hammers; the Holy Spirit uses us for raising His masterpiece, the church. One day, when the work is finished, His flock will rise to meet their Savior in the air. We will go to the mansions He has prepared for us and remain with Jesus forever (1 Thessalonians 4:17). We will share the glory that He won for us during His time on earth (John 17:22). "So God can point to us in all future ages as examples of the incredible wealth of his grace and kindness toward us, as shown in all he has done for us who are united with Christ Jesus" (Eph. 2:7).

God not only rescues sinners and makes them kings reigning above sin, the world, self and the devil, but He also organizes these winners into a great army, where all His children are fighting side by side against all unrighteousness.

20

Homecoming

"When you visit the 'Quakers' you will soon notice that the women will talk and preach. Rightly so. If we put women in the corner we will lose a *Kleinod*, a jewel. It is peculiar that when the Holy Spirit says your daughters will prophesy, we tell them 'no.' How can you explain Galatians 3:28? In Christ we are all equal, and I have always encouraged our sisters to teach and preach in our congregation, and I have put gifted women in key leading positions. When Paul talked about women being silent, he was telling a specific boisterous group of Greek women not to interrupt a service" (Zinzendorf).

(This was revolutionary in the 18th century, and Zinzendorf was attacked by his opponents for establishing a *Weiberwirtschaft*, women dominance).

When the royal court in Dresden heard about the thriving communities of *Gnadenhill* and *Gnadenberg* in Silesia, the Prince Elector of Saxony in Dresden began to question the Count's banishment. After all, the Prussian Emperor in Berlin protected the *Unitas Fratrum* communities. And there was no question that good, hard-working citizens paid tariffs and taxes.

In October 1747, Zinzendorf was overjoyed to receive news of the decree canceling his exile from Saxony. Within three days he was back in Herrnhut, and over two hundred Brethren celebrated with a love feast. Zinzendorf wrote, "I always had the conviction that if reasonable people see a cloud of witnesses who are saved by grace through faith and observe that they are honest, sensible, law-abiding, modest, and hard working, then any philosopher should come to the conclusion, that what I think and preach brings good results."

Shortly after his arrival in Herrnhut, Zinzendorf received another letter of utmost importance from the court at Dresden, "The United Brethren have all the permanent rights of a normal Saxon citizen. They have been granted permanent religious freedom and are free to conduct their own distinctive services and determine their own spiritual leaders." Zinzendorf was jubilant, but he received this news with no trace of pride. He wrote, "If we would find a religious assembly that would be closer to the heart of the Truth, we would be more than willing to affiliate with those Brethren and be content to submit to their deeper understanding."

One of the Zinzendorf's greatest antagonists was Baron von Huldenberg. He had accused Zinzendorf of *Religionszerrüttung*, wrecking religion and fomenting tumultuous behavior. The real reason was that his beer brewery suffered loss of income, since some of his villagers were influenced by the gentle, virtuous, pietistic behavior of the Moravians. It was partly through this man's relentless criticism at the royal court in Dresden that the Count was banished from Saxony. Zinzendorf knew about these senseless accusations against him and the unrelenting denunciations of Herrnhut. He wrote the Baron a letter some time before his exile, "If I would have the honor to meet you personally, you would soon notice that I am not a friend of disorder. If you would really get to know Herrnhut, you might wish your villages to be like that. I take the liberty to enclose a little booklet with the title, "About Christian Assemblies." I beg you as an honorable proprietor to read it at your convenience, and I am convinced you will come to a different verdict about how honestly and uprightly the Herrnhuter Christians live together."

> At times we are all tempted by the evil one to harbor ill will. But the Word of God cautions us to post a guard before our heart because it is from the heart that the choices and consequences of life flow. It behooves us to sometimes pray as David did in Psalm 141:3, "Take control of what I say, O Lord, and guard my lips."

Four years after Zinzendorf's return to Herrnhut, a devastating fire broke out in Baron Huldenberg's estate buildings. They burned down, and his castle was greatly damaged, jeopardizing his financial condition. As the Baron was sifting through the rubble, he came across a letter he had received from Zinzendorf almost twenty years earlier. To his amazement, the letter showed only a few scorched spots. What caught his attention were sentences in the letter that he himself had underlined, in which Zinzendorf begged him to change his opinion about Herrnhut. The Baron had done the underlining as an act of defiance, but now his conscience gave him no peace. Accompanied by a clergyman, Karl Rudolf Reichel, the Baron traveled to Herrnhut. He showed the singed letter to Zinzendorf and explained how God providentially used it, prodding him on to seek forgiveness. Zinzendorf did not hesitate to forget the past and he granted the Baron total forgiveness. Huldenberg became a true Christian. Evidence that he became a new person in Christ was found in a letter he wrote soon after his visit to Ludwig, "I can assure you with unfeigned joy that I have a completely different attitude about your congregation. I did not deserve the humble letter you wrote so many years ago. But the merciful and wonderful Savior used your letter as a reminder about your prophetic words, telling me that if I would find time for a visit, I would change my opinion about the Moravians and Herrnhut. With great shame, but with utmost honesty, I have to confess that my blind, opinionated, and unwarranted attitude towards you kept me from responding to your tract. It is reprehensible that in my stubbornness I swore never to visit your village." For the rest of his life, Baron von Huldenberg maintained a genuine friendship with Ludwig. He held up the Moravian community to the citizens of his villages as an example to follow.

Why would the Baron, a fellow Saxon and German, be so obstinate in his animosity towards Zinzendorf and the United Brethren, even to the point of causing his banishment and the possible scattering of the Brethren and preventing revival and the spread of Pentecostal fire all over the land? The New Testament clearly teaches that hostile spiritual powers work through men and nations, opposing the work of God, His kingdom, and His people. These enemies of God are invisible, cosmic powers that influence all people who do not live in the Kingdom of Light. While Satan and the evil powers are described in the New Testament as already defeated, it is, however, "not yet total defeat." God's enemies are bound, but as one theologian expressed it, "they are bound by a long rope." Paul experienced something similar. "And then, dear brothers and sisters, you suffered persecution from your own countrymen. In this way, you imitated the believers in God's churches in Judea who, because of their belief in Christ Jesus, suffered from their own people, the Jews (1 Thessalonians 2:14). Paul further writes in the same chapter, about being driven out, and preventing them from preaching the Good News. He also had an intense longing to see the Thessalonians. He tried again and again, but Satan prevented him.

Dr. Ed Murphy, in his book, *The Handbook for Spiritual Warfare*, page 359, writes an elucidating passage about Paul's combat with evil forces, "Satan stopped Paul from doing what Paul knew was the will of God. Is that possible? According to Paul, it is. Most of us have difficulty with this dimension of spiritual warfare. We try to ignore it, or we water it down until Satan is seen almost as already bound in the pit and completely unable to effectively oppose believers. Our preachers often tell us, God is sovereign. He always does his will in heaven and on earth. Neither man, nor the devil, nor demons can ever interfere with his will. Therefore as long as we are walking in the Spirit, Satan cannot successfully resist us when we are in God's will. This God would never permit. This sounds pious, but it fits neither the teachings of Scripture nor the experience of God's people. It certainly is a 'truth' unknown to the apostle Paul according to this passage. Though we are protected from serious or total defeat while we walk in the Spirit (if we walk in the flesh he has already a stronghold in us), we can and will suffer setback, and Paul didn't like it. If we call such setbacks the will of God, we deceive ourselves. Indeed, Satan must be delighted when we clean up his dirty work by calling it the will of God. While we are taught to rejoice in everything we are not taught to rejoice because everything is the will of God. We are to rejoice even when God's will is not being done, we are sharing in Christ's suffering for his body's sake, not because the work of Satan is really the work of God. Let's not try to eliminate the mystery of evil by calling it 'good.'

"How do we handle the supernatural opposition when we know we are in the will of God? The answer is simple to say, but hard to do! We stay where we are, serve faithfully, and suffer. We continue to serve and to suffer until, if necessary, we die. That is what Paul did (2 Tim. 4:7-8). So did Peter (2 Peter 1:12-15). So have many of God's saints from the beginning until now (Heb. 11:32-40). At the same time, God's Holy Spirit sustains us with joy (1 Thess. 1:6; Rom. 5:1-5)."

21

Setbacks and Triumphs

"*Gemeingeist,* one heart and one soul, does not mean we are all equal. Every soul is an individual king. You can find the beauty of Jesus in every person, even though the social status, temperament, maturity, and age are different. Do not put anybody under pressure to do certain ministries. Heartfelt ministries only develop in a chamber called freedom" (Zinzendorf).

Many years after the Holy Spirit fell in that "glorious summer," as Zinzendorf called it, the Moravian prayer vigil continued around the clock. The results were inevitable. As their prayer for missionaries continued unabated, spiritual warfare intensified.

Prayer is God's way of giving His church on-the-job training in overcoming forces hostile to the advancement of His kingdom. In our prayer closets, we overcome Satan and his minions. Prayer and faith are formidable and essential weapons in Christ's victory over the prince of darkness. "Those who are victorious will sit with me on my throne, just as I was victorious and sat with my Father on his throne," Jesus explained in Revelation 3:21. On our knees we are overcomers. That God will often make His action dependent on our prayers is expressed in

Scripture many times. The Lord said to Ezekiel, "I looked for someone to stand in the gap" (Ezekiel 22:30). God is almighty; He is the utmost, supreme, sovereign being of the universe. He is judge, jury, executive, and enforcer. It is a baffling mystery, but by His love for His children He allows us to participate in His blueprint of history so that we might share the rewards He has promised to His children (Revelation 22:12). God works through prayers offered by converted hearts to increase His realm and dominion on this earth. "So pray to the Lord who is in charge of the harvest; ask Him to send more workers into His fields" (Matthew 9:38).

For prayer to be effective, God requires that we abide in Him and that His **words** abide in us. Then we can ask anything of the Father in Jesus' name and He will grant it to us. Our guerrilla warfare on this earth brings us to full maturity and prepares us to rule in heaven with Him. Jesus is preparing the church, His Bride, for governing. Prayer and intercession are an essential part of our apprenticeship. John Wesley said, "God will do nothing but in answer to prayer." S.D. Gordon said, "Prayer is striking the winning blow, service is gathering up the results."

Throughout history, men who were inflamed with love for prayer did great exploits for Christ and "learned to know their Creator and became like Him," (Colossians 3:10). These were men who spent much time with God.

John Wesley spent two hours daily in prayer. He began at four in the morning. He thought prayer to be more his business than anything else.

John Fletcher stained the walls of his room by the breath of his prayers. His whole life was a life of prayer.

Luther said, "If I fail to spend two hours in prayer each morning, the devil gets the victory through the day. If I have too much business I cannot get on without spending an additional hour in prayer."

Samuel Rutherford rose at three in the morning to meet God in prayer. John Welch, a wonderful Scottish preacher, prayed up to eight hours a day. He wrapped himself in a blanket when he got up at night to pray. His wife would complain when she found him lying on the ground weeping. He would reply, "O, woman, I have the souls of three thousand to answer for, and I know not how it is with many of them."

The Marquis DeRenty ordered his servant to call him from his prayer vigil after a half an hour. When his servant saw how deep he was in prayer he did not want to arouse him. He waited until three half hours had passed. When he called him, the Marquis arose from his knees and said, "O, what a short half an hour it was."

David Brainerd worked mightily among the American Natives. He lived a life of holiness and prayer. He wrote in his diary, "Feeling somewhat of the sweetness of communion with God and the constraining force of His love, and how admirable it captivates the soul and makes all the desires and affections to center in God, I set apart this day in secret fasting and prayer, to entreat God to direct and bless me with regard to the great work that I have in view of preaching the Gospel, and that the Lord return to me and show me the light of His countenance. I had little life and power in the forenoon. Near the middle of the afternoon God enabled me to wrestle ardently in intercession for my absent friends, but just at night the Lord visited me marvelously in prayer. I think my soul was never in such agony before. I felt no restraint for the treasures of divine grace were opened to me. I wrestled for absent friends, for the ingathering of souls, for multitudes of poor souls, and for many that I thought were the children of God, personally, in many distant places. I was in such an agony from sun half an hour high till near dark that I was all over wet with sweat, but yet it seemed to me I had done nothing. O, my dear Savior did sweat blood for poor souls! I longed for more compassion toward them. I felt still in a sweet frame, under a sense of divine love and grace, and went to bed in such a frame, with my heart set on God."

Jonathan Edward wrote about David Brainerd's prayer life, "His life shows the right way to success in the works of a ministry. He sought it as a soldier seeks victory in a siege or battle; or as a man that runs a race for a great prize. Animated with love to Christ and souls, how did he labor? Always fervently. Not only in word and doctrine, in public and in private, but in prayer by day and night, wrestling with God in secret and travailing in birth with unutterable groans and agonies, until Christ was formed in the hearts of the people to whom he was sent. Like a true son of Jacob, he persevered in wrestling through all the darkness of the night, until the breaking of the day."

There are some amazing stories about the Moravians, losses they suffered and conquests they achieved. One story involves Gottlieb Israel, a limping Moravian weaver, who sailed to the West Indies with a friend and companion. The ship ran aground near Tortola and his comrade drowned right before his eyes. As Gottlieb hung on to a reef and as the waves hammered him, he didn't know how long he could keep his grip. Just in the nick of time, he was rescued. Back home in Herrnhut, when he told the story to the congregation, Zinzendorf asked, "What did you think as you were holding on to the rock?" Gottlieb replied, "I was singing our Single Brother Hymn," a song composed by Zinzendorf, number 963 in the Moravian Hymnal:

You wall destroyer, where are you seen?
On the rocks, in the holes, on the wild plains,
On islands of heathens and on the tempest waves,
Which are your decreed places since eternity.

Friedrich Höcker and Johannes Rüffer traveled to the Guebres, fire worshipers in Persia. On their wearisome journey, Kurdish bandits robbed and beat them. They survived, but when they were attacked again, Friedrich was seriously wounded and almost died. Starving and nearly naked, they stumbled into a British Consulate. Soon the two missionary doctors decided to return home. Again they were attacked and robbed, and this time Johannes succumbed to his wounds and died. Friedrich buried his dear friend somewhere along the way.

In Guyana, the dying of Moravian missionaries was especially heartbreaking. Seventy-five out of the first 160 ambassadors for Christ died within a decade from tropical fever, poisonous snake bites and dysentery. Brother Andreas Rittmannsberger lost his life within six months of his arrival.

Stories like this did not cool the Moravians' desire to bring salvation to a dying world. In 1752, a group went to work among the Eskimos and sailed on the ship *Hope* from England to Labrador. When they arrived, four Moravians went ashore and started to build a house. They wanted to name the settlement Hopedale. The ship went farther north to drop off five more missionaries. As soon as the five evangelists were on land, a group of Eskimos murdered them. The captain of the boat sailed back down the coast in a hurry and rescued the other four missionaries or their fate could have been the same. Zinzendorf was greatly saddened as another outreach failed.

We find an entry in Zinzendorf's diary about his thoughts of conquests and failures, "I am not certain whether the time of massive conversions of heathens is here. But I see small fruits in some countries. But the Savior has seen our labor and sweat. It is conceivable that God could have done it without us. I am also not certain whether we are "mining" permanently or observe only beginnings of short durations. But, oh, even if our soul-gathering time is only of a limited period, and even if we suffer loss of Brethren, and even, by now, we have sent the Brethren over two hundred times on voyages across the oceans, a harvest of hundred souls would be a rich reward."

Melchior Nitschmann, the weaver and Elder who was among the five men of the *Unitas Fratrum* who decided to stay in Herrnhut, traveled with George Schmidt to Salzburg, Austria. On their way they visited several secret house groups to strengthen and encourage the believers. In one meeting, the police interrupted, handcuffed them and threw them separately in jail. Zinzendorf tried several times through the authorities for their release. The Brethren suffered in their cold cells. Within a year, Melchior died of pneumonia. George suffered for six more dreary, lamentable years. Finally, he was so exhausted and feeble that he pretentiously converted to Catholicism. They released him and he traveled, weakened back to Herrnhut. The Brethren were astonished and received him with joy. He suffered greatly with twinges of remorse for denying his faith. In 1736, he sailed as the first missionary to South Africa. When he was chosen, he uttered, "My Savior allowed me, most unworthy soul, to go." He established a school and taught the Knoi natives to read, write, and farm. He told them about the love of his Savior and His atonement for sin on the cross. It was five years before he had the first convert. The local clergy were jealous because George brought to the people prosperity, education, and Christ. The clergymen questioned the Moravian ordination and used their influence to expel George Schmidt.

Almost fifty years later, three missionaries returned to South Africa and located the ruins of the original house George Schmidt built. In the garden was a giant pear tree that grew from a tiny shoot that George planted. They also met a remnant of believers and an old woman named Magdalena. She still had a Bible and could read the Word. Within ten years, there were over 1,500 believers who lived in a village called Valley of Grace that this second group of missionaries established. They were self-sufficient, could read, and had a strong spiritual life. In 1838, they established a teachers' training college.

William Wilberforce, the great evangelical English reformer wrote about the Moravian missionary passion, "They are a body who has perhaps excelled all mankind in solid and unequivocal proofs of the love of Christ in them through an ardent, active zeal for His dominion. It is a zeal tempered with prudence, softened with meekness and supported by courage which no danger can intimidate, and a quiet certainty no hardship can exhaust."

Mission work in the West Indies eventually thrived and over 4,000 slaves were baptized. Even though twenty Moravians died on the islands, the fruit of the first two young men, Leonard Dober and David Nitschmann, was blossoming. The slave owners never again feared an uprising of the slaves. This is what the governor of St. Thomas Island declared in 1749, "The church of the Brethren has brought about a better spirit on the island. It is now a stronghold of peace. In the past I would have not dared to sleep anywhere but in my fort. Now I can sleep anywhere on the plantation without fearing for my life. If there would ever be a plot, which I think would be most unlikely with the new prevailing attitude, I am sure some slaves would pass that information along to me."

In Amsterdam, the Moravians did a mighty work among Jewish people. Many Christian churches had anti-Semitic sentiments, but the Moravians shared the Gospel with Jewish people and followed Ludwig's example with Rabbi Abraham. A true Christian loves the Jewish nation. "For Christ Himself has brought peace to us. He united Jews and Gentiles into one people when, in His own body on the cross, He has broke down the wall of hostility that separated us" (Ephesians 2:14).

Johannes Beck, Matthäus and Christian Stach, and the diehard Christian David, the carpenter who was building their homes, worked among the Eskimos in Greenland. Their missionary zeal was tested with patience. It took six years before the first Eskimo family was baptized. In their language was no word for God, devil, sin, or justice. These strangers were peculiar to them and there was no interest at first in the afterlife when they heard, "No sea lions in heaven." Eventually over two hundred Eskimos were saved. Matthäus was one of the first missionaries to visit Greenland. He brought two Eskimos back to Herrnhut and told wonderful stories of continued growth.

Setbacks and Triumphs

Zinzendorf wrote a hymn about Greenland,

Trotting through ice and snow,
For one poor soul Christ to know,
We gladly bear all grief and pain
To make known the Lamb once slain.

Abraham Richter, a merchant from the city of Stralsund who joined the Brethren, worked among the Arabs in Algiers. He wrote inspiring stories of success to Herrnhut. He never saw his homeland again. The Black Death plague took his life. The congregation supported these missionary efforts with prayer and looked forward each week to hearing letters read that came from around the world.

In the state of Georgia, it seemed the enemy was winning the spiritual battle. The Spanish army invaded from the south, hoping to claim the area for Spain. The governor of Georgia warned the colonists to prepare for war. When the Moravians refused to bear arms, they were expelled. Evangelist George Whitefield heard about their plight and helped them travel to Pennsylvania. Communities in Nazareth and Bethlehem were flourishing, and the governor of Pennsylvania was amicable towards the Moravians. The governor even came to the aid of David Zeisberger and Friederich Post, missionaries who worked among the Indians in the Hudson River Valley. Because some white settlers were unhappy that Indians were becoming Christians, the Brethren were arrested on some false charges, transported to New York and thrown in jail. However, the Pennsylvania governor secured their release.

David Zeisberger (1721-1808) was for sixty-two years relentlessly laboring for Christ among the Iroquois and Hurons. He was also with the pioneers who built Bethlehem settlement. In 1750, he went on a dangerous, wearisome trip to secure permission from the Iroquois for missionary outreaches. The Indians soon adopted him as a member of their nation, and many were adopted into God's family through his work. He married when he was sixty years old and 400 Delaware Indians attended his wedding, almost all of whom were counted as Christians.

Lord Granville, an English aristocrat, offered Zinzendorf a real estate bargain, 100,000 acres of North Carolina land. Zinzendorf was ecstatic and deeply grateful to the Lord for all He was doing. With the help of Thomas Penn and James Oglethorpe, he secured the right for the Moravians, like the Quakers, to be exempt from bearing arms. In England, Parliament passed a bill in 1749 freeing Moravians from obligatory military service.

In November of 1755, Zinzendorf received the most heartrending news from Pennsylvania. Twenty miles up from Bethlehem, a mission called *Gnadenhütten*, refuge of grace, was burned down and ten missionaries and one child were murdered. The perpetrators were incited by soldiers with false propaganda, as so often is the case in the intrigues and politics of wars. Zinzendorf preached a sermon about turning the other cheek, and he prayed with the Brethren that the slayers would have the grace to accept the Gospel of Jesus before their death. Shortly afterwards, Zinzendorf was able to send fifteen Moravian volunteers to Pennsylvania as a replacement for the martyred missionaries.

In 1759 Zinzendorf again received more dismal news. In the Seven Years War, Russian soldiers burned the buildings of *Neusalz,* new salt, and the refugees had to flee to neighboring *Gnadenberg,* hill of grace.

Despite setbacks, missionary work continued, and by the end of Zinzendorf's life, 226 Moravian missionaries had gone into the world. They shared the Good News that we so take for granted, that through Christ we can become a new person and can throw off the old nature we received from Adam. In 2 Corinthians 5:18-20 it says, "And all of this is a gift from God, who brought us back to Himself through Christ. And

God has given us this task of reconciling people to Him. For God was in Christ, reconciling the world to Himself, no longer counting people's sins against them. And He gave us this wonderful message of reconciliation. So we are Christ's ambassadors; God is making His appeal through us. We speak for Christ when we plead, 'Come back to God!'"

When Paul urges his readers to be reconciled to God, it is not a casual request, as if he was saying, "Do me a favor," but he is beseeching, as though Christ Himself is pleading.

By the end of the eighteenth century, over one thousand missionaries had been sent from the small village of Herrnhut and other Moravian settlements. The secret of their success was fervent, heart-felt, day-and-night prayer, a disciplined Spirit-filled lifestyle, and obedience to the Word of God. "You are truly my disciples if you remain faithful to my teachings" (John 8:31). The Moravians learned from their leader principles of how to tell heathens about the cross and the Lamb of God. In his epistles, Paul focused on Christ crucified and said he didn't want to boast about anything except the cross. He avoided clever speeches for fear the message of the cross would not be understood. However, the cross is always controversial, and the scars on his back were the result of his teaching that the cross of Christ alone can save.

22

Christian Renatus

"A congregation which is full of life, speaks, prays, and sings daily together is a mighty fortress against the continual danger of lukewarmness" (Zinzendorf).

Zinzendorf loved England and often spent time there. In all, he stayed there over six years. With the help of Peter Böhler and August Gottlieb Spangenberg, he established communities in London and Yorkshire. Böhler was the Moravian who preached out of Romans when John Wesley was so wonderfully assured of his salvation.

Spangenberg was a Pietist and a theologian from Jena, Thüringen. He had a master's degree in theology and became enthusiastic about the Moravian Brethren. Zinzendorf personally liked Spangenberg, and he valued his counsel. Spangenberg's career was occupied with one special assignment after another in the service of the *Unitas Fratrum*. He first heard about the Moravians when two simple men from Herrnhut, Andreas Beyer and Gottlieb Wried, visited the university in Jena and gave an anointed testimony about changed lives, a transformed community, and the visitation of God's Holy Spirit. Spangenberg wrote, "I was a quiet listener, but my heart began to rejoice."

Christian Renatus, Ludwig's only son to reach adulthood, helped his father while he lived in London. Father and son grew very close during this time. His father observed the Holy Spirit working in Christian's young life, helping him to fall in love with Jesus. "Christel" had been caught up in the frivolous living in Herrnhaag, and the pain of that memory cut a deep wound that worked to mature him. Zinzendorf knew that even young people who grow up in a sheltered Christian environment, protected from open sinfulness, still have what he called a *Grundverderben,* or underlying deep corruption, rooted in the Adamic nature. This means the old nature has to be regenerated through grace by faith in Christ. Ludwig prayed a great deal for his son while in America, that he would become a true child of God and a servant of Christ.

When Ludwig came back from America in 1743, his heart was joyful when he learned that Christian Renatus had totally given his heart to the Savior. When he returned he barely recognized his son. He was much more serious and totally committed to Christ. His heart burned, and all his efforts were toward igniting Jesus' love in their gatherings of single men. He prayed for them, encouraged them, and the Lord used him to save souls.

A year before his untimely death, Christian Renatus grew weak and began to cough. Soon his lungs were destroyed by the TB bacillus and he died. The Brethren wept at his grave. It was a great loss for Ludwig, since his son worked tirelessly to help him, often through the night.

Christian was engaged to marry Anna Johanna Piesch, an Elderess in the single sister choir. Later in her life she married Nathanael Seidel, but throughout her life she kept on her finger the engagement ring that Christian gave to her. Ludwig's wife, Erdmuthe Dorothea, was so crushed by her son's death that she slowly lost the will to live. When Christel, as she called him, left for England just a year before his death, he jumped out of the carriage three times to hug his mother tenderly "one more time." When she heard that he was sick, she was delayed by her own illness from visiting. As soon as she gained enough strength, she started the journey, but the news of Christel's death reached her in Zeist, Holland. She lay ill for weeks and wrote in a letter to her family, the Reuss, "I must return with empty hands and leave behind my precious Christelein. [Adding a *lein* to a German name makes it especially dear]. How deeply it cuts. No day have I been without tears. To Papa Ludwig I have to put on a brave front. It is amazing how heaven draws me where my chosen little Christel is so happy. He must be thinking about me, and I am sure he is asking our dear Lamb of God to comfort me. During his life he never wanted me to worry about him, as he wrote in his last letter. I see now that he wrote *adieu*. This was never his usual closing. But I must stop, tears well in my eyes. Why do you think I am still here?"

Several times she visited Christel's grave in God's Acre called *Sharon*. She wrote, "It is a painful but an amazingly comforting place." When she returned to Herrnhut, she was stooped with grief, and everyone felt compassion for this deeply afflicted woman who was broken and had no will to live. She told the congregation not to mention Christel and wrote, "I cannot describe how weak I feel almost every day in my innermost being." The impact of losing her son is certainly understandable, considering that the Zinzendorfs had twelve children, and nine of them died young.

Zinzendorf did not fare better. His grief was profound. Some years before at the funeral of one of his own children, he told his congregation, "From the moment of birth never regard children as your own, but resign them wholly to the Savior as His property." Nevertheless, Zinzendorf's heart was full of sorrow. His friend, Spangenberg, wrote this observation revealing Zinzendorfs condition: "I cannot describe how his father felt, who was so brokenhearted when the news was brought to him. When he reflected what his son had been to him, his eyes overflowed with grief. When he read his son's papers and noted his daily communion with his Savior, his tears flowed still more. Renatus was loved not only by his father, but also by other members of the Brethren."

Paul gives this comfort in Romans 8:23, "And we believers also groan, even though we have the Holy Spirit within us as a foretaste of future glory, for we long for our bodies to be released from sin and suffering. We, too, wait with eager hope for the day when God will give us our full rights as his adopted children, including the new bodies he has promised us." In his suffering, Job gave an excruciating cry of anguish, recorded in Job 30:16-19, "And now my life seeps away. Depression haunts my days. At night my bones are filled with pain, which gnaws at me relentlessly. With a strong hand, God grabs my shirt. He grips me by the collar of my coat. He has thrown me into the mud. I'm nothing more than dust and ashes."

The truth is that all of us face adversity in various forms. We sometimes wonder where God is in all of this. Can we really trust Him when our life is filled with pain? How difficult it is in our travail to believe the Word of God in Psalm 50:15: "Then call on Me when you are in trouble, [affliction, hardship, adversity] and I will rescue you, and you will give me glory." In our suffering we may not feel His presence; He may be completely silent and we may agree with Job that we must hunt for God. "I go east, but He is not there. I go west, but I cannot find Him. I do not see Him in the north, for He is hidden. I look to the south, but He is concealed" (Job 23:8-9).

When darkness fills our soul, we might wonder, does God truly care about our tribulation? For a time, it may be more difficult to trust God than to obey Him. When it comes to obedience, our loving God has given defined boundaries of His revealed will. Through the power of the Holy Spirit we are able to obey Him progressively more and more. But trusting God is an arena that has no boundaries. We don't know what is ahead or the duration of our suffering. We don't know the extent of what we will suffer, whether it will get better or worse. David lamented, "O Lord, how long will you forget me? Forever? How long will You look the other way? How long must I struggle with anguish in my soul, with sorrow in my heart every day? How long will my enemy have the upper hand?" (Psalm 13: 1-2).

As we deal with these waves of heartache, we have no idea how often they will come. We are coping with the unknown. But the Word often exhorts us to trust God just as we obey Him. If we don't trust as we go through trials, we will inevitably sin against His commands and fail to venerate His holiness. Doubts about His sovereignty will arise and we may question His character. We can only trust God through the lens of faith, not through the perspective of circumstances. In God's Word we find assurance that God is actually present in our agonizing circumstances. The Holy Spirit helps us, comforts us, guides us, and we receive wonderful assistance when we trust God in the midst of our adversity.

We are not to become prisoners of our feelings. Trusting God is a matter of the will, a decision to believe God's Word and His promises. We must cling to them despite the adversities that at times seek to overwhelm us. Struggling through my own difficulties, I've chosen to have confidence that the Father has infinite wisdom and knows what is best for me. He has an immeasurable love towards me, and He is the Supreme Ruler. In His love, He always wills what is best for us. In His wisdom, He always knows what is best. Through His sovereignty, He has the power to accomplish it.

John Newton, reformed slave trader and author of the hymn, "Amazing Grace," watched as his wife died slowly and painfully of cancer. He wrote, "I believe it was a few months before her death, when I was walking up and down the room, offering disjointed prayers from my distressed heart, when a thought struck me with unusual force. The promises of God must be true that He surely will help us in time of trouble, if I am willing to be helped." John Newton chose to be helped. He realized his need to rely on the Lord rather than give in to overwhelming sadness. In facing the inevitable losses of life, grieving is absolutely crucial for our healing, yet, it is sinful to wallow in self-pity continually. So, during times of testing, there is a choice. We can choose resignation and feel sorry for ourselves, which is a form of narcissism, or we can trust what God says in His Word, that He has a good plan for us. "For I know the plans I have for you," says the Lord, "They are plans for good and not for disaster, to give you a future and a hope" (Jeremiah 29:11).

Prayer is an effective tool in our decision on how to handle suffering. David wrote, "But in my distress I cried out to the Lord; yes, I prayed to my God for help. He heard me from His sanctuary; my cry to Him reached his ears" (Psalm 18:6). We are urged to trust Him in our adversities and we also need expectant faith that the Holy Spirit will enable and strengthen us. We may often say, "God, I don't understand, but I trust you."

In Hebrews 13:5, God assures us, "I will never fail you. I will never abandon you." These words are balsam for the heart. In Isaiah 43:2, God promises, "When you go through deep waters, I will be with you. When you go through rivers of difficulty, you will not drown! When you walk through the fire of oppression, you will not be burned up; the flames will not consume you." Peter urges us to give all our worries and cares to God, for He cares what happens to us (1 Peter 5:7). His care is infinitely wise and good.

John Newton reflected, "If it were possible for me to alter any part of his plan, I would only spoil it." Trust is a vigorous act of the soul by which we choose to lay hold of the promises of God and cling to Him despite calamities that, at times, seem to overwhelm us. "Who can command things to happen without the Lord's permission? Does not the Most High send both calamity and good?" (Lamentations 3:37-38). Rather than being offended by God's sovereignty in times of calamities, be comforted in the knowledge that our Father has a loving purpose in everything that happens. "Sing for joy, O heavens! Rejoice, O earth! Burst into song, O mountains! For the Lord has comforted his people and will have compassion on them in their suffering" (Isaiah 49:13).

To trust God, we must know Him personally and intimately. David wrote in Psalm 9:10, "Those who know Your name trust in you, for You, O Lord, do not abandon those who search for You." To know God's name is more than just knowing facts about Him. When we have a deep, personal relationship with Him, we feel His comfort in the midst of our pain and discover that He is trustworthy. With the Word of God dwelling in us richly, the Holy Spirit reveals that the Father in heaven is full of love and wisdom and we should be more than willing to submit joyfully to His sovereignty. After all, Jesus also promised us that He has us in His grip, and nobody will snatch us out of His hand (John 10:28).

23

Zinzendorf's Wife: A humble helpmate

"Now I am alone here. You can easily imagine what a difficult test this is for someone like me to see my dear lord [Ludwig] begin such a long and dangerous journey. I could not bear it if I were not sure it was the Savior's will and not a venturesome act. I believe the Savior will bring him back to me if it is His will and He will not place more on his shoulders than he can bear" (Erdmuthe Dorothea).
(In a letter to her brother when Zinzendorf left for a year-and-a-half on a mission trip to America).

In 1756, four years after their son died, Ludwig lost his beloved wife, Erdmuthe Dorothea. The Lord had shown his goodness to Ludwig by giving him such a *Lebensgefährtin*, life-long companion. Being Zinzendorf's wife was surely not an easy task, but she proved to be indispensable to his work. Essential to the success of their marriage and mission was her willingness to give up riches, comforts, and worldly honor. She wrote more than sixty hymns, and from these we catch a glimpse of her heart. In these songs, she revealed her strong faith in Christ's blood, shed for her as the only reason for her hope. She poured out her feelings about remaining silent in tribulations and her unshakable trust in accepting all that came from the Savior's hand.

Erdmuthe possessed a keen and astute understanding of her husband's daring enterprises. Knowing he was both extravagantly generous and a poor economist, she was the one who kept them out of the poor house. She was thrifty in managing a large household and expertly handled financial affairs. She received 20,000 *Talers* from her godmother, which was a large amount of money. Because she knew how to do a lot with a little, the money was wisely spent. Her work included helping new Moravian settlers, supporting orphans, and hiring poor people.

Household staff included a housekeeper, three chamber maids, two footmen, a house servant, a laundry girl, six maids, and a coachman for eight horses. Tobias Friedrich was the house steward and the music master. All those employed belonged to the congregation and received a small salary, plus free room and board. Her motherly affection and godly character had a powerful impact on everyone around her. She had a joyful spirit and Ludwig once wrote, "She spread the teachings of the blood and wounds of Jesus within her circles and also diligently assisted me in preparing the *Losung*, the watchwords for the year."

Erdmuthe was a wonderful storyteller, with an ability to captivate her audience. She was also a cherished friend. Sisters in the choirs and small groups gladly accepted her insights and wise counsels. Her sister-in-law, Theodora von Reuss, wrote in her diary, "I could always speak with my dear friend Erdmuthe about all my spiritual and physical circumstances. I accepted her instructions with love and learned many insights about marriage and how to live sacredly before the Lord."

Before Erdmuthe married Ludwig, they had long, spiritual conversations. He wrote to her that although his love for Jesus was paramount, he loved her with all his heart. He envisioned a *Streiterehe*, a marriage of warriors, meaning they would fight to expand the Kingdom of God. Erdmuthe willingly fit into her husband's plans and shared his zeal for Christ in suffering and in joy. They had their wedding rings engraved, hers with "Let us love Him," and his with "He first loved us."

Erdmuthe certainly had her portion of tribulations. She especially suffered from all the tension in Herrnhut before the Moravian Pentecost. Undoubtedly, her greatest heartache was the loss of nine out of twelve children. Most died at a young age. When she received the sad news on one of her mission trips that her four-year-old son, David, had left this world, she grieved for a long time. In a heavy-hearted mood, she wept as she composed a lamenting hymn. Her five-year-old daughter, Johanna Salome, noticed her tears and wanted to comfort her. She said, "Mama, will you also cry for me when I die? When you have neither David nor me, we shall be with the Lamb and sing. There it is much better than here." Johanna Salome's utterance was prophetic. She joined little David six months later. Another daughter, Anna Theresa, also left this world when she was four years old. Ludwig was not with Erdmuthe when she gave birth to Anna Theresa. He wrote, "I am sure you can easily imagine, my beloved wife, that it is a great joy to me that your Savior has so graciously helped you. I had all along the faith that would be the case. The Savior has been very merciful to us. Let us grow daily more in His likeness. I am doing well on my journey as a witness."

Then there was the two-year-old Theodora Charitas. Her preferred place was sitting on Papa's lap, singing with him her favorite hymns. She loved her dad *zärtlich*, tenderly. Once her mother asked her, "Where have you been?" She answered in a matter of fact voice, "I was with the Savior and Papa."

"Oh," inquired her mother curiously, "you have been with the Savior?"

"Yes, Papa was speaking to Him."

She caught her dad praying in his audible voice, which was Zinzendorf's preferred style of prayer. Theodora Charitas did not celebrate her third birthday; she joined the other Zinzendorfs' children in the land of glory. It is there that Jesus will fulfill His pledge to keep on revealing the Father to her and to us throughout eternity (John 17:26).

Erdmuthe also suffered greatly when her adult son, Christian Renatus died. She lost her zest for life. She slept more and more, and one day, without any apparent sickness, she just didn't wake up. All the brothers and sisters mourned for her and shed many tears. A relative, Heinrich Ignatius, wrote in his diary, "She went like a feeble candle that is easily blown out." Friedrich von Watteville wrote, "Our honorable sister and dearest mama, the congregation's faithful nurse and foster mother, has passed into the arms of her Bridegroom." Friedrich personally brought her husband the news of Erdmuthe's death. It came so unexpectedly that Ludwig told his best friend rather abruptly, "Now let me be just by myself," and he shut himself away and wept for hours.

Around 2,000 mourners attended her funeral. All the sisters wore their white festive clothing. At her funeral, Zinzendorf said, "The Lord through His great power accomplished many glorious deeds through her. She gave wise advice and had deep insights into Scripture. People will speak of her wisdom and the congregation proclaims her praise. She was **'God's princess among us.'**" (The last four words are also chiseled as an epitaph on her granite flat gravestone next to Zinzendorf).

Some time later, Ludwig revealed the pain in his heart before the Brethren in a Berthelsdorf Synod. "I can say in all my life I have never endured such anguish. When my son Christel who toiled so faithfully with me departed from this earth I travailed a lot. But the home-going of my wife was even more agonizing."

Long afterwards, he reproached himself and complained, "In many respects I failed to do the things rightly expected of a husband who attempts to model his marriage on Christ."

In the last few years, before her death, Ludwig and Erdmuthe lived in separate places. Zinzendorf lived in the mansion in Berthelsdorf and Erdmuthe in the manor house in Herrnhut. She was still the *liebe Mamachen,* affectionate mama. Her daughters and some close Moravian sisters in the Lord visited her often. Her widowed sister-in-law Theodora, who Zinzendorf so passionately pursued almost forty years ago, was always close by. Erdmuthe had her corner in a comfortable sofa with a little table. She dressed like all the sisters in Herrnhut, but kept a certain distance as an aristocrat.

One source mentions that his frequent travels put a rift between them, however, the reason for them being apart isn't made clear in the old books. It is possible that in her grief she may have chosen seclusion.

Zinzendorf and his wife both demonstrated humility in different ways. He introduced foot-washing for all the *Unitas Fratrum*, sisters with sisters and brothers with brothers. Erdmuthe could not bring herself to do it with one particular woman. Ludwig wrote to her, "I have followed you often in your wisdom, and now could you obey me with my advice and wash the feet of this sister? You can follow Christ in His humility." A short time later, Erdmuthe progressed spiritually and washed this woman's feet. Afterwards, she could live with that sister in a new, genuine relationship, and she even allowed the woman to address her informally. Members of the congregation reported, "Our Sunday services have never been like they are now, praise be to God. Our honorable Countesse now considers foot-washing a noble service, and she is very cordial to us." Zinzendorf wrote to her when he heard about the foot washing, "Dear Sister, you are truly the half of my heart in Christ. I embrace you with fervent and pure love in the eternal all embracing and penetrating Spirit of my Savior. I kiss you with passion for you are my true honor."

On another occasion, Ludwig suggested that Erdmuthe stop wearing her special clothing and dress like a plain sister. This meant giving up a train, a crinoline, and a contouche, which is a wide, comfortable outer garment. In a letter to Ludwig, she explained that she was willing to give up everything but the outer garment. She wrote, "I believe you would not like to see me without the contouche." She was self-conscious about her back, which was slightly bent because of her weak constitution as a child.

Erdmuthe was present when several commissions from the royal court in Dresden arrived with orders for an investigation. Some very critical matters hung in the balance. Would the Moravians be forced to leave Herrnhut? Would the Count be exiled? For eleven days, commissioners examined all aspects of their lives. They were particularly suspicious of the hourly intercession and asked the prayer warriors if they were praying against the Prince Elector. Apparently, they feared those prayers as they would a conquering army. Erdmuthe was interrogated, and she later wrote about this experience, "The time of suffering is a glorious time. There is a certain gentle, powerful feeling that cannot be described when you have a union with the heart of Jesus. We are together almost the entire day."

Years earlier, when another young son, Christian Ludwig, died of dysentery, Erdmuthe Dorothea opened her heart: "We have to endure these trials in our pilgrimage. I pray that the Savior might achieve his purpose in bringing me through this fire. He was only ill for six days. He was healthy and exceptionally clever. My mother's heart is deeply wounded, but Christian Ludwig is happy now, and he knows the One who made the wound, 'Is Love.'"

The Love of God!

"Could we with ink the ocean fill,
And were the skies of parchment made,
Were every stalk on earth a quill,
And every man a scribe by trade,
To write the love of God above
Would drain the ocean dry,
Nor could the scroll contain the whole,
Though stretched from sky to sky.
O love of God, how rich and pure!
How measureless and strong!
It shall forevermore endure
The saints' and angels' song."
                    (Frederick Lehman).

24

Heimgang, Home Going

"Do not digress even for a quarter of an hour from the loving Lamb of God. Name no virtue except in Him. Preach no commandment except faith in Him. No other justification but that He atoned for. No other sanctification but the privilege to sin no more in Him. No other happiness but to be near to Him, think of Him and do His pleasure. No greater loss but to be deprived of Him. No greater calamity but to displease Him. No other life but in Him." (Zinzendorf).

After his wife died, Ludwig withdrew for days and mourned for the rest of the year. One of his retreats was an attic room in the Diaspora house at Herrnhut. Spangenberg wrote, "Of the one thousand residents in Herrnhut only a few were aware of it." There were periods of inaction followed by whole nights of exhausting, all-out efforts to catch up on correspondence. Part of the Count's sorrow may have been compounded by remorse. In his relentless endeavors for his Savior, he had forgotten that Erdmuthe was a wife, and a mother.

August Gottlieb Spangenberg (1703-1792) was perhaps Zinzendorf's closest friend and his mentor. Spangenberg was a great scholar and theologian. He studied at the university in

Jena, Switzerland. When he was a student he had moments of doubts about his faith and battled many temptations. He was saved by two plain Moravians. Spangenberg wrote, "These Brethren from Herrnhut were angels sent by God. These fellows believed *schäfleinsdumm,* simple as a sheep, truly and entirely in their hearts what the Bible says without interpreting it through the lens of the flesh or through intellectual reasoning."

Benjamin Franklin called him, "My very much respected friend, Bishop Spangenberg." He tutored Zinzendorf when he was preparing for his Lutheran ordination. When it looked like the Brethren might have to leave Herrnhut, he negotiated a grant from the king of England for a Moravian settlement in Georgia. In 1735, he led a group of nine Moravians to Georgia and also did some evangelistic, soul-saving work in Pennsylvania. He surveyed and settled Moravians of Wachovia in North Carolina. After he was consecrated as a bishop in 1744, he assumed all responsibilities for the ministries in North America. When Zinzendorf died, he was called back to Europe where his executive experiences proved crucially important for thirty years in helping the over-extended Moravian ambitious undertakings. Some years later, he wrote in his memoirs about this period in Zinzendorf's life. "For many hours he often went into seclusion and placed himself in the presence of the Lord. He reflected about his thirty-four years of marriage. The faults he detected in his heart gave him great humility. He went several times through a deep self-reproach for leaving Erdmuthe alone for long periods of time. The lamentation over this realization was deep and bathed in many tears, and he frequently asked his Savior for full forgiveness."

In the year of mourning he was not totally inactive. He still preached with endurance. Every month at the congregation day he preached from morning to evening. Many people from outside Herrnhut also came to hear his stimulating and anointed sermons, which were peppered with impromptu poetic songs and poems. Word pictures out of the Bible were compelling, and narrated with a gush of effective words. He was truly a master of the German language. People were so riveted; they did not want to go home. More than once a person fainted for lack of nourishment. It was startling to Zinzendorf, since he did not feel any exhaustion.

He also traveled on Christ Ascension Day in 1757 to the settlement *Gnadenfrei,* "Freed through Grace." They all expected him with joy and he held a *Festrede,* a festive celebration sermon, in the packed out large community hall.

After a year of mourning, the Elders in Herrnhut came up with a plan. They knew that Ludwig held a certain woman of the congregation in high esteem, Anna Helena Nitschmann. She was born in Moravia and was twelve years old when the congregation experienced the Pentecostal fire in Berthelsdorf. The Lord used her mightily as she worked tirelessly among the children. One evening, for instance, she gathered many children on the Hutberg, a hill close to Herrnhut, and they sang happy songs to the Lord. After a while, they travailed in prayer about lost souls and cried out to the Lord. A woman in Strahwalde, about a mile away, complained about the noise at such a late hour. Some time later, the complaining woman was converted and she apologized.

When Anna was fifteen years old, she was already an Elderess of eighteen girls in the single women's choir. When she was twenty, she sank into a deep crisis of faith, and wanted to resign her position as an Elderess. Zinzendorf stood close by her as a counselor. To counteract rumors of being so much with her, he came up with a unique plan. He asked Anna Nitschmann's father to adopt him in 1737. Anna then became his sibling. Anna had remained single and was a virtuous disciple of Christ. It was said of her, "When she spoke or prayed or sang, all hearts opened up to her, and she filled her role with zeal and devotion until her death."

Anna sailed to America when she was twenty-five years old and spent several years as a key member of the "Pilgrim congregation." She was instrumental in the evangelization of German settlers.

Zinzendorf's blood and wound hermeneutics of the crucified Savior were frequently adorned and beautified in his pictorial sermons. The side wound of Jesus was mentioned in hymns, prayers, and even in plays. We find his point of view in his writings: "The love and *Zärtlichkeit*, tenderness we have for Jesus allows for a hundred expressions and word pictures. If you cannot find enough words to verbalize this love it is a proof of your affection for Him."

In the 18th century, mystics like Madame Jeanne Guyon (1648-1717) used sentimental imagery, romance and poetic expression to describe interaction with God in human words. Mystics depart from theologians, they may not be teachers. Their words are the experiential outbursts of love and divine exhilaration. Anna undoubtedly was influenced by Zinzendorf and by some of his mystical theology, as we read in her writings and in a letter from America, "Like a poor little worm, I desire to withdraw myself into His wounds and nail prints. I swim in the sea of grace that is the blood of Jesus. It is well with me when I rest in the side wound of Jesus." This love language seems strange to us now, and we brush it away as intense, fervent embellishment, but many books written by mystics in those centuries were saturated with sentimentality. She composed a lovely hymn,

> *Jesus, Thou wouldst have us to be*
> *In everything conformed to Thee,*
> *Though we oft are filled with shame,*
> *Because Thou alone dost know our frame,*
> *Thy patience, love and grace we claim.*

Celibacy was never held up as the ideal state, but young brethren and sisters quite frequently pledged themselves to wait with matrimony so they could go more easily as missionaries, or on extended special assignments. Zinzendorf encouraged marriage, and most Moravians eventually ended up hearing the "ringing of wedding bells for their own marriage."

Anna lacked an aristocratic title. By this time, it seemed, Ludwig placed no significance on worldly titles. He must have known the wonderful title God has given us in 1 Peter 2:9, where all believers are described as a "royal [aristocratic] priesthood." Anna held Zinzendorf in high regard. In fact, Ludwig once said, "Anna is putting me too high on a pedestal."

As mentioned before, the Elders had a plan and a meeting. Zinzendorf's close friend, Friedrich von Watteville gave a speech, "Almost a year has passed since our beloved Mama went home. Dear Papa needs to become part of our choir again. We can think of no one else but the *Jüngerin*, disciple, Anna." All the Elders joined in Friedrich's sentiment. He was chosen to be the matchmaker and to inform Zinzendorf about their unanimous decision. Shortly afterwards, he asked Anna whether she would consider exchanging wedding vows with Ludwig, and then he asked Zinzendorf about the possibility of marrying Anna. Both were agreeable to his suggestion. Bishop Leonard Dober married them, and eleven friends witnessed the private ceremony. Zinzendorf asked them, for reasons of his own, to keep it a secret for a while. The marriage was announced a year-and-a-half later.

Johannes Nitschmann penned his thoughts about this unconventional situation: "Because his mother was still alive and living in Berlin, he wanted to bring the news of their marriage to her personally, and he did not know what she would say." Zinzendorf needed time to tell other family members, relatives, and his aristocratic patrons about his marriage. It was one thing to defy the sentiments of aristocrats to become a minister of the Gospel. It was quite another thing to marry a peasant and a former *Kuhmagd und Weberin,* milk maid and weaver. Zinzendorf wrote, "Annel, (her pet name) has an extraordinary mind, a good disposition and many spiritual gifts. Without any hesitancy can I introduce her to the world as a Countesse."

The secret was well kept. That Ludwig and Anna could minister and travel together as man and wife without causing any rumors shows how far removed the private life of the aristocrats were from the commoners in the 18th century. Sadly, the marriage was of short duration.

Zinzendorf's last years were full of ventures. We get a glimpse of his activities when we read at random a sample page in his diary:

* *A night spent in deep humility in His presence. Prayed for every family in Herrnhut.*
* *On a journey to Zittau, brother Christoph told me his testimony. He is spiritually far ahead of me.*
* *Prayed on the Hutberg* [a hill just outside Herrnhut] *for 130 cell groups in other places. I received inner leadings from the Lord.*
* *Tuesday, I preached in Hennersdorf about committing our lives to the Lord in childlike faith and to abolish any temporal longing. I was so carried away in my preaching that I added personal experiences which I should have kept to myself.*
* *David Nitschmann* [the first missionary to the Caribbean] *and Christian David visited me for brotherly discussions. We examined ourselves. We told each other things in our lives that mar the image of Christ. They told me my weaknesses, and I told them what they lacked.*

This sounds like what we men call accountability, and it shows the humility and brokenness of Zinzendorf. I ask myself, would I be able to take correction from a man like Christian if he had once called me "The Beast"? And yet, on the salutary side, Jesus calls us **true** children of the Father in heaven when we are able to **forgive** (Matthew 5:45). On the foolish side, if we don't forgive, we will experience divine chastening. "There will be no mercy for those who have not shown mercy to others. But if you have been merciful, God will be merciful when He judges you" (James 2:13).

The second question is: Why are some members in the Body of Christ so joyless, and as a consequence, unsatisfied? Could it be that they are under the reproach of the Lord for harboring unforgiveness in their hearts? Only after a full confession of his sins did King David dare to ask the Lord, "Restore to me the **joy** of your salvation, and make me willing to **obey** you" (Psalm 51:12).

Zinzendorf showed great concern for his flock, every missionary and each individual. He often said that the congregation is only as high and holy as each individual's heart is with the Savior. The choirs received new goals, and he watched their growth in sanctification with keen interest. Revived souls in nearby villages received his attention and care as well. This was Zinzendorf's finest hour. The Brethren loved him more than ever. Zinzendorf and Herrnhut belonged to each other. He made two more *Pilgerreisen*, pilgrimages, with his new wife, Anna, with his two daughters, Henriette Benigna and Marie Agnes, his son-in-law, Johannes von Watteville, his secretary and some Brethren. They traveled in two coaches to western Germany and Switzerland. The Count preached to large audiences in Basel, Montmirail, Geneva, and Lausanne. He greatly encouraged many Brethren to become missionaries to Greenland, the American Colonies, the West Indies, Surinam, Tranquebar, Abyssinia, and the Near East. He exhorted them with the finest mission theory, "A missionary seeks nothing else, day and night, but that the heathens find joy in their Savior and that the Savior may find joy in the heathens." He wrote in his diary when he reflected on all his impressions on this trip, "If you depend on one man or on one family they will disillusion you. But if you show me a vibrant community I can promise you enduring success. This is the blessing of this current time, Spirit-filled communities by the hundreds."

When he returned to Herrnhut, he spurred the Brethren to return to their first love. Daily preaching and conferences with Elders, choir leaders, teachers and missionaries kept his calendar full.

Frequently, he invited Lutheran pastors to his mansion, exhorting them to personal holiness, to sound doctrine, and devout teachings of the Word. He earnestly pleaded with the pastors, "It has to be the burning longing of your heart that the suffering of Jesus is not lost on a soul. If a person gets converted, the entire honor has to go to the Savior, because salvation is the result of His passion on the cross. Narrate pictures to them how our Savior bled for us to death. Tell them not to run from Him as Adam did, but to run always toward Him. The friendship and intimacy with Christ will help them not to sin. It is the best means; yes it is the only avenue to become blissful and holy. Augustinus expressed that so beautiful in his meditation, when he wrote the hymn, 'Jesus, your deep wounds.'" Over one hundred pastors were under his tutelage.

A group of revived Slavic people, called Sorbs and Wenden, lived near Herrnhut. Many of them came often to Herrnhut to hear Zinzendorf preach. After hearing a sermon, one member of this group approached the Count and said, "I cannot fully understand your language, but for twenty years I have thought exactly as you do but could not express it. While you spoke I said to myself, this is it, this is it."

When a preacher such as Zinzendorf is Spirit-filled, an irresistible grace leads others to Christ. Through the supernatural operation of the Holy Spirit, people see and feel the reality of the indwelling Christ in that person. Preaching is the outward calling, and when the carnal hear that call, they must choose to resist or respond. If they respond, the effectual calling makes them children of God. If they resist, it will lead them to a spiritual death. Pride, rebellion, and self-righteousness are the biggest obstacles to a true conversion.

Zinzendorf, his wife and his household journeyed one more time to his beloved Holland. He stayed for a year in a large manor house in Heerendijk. His robust health was declining. He gained weight, had frequent colds and coughs, and his voice was often hoarse. He took leisurely walks, went earlier to bed, and ate regularly.

Moravian missionaries came back from countries and continents such as Greenland and South America and told him inspiring stories of continued growth. Zinzendorf listened eagerly, discussed and prayed with them about problems, and invited them to his three daily home groups and conferences. When they bade him farewell, he blessed them with "love and memory" from the Brethren.

On the 24th of December 1759, he returned home to Herrnhut. Anna was exhausted and sick from the long journey. She could not fulfill her obligations as an Elderess of her choir anymore. His long-standing, active and tireless consort was spent. She was not the youthful enthusiastic companion anymore. His faithful student, whom Zinzendorf called thirty-three years ago, when Anna experienced the Baptism with the Holy Spirit, "His first great girl" had a lingering sickness. She always admired and followed his lofty ideas. She climbed on his high reaching flights with fervor. Now she sometimes voiced publicly her different opinion, pulled back, became at times irascible, and sought stillness.

Zinzendorf did not know, but Anna was quietly suffering from a fatal disease.

At the beginning of 1760, Zinzendorf could still preach up to eight sermons a day. An anointed sermon from Luke 24:36 was based on one of Jesus' appearances after the resurrection: "And just as they were telling about it, Jesus himself was suddenly standing there among them, and He said, 'Peace be with you.'" Zinzendorf ended this sermon with a song he composed, "What would you think? How would you act, if our Lord suddenly came? Would you be afraid? Oh, no, with tears flowing from your eyes, you would fall before His feet and say, 'Bridegroom, we are here.'"

During the last few months of his life, his eyes quite often filled with tears. One brother was walking behind him and heard him talking to his Savior, "Oh, I wish I could personally tell you all my plans." On another occasion he said, "Nobody will be called home unless the Savior decrees that the person is expendable." He also admonished his Brethren, "Children, we have to be diligent, the time is short."

In one of his last discourses before his departure from this earth, he said, "We always have to have the expectancy that the Savior comes soon and takes us into His rest. This is a sublime, blissful, tender and *herzhinnehmender,* heart capturing thought. When people have this hope and longing in their thought life and it becomes a solid anchor, then it will give them a helping hand to truly become a 'people of God.' Soon they will be noticed by the traits and quality of their behavior that they belong in the 'family of the Savior.' They will keep on walking towards Him year after year and at the same time feasting on His merits. At last, they will see the One they believed in and always had in their hearts."

Zinzendorf's constitution became weak in the spring of 1760. Zinzendorf must have felt that his pilgrimage on this earth was coming to an end. He gave himself no rest and worked late hours to finish the *Losung* for 1761. The last entry Zinzendorf chose was prophetic ..."We bless you from the house of the Lord" (Psalm 118:26). "Then the king turned his face and blessed the entire community" (1 Kings 8:14). "And let the peace that comes from Christ rule in your heart. For as members of one body you are called to live in peace. And always be thankful" (Colossians 3:15). "But the love of the Lord remains forever with those who fear Him. His salvation extends to the children's children" (Psalm 103:17).

Then on Sunday morning, May 4, he visited all the leaders of the different choirs and he expressed his tenderhearted love for them. His wife, Anna, accompanied him, even though she was feeble. In the afternoon he went into seclusion to pray, as was always his habit. In the evening he celebrated the end of seven sessions for the 'Synod of the Single Sisters,' which he began in April. Some Brethren urged him to cancel the ceremony, as they noticed that he felt uncomfortable in the big, cold assembly room. But he was determined to finish his curriculum. Later in the evening he felt exhausted and went to bed early. His sleep was fitful and he developed a fever. In the morning he got up with some effort, and with great diligence he finished a manuscript. Then he mentioned to a brother, "Now I can rest in peace." He did not eat at the dinner table but drank several glasses of water. He remarked that he felt a great heat in his body. He was very cordial with all the houseguests.

In the afternoon, he visited his beloved, ailing wife and composed a poem of thirty-six stanzas for the single sisters choir, which he recited in the evening after the *Liebesmahl,* love-feast [Holy Communion]. His voice was so weak that many verses were not understood. After the celebration he went to bed without delay, but did not sleep. Soon his fever became *hitzig,* even hotter, and he developed a fierce cough. Dr. Hasse was called and he diagnosed catarrhal fever. On Tuesday, he asked that someone would read all the letters and correspondence to him. In the evening, his three daughters

Heimgang, Home Going

Marie Agnes, Elizabeth and Henriette Benigna came for a visit. They had an intimate and lovely conversation. It was a great delight for him once again to see his daughter, Henriette Benigna von Watteville. She had arrived after a lengthy stay in England and Ireland. He told his daughters, "Whenever I was sick in my life I asked the Lord what was the cause and what did He want to tell me? Whatever the Lord laid bare to me, I made it known to my close friends. Then I did not hesitate and I openly revealed my transgression and confessed that I was a repentant sinner. Sometimes people abused this openness, but I was never discouraged not to admit my wrongdoings. This time, however, the Lord has no message for me in my illness."

News spread quickly that the Count was ill. Many close friends came and visited him. Count Heinrich Reuss, the brother of his late wife, Erdmuthe Dorothea, was also present. Ludwig was very cordial and warm with all his friends and visitors. He did not sleep at night, and his physical condition deteriorated rapidly. On Wednesday, his fever rose again and he developed prolonged coughing spells. Although he still had a joyful spirit, his voice was too weak to speak, and he was drifting in and out of consciousness. On Thursday, the last full day on this earth, he regained a remarkable strength. He had long conversation with his three daughters and some very close friends. He mentioned to his closest school friend, Friederich von Watteville, that he felt jubilation in his heart, and he was totally at peace with his Lord's plan for him.

Anna came to see him for the last time. She was also suffering from a fatal illness, possibly cancer, and could only visit him with great effort. His son-in-law, Johannes von Watteville, was also with him, and many other Brethren. With a friendly and joyful countenance he said, "I cannot express how much I love you all. Aren't we already as in heaven and love each other as angels? The prayer of the

Lord in John 17 that we all become one is manifesting itself among us."

He started reminiscing about many of the brothers and sisters who were already in heaven. He still remembered many names. The oil painting must have come to his mind that Brother Valentin Haidt painted in Herrnhaag. (This painting is now in the Herrnhut archive). The oil painting shows twenty-two converts in their native costumes, all standing before the throne of God and the Lamb, representing the first fruits.

He also mentioned all the great blessings the Lord granted him and the Brethren in thirty-three years. He spoke to all of them present in the chamber. "I thought in the beginning the Lord would only grant us a few heathens, but now there are thousands saved." Then his voice became stronger and he cried out with enthusiasm and fervor, "Brother Nitschmann, did you ever imagine at the onset of this outreach how much the Lord would do? What a formidable caravan is already standing around the throne of the Lamb!"

At midnight, his tongue became heavy and he was drifting into periods of unawareness. His speech returned in the morning and he was grateful to his Lord. He motioned to his son-in-law, Johannes, to come close to him. He whispered, "Now my good and best Johannes, I go to my Savior. I am ready, my heart is totally resigned to the will of my Lord, and He is satisfied with me. If He cannot use me here any longer, I am ready to go to Him; nothing is in the way."

Baron Friedrich von Watteville and David Nitschmann came again for a visit, and Ludwig spoke a few words to them. However, his voice was too weak to be fully understood and he fell silent. For almost an hour he could only look at them with an affectionate, happy expression. Moravian missionaries were all around him and in the surrounding rooms. Brother Seidel was home after years in the West Indies and Denmark. Brother Töltschig [he was among the five Brethren who were present when they laid the foundation stone for the community center] was also present after twenty years in America, Holland, and England. Spangenberg wrote later, "The peace of God in the chamber was so consoling."

Around ten o'clock in the morning, Zinzendorf lifted his head slightly, took a few deep breaths and laid his head peacefully back on the pillow. His eyes were clear and discerning. Watteville prayed out loud, "Now let your servant depart in peace." He was completely at peace as he went home to be with the Lord. "Those who are wise will shine as bright as the sky, and those who lead many to righteousness will shine like the stars forever" (Daniel 12:3).

Count Reuss wrote in his diary, "There was such a wafting of *Gottesfrieden,* peace of God, that all our hearts were comforted. Many embraced each other with a paroxysm of tears." Paul said in 2 Tim. 4:7, "I have fought a good fight, I have finished the race, and I have remained faithful." In a hymn Zinzendorf composed, he wrote, "Oh, Lord, grant to me, in my hour of death, a sign of your peace."

The Lord granted him this favor. In another hymn he expressed his sentiments about the last moments of saints on earth,

> *When you are alive, you are a witness*
> *Of the power of Christ in you.*
> *This power is like a barb in your heart.*
> *When you leave this earthly tent*
> *To go and kiss the Lamb,*
> *The last expression on your face*
> *Should testify that you had saving faith.*

The *Losung* for the day Zinzendorf died was, "They weep as they go to plant their seed, but they sing as they return with the harvest" (Ps. 126:6). The same day, Johannes Nitschmann wrote in his diary, "When he was gone, we thought it was only a dream. We were not worthy to have him among us. We loved him so much. He sometimes suffered among us because we could not rise to his lofty principles. He had a *Gemüt,* heart and soul, soaring upwards with wings of an eagle and he was striving to accomplish the highest goal in all divine admonitions. It seems that at his departure even nature is mourning because the fog is even denser than in the winter."

Count Reuss, Zinzendorf's brother-in-law, wrote in his journal, "I thank my Savior for the blessing and grace that I could be with the honorable Count. I enjoyed his company and I learned so much from him. I cannot describe my sadness when I saw him so quietly resting there. He was such an enterprising servant of the Lord who stimulated us all to action. I could not look long enough at his face as his honorable remains lie there. The hymn he wrote and sang for the Passion-Week of Christ came to my mind, 'Wonderful countenance of Jesus, when I finally lay down, will my face ever look like Yours?' We allow him now to rest from all his astonishing achievements. We were consoled by our perception that he is jubilant and he feels overjoyed to be home with the Lord."

News of his death spread rapidly, and a stream of visitors came from all over the neighboring villages. Johannes told the congregation of their leader's last days. Herrnhut had never seen such a crowd! Many tears were shed as his body was laid in a purple casket. General Freiherr von Beck in nearby Zittau even sent a detail of soldiers for crowd control. At 3 o'clock in the afternoon, the big hall in the white church was crowded. Johannes von Watteville, the husband of his daughter, Henriette Benigna, knelt down beside the casket and offered up a fervent petition, "Most lovely Savior, You are the Elder of Your church, we are lying in the dust before You. We entrust all our Brethren into Your care again. O Jesus, You are the head of the congregation, You established us, we thank You that You gave us this disciple of Yours for so many years. You used him as Your servant and we received many blessings through him. We thank You for all his sweat and toils, and for the blessed founding's You did through him. You placed Your Spirit upon him and we received grace and anointing. Most lovely Savior, forgive us, because of Your wounds, as a congregation and as individuals that we gave him grief in the days when he walked among us. Console him now and send him a friendly twinkle from us. He is home with You now and resting from all his labors at Your wounds. We know and we have felt that You always loved him, You were at his side and Your presence was with him. He was a tool in Your hand and You worked with him according to Your grace. You are his Savior, his One and All, You were his familiar Lord, You gave him from Your merits, he never wanted more.

"Now, lovely Savior, look at us all in Your grace. Without You we would feel as orphans, because You took Your disciple from us. But You are our Elder, You will not forsake us, You will bring us through. Help Your people, Lord Jesus Christ, bless what is Your inheritance. Our hope is in You, dear Lord. You have promised us to be with us all the days until the world ends. Keep Your congregation in their walk of grace until You personally come. Preserve them in their awareness and in their faith of Your holy merits. Let Your merits be in our teachings and let us not walk from the foundation principles which You gave Your blessed Apostles. We want to proclaim Your death until You come again.

"Let us also remember Your disciple, Zinzendorf, Your loved one, may he have always a blessed effect upon us in the future by Your grace. We are certain he will whisper many good words to You in our behalf, since he is standing now before Your throne. Look at us by Your grace and give us grace, simplicity, warmth, unity and brotherly love. We again present our whole congregation to Your care."

In the Herrnhuter chronicle we read, "It was not possible to express more of the emotions. The tears of the Brethren flowed so freely, and there was such a heart melting feeling of grace and sorrow, they all preferred to just let the sobbing express their loss."

Six brothers were continuously on duty as watchmen over the casket. On the day of the funeral, all the women wore their festive, white dresses. Trombones were blown and a total of thirty-two brothers rotated carrying the precious casket for short distances. Two thousand mourners followed the casket to God's Acre. Johannes Nietschmann started a hymn, and the whole congregation sang antiphonally with him:

> *Oh, what blissful joy your dream must be,*
> *When in your visions you do see*
> *The matchless Lamb of Calvary.*
> *The Man of Sorrows has set you free,*
> *When to His wounded side you flee,*
> *For He has fully paid your penalty.*
> *The cross that showed His greatest love,*
> *Has guaranteed your place above,*
> *Where you are nestling as a dove.*
> *Would we awaken this noble soul,*
> *And force him to stay with us below,*
> *When now at last he's been made whole?*

His wife, Anna, was too weak to attend the funeral, but she looked out the window from the manor with tearful eyes as Ludwig was laid in a walled crypt. When Johannes von Watteville had brought to Anna the dismal news that her beloved husband died, she said, "I have the joyful prospect that I will be the first to see him again." Anna passed away twelve days later. Zinzendorf was buried next to his first wife, Erdmuthe Dorothea. On the flat granite gravestone was chiseled:

> Here are resting the mortal remains
> of the unforgettable man of God,
> Nikolai Ludwig, Count and
> Lord of Zinzendorf and Pottendorf.
> Through the grace of God and through his
> faithful and tireless service
> He became the honored Ordinarius of the Brethren's Unity,
> Renewed in this 18th Century.
> He was born at Dresden on May 26, 1700,
> And departed into the joy of his Lord on May 9, 1760.
> He was destined to bring forth fruit,
> fruit that should remain.

Count Reuss wrote in his diary, "As the casket was lowered into the earth, my heart was cut in two. This prince of the people was sown into the ground. The liturgy was unequaled and I felt that I could stand at the grave for hours with the thought, 'I wish I could go with him into the tomb.' We all had the awareness of his nearness. A thousand tears flowed. The congregation sang hymns of blessings upon him and the peace of God was over all of us. This hour will never be forgotten. This scene had such a liturgical ambience, I am sure that our blissful departed one would have looked on with joy. We said to one another, 'Who knows, he may have been with us.'"

"Our dear departed one wanted to go to Holland on this day of his final journey, but I am certain that in all his wanderings he never had such an entourage as today. If he would have given us permission, many of us would have joined him on his last journey to the place he is now."

25

Count Zinzendorf's *Lobrede,* Oration of Praise

"When you produce much fruit, you are my true disciples. This brings great glory to my Father" (John 15:8).

Some time later, Pastor Burkhard Georg Müller from Gross-Hennersdorf [a village by Herrnhut], who knew Zinzendorf very well, preached a memorial service filled with accolades for Zinzendorf. He chose the text, 1 Corinthians 15:10, "But whatever I am now, it is all because God poured out his special favor on me–and not without results, ...yet it was not I but God who was working through me by his grace."

Here are some highlights from that service: "Zinzendorf's whole foundation of his faith, which was established in the heart of his young life through the illumination of the Holy Spirit, became more and more delightful. It was like a magnet which drew him ever closer, to his Creator, his Brother and Savior who gave His blood and life for him. He hung on with body and soul to his dearest 'Man of Sorrow' and 'Enabler of Salvation' revealed in the flesh. This Divine Man endured the death on the cross for him and that was ever so clearly painted before his eyes. His soul fell more and more in love with the most Beautiful of all mankind. I cannot express that fact, as a preacher, with my limited words. He also had a revelation of Christ's eternal merits for him, and his heart was so full of that vision that he continually gave testimonies about that. Oh, this Person above meant everything for him, this Man of Sorrow. His bleeding wounds gave him merits, consoled him, made him overjoyed and sanctified him. This great drama, the Son of God, creator of all things, took the form of a slave, lived poor and despised in this world for over thirty years and offered Himself up for mankind and was slain on the trunk of a cross.

"Zinzendorf realized in his heart the magnificence, lowliness and miracle of the cross and discovered God's justice in that. This understanding became a meadow he was feeding on; it was his bliss and gave him strength and power to live in a godly manner. He lived in that awareness and his heart was burning. That is why he could not live without Him and he was drawn into an intimate union with Him. This union with his most Beloved was tender and childlike. It was his treasure above all treasures. Christ was his other I. Like a child he could talk to Him in this manner, 'You know all things; You know I am glued to You with my heart, my mind, my life, as you surely live.'

"I cannot find the right words to tell you how his heart was full of love toward Jesus. Yes, but above all, he was afraid to ever hurt the heart of his highly esteemed Savior. Out of this love-fervor came his burning desire to work for the Lord. Therefore, it was easy for him to leave position, honor, yes, even possessions, and to give it all willingly to his Lord. Nothing was as precious to him compared with the grace to be a bond-servant for his Lord. That is why he prayed so often the breath prayer, 'Lord, through the shedding of Your blood, make me to be Your own, then I have everything I need on this earth.' Right now in heaven he cannot find anything better than to seek His countenance.

"He had the mind of the Apostle Paul in Philippians 3:8, "Yes, everything else is worthless when compared with the infinite value of knowing Christ Jesus my Lord. For His sake I have discarded everything else, counting it all as garbage, so that I could gain Christ.

"Through the closeness with the 'Groom of his soul' the Lord transferred to him a Christ-likeness in his daily walk, in his mind and disposition. This became his heaven on earth. He spent many hours in the nearness of Christ in prayer. Day and night his Savior was hovering before his spiritual eyes. Was it then really a miracle that what he thought, spoke and did was sanctified with Christ's blood and mixed with His merits and suffering? All what he did was done in the mind of Christ! Christ was his foundational thought and in his manners and practice. The purity of the Lord mirrored in him and the Spirit revealed to him one insight and understanding after another.

"He learned from Jesus to love everything Jesus loved. Because of Him he could love all men walking in the Truth. To comply with God the Father's admonition in 1 John 3:23, was predominantly in his thoughts, "And this is His commandment: We must believe in the name of His Son, Jesus Christ, and love one another, just as he commanded us." If he failed in that it became a bitter pain and a heart sorrow for him.

"To forgive others when they offended him was easy and natural for him. When he thought he was the cause by his conduct, his heart was immediately ready to blame himself and to ask for forgiveness. He was seeking every occasion to do good, to open spiritual eyes, to become the feet for the lame. He could hardly ever say no to anyone. To make it short, he was truly a friend of mankind after the example of his Lord.

"He enjoyed the love of Christ, the mystery of Christ and the expectant blissfulness of heaven and it transformed him gradually into childlikeness in his later years. Simplicity and 'boyish' behavior was his beauty.

"Some years ago I personally heard about the honorable Count, and I was familiar with some of his truthful writings. So I decided to travel to Herrnhut with an open mind. I was immediately impressed by his humility and by his gracious sweetness in his liturgy and sermons. I can assure you, I told myself, the journey was worth it and I traveled home with joy. I agreed with the queen of Sheba, truly, I had not heard the half of it.

"Zinzendorf worked steadily and tirelessly. I do not intend to take away from the other co-laborers, but Ludwig was admired for his discipline and work habits. He mentioned so often, if the days would only be longer. He traveled twenty-five times across oceans and crossed Europe several times. On Sundays, he preached up to ten times, not only in Herrnhut but among the different choirs and in the big white church, and in the nearby villages.

"He gave away his land, including an Austrian *Lehnhof,* an estate he inherited from his deceased older brother, which he turned over to a nephew. He wanted nothing to stand in the way of full time ministry and expanding the kingdom of God.

"Very few men have suffered so much as this bond-slave of Christ. Enemies constantly reviled and belittled him, and printed venomous articles about him. They accused him that he had a low opinion of other parts of the Scriptures and that he was mainly obsessed with Christ crucified. His answer was that he also agreed with the Apostle Paul, that all treasures and wisdom were in the revelation that God came in the flesh. He believed that was the key to open up all other veracities in the Word of God. Eventually, he expected such attacks and realized he was not fighting against flesh and blood.

"Zinzendorf's extraordinary love for the Scriptures was shown by his ability to quote from memory large portions of the Bible. He loved the golden nuggets he continually discovered in the Word. His mind was invariably in the treasure house of the sacred writings. For him the Scriptures was like gold refined seven times in a furnace. He constantly read the Bible from cover to cover. He talked daily about one or more divine revelations that he discovered. The Holy Spirit gave him many enlightenments and his heart lived in the truth of the Scriptures. When he was eight years old he already resolved in his mind to believe it all as divine truth. He always said that the Word was paramount above all erudite, scholarly reasoning. His first and last proof was always, 'It is written.'

"Yes, all of us enjoyed the great gifts of this bond-slave and witness of Jesus Christ, and we are so thankful that his work goes on. We witnessed that he fulfilled the will of God to build His kingdom on earth. He was a friend of the Bridegroom, and as a *Brautwerber,* a recruiter for the bridegroom, he led many pure 'virgins' to Jesus, washed in Jesus' sin-atoning blood, clothed with His righteousness, and anointed with His oil of joy. All this came through the grace of God and through the nursing of the Holy Spirit.

"Now, he is resting on the side wounds of Jesus. It pleased his Lord and Master to wave at him while he was so busy and to call him into eternal joy. He willingly laid his work down as obedient as a child and yet he was a prince. His blessed departure was like a seal upon all his work.

"We look and turn our eyes upon his departure and we want to follow him in his faith. May his remembrance cause to spring up and sprout, and cause an imitation in thousands of hearts among the Brethren, the children of God in the diasporas [far from homeland] and among the heathens.

"We, I say, all of us, come before our Savior, the Head and Bishop of His church, who is with us all our days until the end of the world, want to renew our pledge to Him. We want to dedicate ourselves again to comply with His 'Love-wish' to lead all the people on earth by His grace into His eternal home. Whoever has this wish and desire, let him say 'Amen.'"

26

The Moravian spirit

"I have heard all about You, Lord. I am filled with awe by Your amazing works. In this time of our deep need, help us again as You did in years gone by. And in Your anger, remember Your mercy" (Habakkuk 3:2).

Some time ago, when I told our pastor, Jason Hubbard, director of the "Light of the World Prayer Center" in Bellingham, Washington, that I wanted to write a book about Zinzendorf and the Moravians, he gave me his enthusiastic blessing. He wanted me to find out more about the Moravian spirit. Here are my observations and discoveries.

* Harmony was restored in Herrnhut among the quarreling Moravians through **prayer, forgiveness** and by the **unifying** meditation for all the Brethren, the atoning, efficacious, "Look! The Lamb of God who takes away the sin of the world!" (John 1:29) This was the foremost subject matter of Zinzendorf's pleading to them to reunite and restore fellowship when he visited the Brethren from house to house for several days and nights.
* Only then did the small group of Moravians have a blazing encounter with the Holy Spirit and became aglow.

The Moravian spirit

* A few days afterwards they started a prevailing, intimate, day and night prayer vigil, which lasted for over 100 years.
* Revival began in many regions through the anointed preaching of Zinzendorf, and the Spirit filled wandering Brethren to impart an enthusiastic, "Life in Christ" (Acts 17:28) to people in Germany and other parts of the world.
* Five years later, they started to send missionaries into many continents. The Brethren did not fear prison, shipwreck, persecution, ridicule, plagues, poverty, or threats of death.
* Through the leading of the Holy Spirit, they became outwardly centered, and realized that it is a personal responsibility of every member in a Christian community to evangelize.
* For the most part, they were men of little formal education. What they lacked in knowledge, they made up for in piety and passion.
* Zinzendorf was a resourceful, energetic, strong leader, but he did not dominate the congregation and community. He gave room for full participation by all. Therefore, the community lifestyle was not cultish, based on a domineering personality who would draw allegiance to himself. Neither Zinzendorf and nor any other Moravian ever acted that way. They all promoted devotion and loyalty to Christ.
* Centuries of persecution against the Bohemians and Moravians uniquely prepared them for a fervent motivation to send out missionaries.
* Their experience being refugees themselves gave them an unusual compassion for oppressed people.
* They had a deep sense of community discipline but readily accepted group decision-making regulations and policies. For instance, Leonard Dober and David Nitschmann had to wait a whole year before the congregation would decide the right timing and who to send by lot. (They wanted to go immediately after listening to Antonius from Denmark, the former slave in the Caribbean Islands.)
* Their resolution and commitment were such that they were willing to become slaves themselves, if necessary, to reach the plantation slaves for Christ. Faith and love were not idle in their lives. They displayed it in their unselfish service to God and man. Their magnanimous exertion

was prompted by love, not by law. "Faith expressing itself in love" (Galatians 5:6).
* The matter of the casting of lots became a point of controversy. But it was not a matter of 'roll the dice.' It was based on biblical precedents in the Old Testament and in Acts. It was used in a reverent way. After long discussions, consideration, and prayer, when no consensus was reached, the community agreed to be bound by the lot.
* They were perceptive of the leading of the Holy Spirit in their decisions and enterprises. For instance, Anna Nitschmann was elected head of the single sisters and chief elderess as a teenager.
* The theology for missions was different than the traditional methods of telling heathens about the existence of God. Zinzendorf's theory was, "You must go straight to the point and tell them about the cross, the agony and death of Christ."–"There is salvation in no one else! God has given no other name under heaven by which we must be saved" (Acts 4:12).
* Zinzendorf assumed the heathens already knew about a god by intuition and through nature, but needed to know of the Savior, particularly about His blood and wounds on the cross. The annals of the missions are marked with reports of persons who were moved by this message in a way that no other previous religious talk had ever affected them.
* He also told the Brethren, "You are not to aim at the conversions of whole nations; you must simply look for seekers after the truth who, like the Ethiopian eunuch, seemed ready to welcome the Gospel."
* The Moravian missionaries did not go out with exaggerated expectations. They had the freedom to depend upon the Holy Spirit, who as the real evangelist would lead them to souls like Cornelius or the Eunuch.
* They rejoiced whether fruit came extremely slow, or when large numbers appeared ready to embrace Christ.
* The Moravians became popularly known as **"God's happy people."**
* Zinzendorf's conviction was that the Holy Spirit awakens religious longings within unbelievers and then sends a missionary to them. The preaching of the missionary fulfills the seeker's search for spiritual truth. Christ meets them through the work of the Holy Spirit. The Holy Spirit is the only true missionary. Humans are the agents of the Holy

Spirit. They follow the Savior in bringing the Gospel to those whom the Savior, through the Spirit, has already prepared to hear it.
* They had gone to some sentimental excesses but caught themselves and corrected themselves from within.
* The spiritual burden of night and day prayer was lying heavily on their hearts. It was not a part-time preoccupation. They did not put their burden down at leisure and took it up again at a later, more convenient time. Prayer became part of their lives. Their prayer was fueled and driven by love. Love for the lost, love for their Brethren on the mission fields, love for their families. Their love and concern did not diminish It was stoked by the fiery furnace of heartfelt prayer. **Love and a burden dwelled side by side in their hearts.** Love is a burden's supply source. If love is deficient, the burden will grow cold.
* They also had the grace and ability to endure. The chronicle shows that they had the strength and tenacity to keep their focus. Their endurance withstood the test of time. It defied the ever-changing seasons, they scorned the going down of the sun, and they were not discouraged by the coming of a new year. A true burden lives on as if time were something that did not exist.
* They knew no boundaries. Physical and cultural barriers were overcome by their impartiality. They looked past the difference of race, color, education or social rank. All these hindrances appeared to them as merely ice cubes tossed into the blazing fire of persistent night and day prayer vigils for the lost. Their God-given care and burden did not halt for any foe or obstacle. They knew that their unrelenting prayer would eventually conquer souls for the glory of Christ.
* They were not selfish. When their own self was at risk, they would not slink away to escape the responsibility of their burden. They denied themselves sleep, took discomfort, pain, and adversities readily. They stayed focused on the will of God to send out and pray for workers to be fruitful in the harvest field. All else was far distant and irrelevant. They knew that self-love is not conducive to a prayer life, and it could be detrimental to an active burden. Death to self gives life to a burden. A burden must be worth dying for, or it is not worth living for.

* They resolved that the only time they could lay down their burden forever was when they safely arrived at His home and heard the words, "You have been a good and faithful servant."
* In summary we can say, because of the persevering night and day prayer vigils, and the daily one-hour communal prayer, several wonderful biblical fruits were evident in the lives of the Moravians:

1. **Dependency on God.**
2. **Unrelenting mission ventures.**
3. **Growth in personal holiness.**
4. **Pleasurable, gladsome community living.**

* They also safeguarded the Pietistic creed *ekklesiolae in ekklesia*, little church within the church. (Meaning house groups called *Banden* for Bible study and prayer within the corporate body to **combat lukewarmness,** as Zinzendorf said).
* They showed diligence in their attendance of numerous communal services with singing and sermons during the week. One historian wrote, "If we would have emulated the spirit of the Moravians in the 18th century, Christianity would be much further advanced today." (From 1732 to 1752 the Moravians went to twelve different countries. They were seized with a missionary passion that has never left them. One hundred years later, in 1832, they had forty-two 'Moravian Mission Stations' around the world. One hundred fifty years later, around the year 1882, a total of 2,158 missionaries had been sent into the world).
* Sending out missionaries was a natural expression of their Christian life and obedience. It did not call for a widespread heralding as if something marvelous or unusual were at hand.
* Ignatius LaTrobe, the British secretary of the Moravians, wrote, "We think it is a mistake when, after their appointment, missionaries are held up to public notices and admiration. We rather advise them quietly to set out, recommended to the fervent prayers of the congregation. No clamor, no platform heroics, no publicity, but a fervent, unostentatious desire to make Christ known wherever his name had not been named. This became knit into the ongoing life and liturgy of the Moravian

church, so that, for example, **a large portion of public prayer and subsequent hymnology was occupied with the subject of sending out missionaries."**

* The members lived in like-mindedness, and they knew that Jesus was the center of their lives. He was in their conversations, their sharing, their ministry, their meetings, their hymns, and their lives. They lived as a community of saints who possessed divine life because they enthroned Jesus Christ and lived joyfully and in **obedience under His Kingship.**

* They understood that God is not just saving individuals and preparing them for heaven. God is also creating a people among whom He can live and produce His life and character. They actually experienced a foretaste of the complete future happiness. "They had been permitted to understand the secrets of the Kingdom of Heaven, but others are not" (Matthew 13:11).

* The Brethren came together many times during the week in cell groups. Brothers with brothers, and sisters with sisters. They were seeking the Lord together in groups of five to seven. They allowed Jesus to love them and they returned that love back to Him and to each other. "They were carefully joined together in Him, becoming a holy temple for the Lord" (Ephesians 2:21).

It is truly on the heart of the Father in heaven that we exhibit and manifest His love in us here on earth, how we treat **one another.** Numerous times we find the phrase **one another** in the New Testament. I believe the Moravians displayed the admonition of **one another** in many ways.

*After the Baptism with the Holy Spirit, they lived in peace with **one another** (Mark 9:50) and lived in harmony with **one another** (Romans 12:16).

* As we read on the back cover, they exhibited their love for **one another** with a holy embrace (Romans 16:16) and greeted **one another** with a holy kiss (1 Corinthians 16:20).

* They took care of the elderly and the sick. They served **one another** in love (Galatians 5:13.)
* In their cell groups (100), they submitted themselves to **one another** (Ephesians 5:21) and they received instructions and directions from **one another** (Colossians 3:16). And they learned to be accountable to **one another** (1 Peter 5:5).
* Through the daily *Losung*, they edified **one another** (Thessalonians 5:11) and exhorted **one another** (Hebrews 3:13).
* As we read in Zinzendorf's diary, they had round table discussions. They took guidance and advice from **one another** (Romans 15:14), confessed their faults to **one another** and prayed for **one another** (James 5:16).
* Because of their relentless passion for mission outreaches, they must have provoked **one another** unto acts of love and to good works (Hebrew 10:24).
* They learned to practice the presence of the Bridegroom dwelling in their hearts. His love inspired the communion of saints to pray, meditate, worship, send out missionaries, and celebrate the Lord's Supper. They knew that the glorious Jesus indwells His Church.
* The Moravians had discipline in their spiritual lives. Young men and women lived in separate groups, called choirs. No scandal was ever reported. Holiness was a strong desire. Can you imagine a church Elder from time to time asking couples whether their marriage was honoring God?
* The Moravians realized the opportunity of the hour to bring the Good News to the people who were enslaved by the Christian nations of Europe. The Brethren had no political motivations. Their only motivation was their determination to bring the 'spiritual freeing power of Christ' to other oppressed people.
* The Moravians developed a militant spirit to bring the Good News to a dark world. This aggressive spirit, called *Streitergeist*, did not go unchallenged. When it became known in 1735 that so many young single Brethren had died in the Caribbean of tropical diseases, a *Generalrevolte*, a general revolt, broke out. (Later on in Guyana, for instance, the dying was horrendous in the beginning and in one decade

they lost seventy-five Brethren). There were heated discussions and divergent opinions for days about the effectiveness of outreaches versus the loss of young lives. After days, calmness settled in their hearts. The conclusion was to maintain the uncompromising consensus to keep on sending harbingers of the Good News to "the least of the people" who were living in utter spiritual *Elend*, wretchedness. After this decision, one historian wrote, **"The Brethren received such godly love in their hearts for missionary work, it is doubtful it was ever matched by other denominations."** Zinzendorf composed several poems about this era:

In these days we dare to challenge inactivity.
We want to work where there are exertions.
We don't want to faint and lose hearts.
We want merrily to toil away,
And carry our loads up to the scaffolding.
Inactivity is not our attractiveness,
Working and sweating refreshes and makes you rocklike.
Our eyes are clear; our minds are in high spirits.
There is nothing more beautiful than a dusty worker.

About the young lives lost in the Caribbean, Zinzendorf wrote:

Now there are souls sown,
It seems their cause is lost,
But on their graves it is written,
This is the seed for the Mohren. [Black people].

The *ekklesia* is the visible image of the invisible Christ. Dietrich Bonhoeffer called this, "Christ existing as community." We have to remember it is not the individual Christian who has the fullness of Christ. Paul might have written to the United Brethren in Herrnhut, all of you together are Jesus Christ in your community. Remember who you are and walk in this knowledge. "To you who have been called by God to be His own holy people. He made you holy by means of Christ Jesus, just as he did for all people everywhere who call on the name of our Lord Jesus Christ, their Lord and ours" (1 Corinthians 1:2). The church is the body of the ascended Lord. The body of Christ is not **like** His body, it **is** His body. ... "I will live in them and walk among them. I will be their God, and they will be my people" (2 Corinthians 6:16).

Compared to the Moravians, the church today is weak because we flirt with sin. The Word of God makes a concession for occasionally missing the mark and for stumbling, because we know the blood of Christ cleanses a contrite sinner (1 John 1:7). But if the church does not cry out against abortion and homosexuality and trifles with the lures of the world and persists in habitual sin, we cannot claim we are a new person in Christ (2 Corinthians 5:17).

I was disturbed when I saw an Anglican Bishop kiss his live-in partner on the mouth and then gave him Communion. It saddens me when churches lose the clear vision between historical biblical Christianity and the anything-goes universalism. Many churches now experience what happened to the wife of Phinehas, when she died in childbirth delivering a boy. The midwife named the child Ichabod, "Israel's glory is gone" (1 Samuel 4:2).

Are we living in the time to ponder the indictment Jesus has for His church in Laodicea? "I know all the things you do, that you are neither hot nor cold. I wish that you were one or the other! But since you are like lukewarm water, neither hot nor cold, I will spit you out of my mouth! You say, 'I am rich. I have everything I want. I don't need a thing!' And you don't realize that you are wretched and miserable and poor and blind and naked" (Revelation 3:15-17).

The late scholar, William MacDonald, wrote in his commentary,

"Whatever interpretation we take of the Book of Revelation, it is undeniable that the church of Laodicea presents a vivid picture of the age in which we live. Luxury-living abounds on every hand while souls are dying for want of the Gospel. Christians are wearing crowns instead of bearing a cross. We become more emotionally stirred over sports, politics, or television than we do over Christ. There is little sense of spiritual need, little longing for true revival. We give the best of our lives to the business world, and then turn over the remnants of a wasted career to the

Savior. We cater to our bodies which in a few short years will return to dust. We accumulate instead of forsake, lay up treasures on earth instead of in heaven. The general attitude is, 'Nothing too good for the people of God. If I don't pamper myself, who will. Let's get ahead in the world and give our spare dollars and evenings to the Lord.' This is our condition on the eve of Christ's return."

The snare of antinomianism goes back to the New Testament. It is the false belief that we are free from the law in our actions. Paul vehemently refutes the suggestion that justification by faith alone leaves room for persistence in sin. An excellent book written by John McArthur, *The Gospel According to Jesus*, deals with this pervasive problem of flirting with sin and the world. The apostle John writes in 1 John 3:9, "Those who have been born into God's family do not make a practice of sinning, because they are children of God."

Hans Denck, a German Anabaptist was a bold and an anointed preacher. Thousands came through his preaching to a true faith in Christ. He suffered terribly for his faith and was emotionally and physically spent when he wrote shortly before his death in November 1527, "He who accepts the redemptive work of Christ but continues living in a fleshly, animalistic manner does not show respect to Christ. He reveres Christ in the way the pagans did their gods. That is blasphemy, of which the world is full." A good axiom to remember is this: We never become sinless, but we should sin less and less.

William MacDonald, a theologian who wrote over seventy books, was my mentor for many years. He passed away on Christmas Eve, 2007. In his booklet, *True Discipleship,* he lists seven principles of a true Disciple of Christ, according to Luke 14:26, 14:33, Matthew 16:24, John 8:31, 13:35.

* All of these were evident in the life of Zinzendorf and the Moravians he inspired.

> A supreme love for Jesus Christ
> A denial of self
> A deliberate choosing of the cross

A life spent following Christ
A continuance in His Word
A fervent love for all who belong to Christ
A forsaking of all to follow Him

* The secret to the power of the Moravians' spiritual life is that when the Holy Spirit fell on the congregation in 1727, the Brethren were set on fire. A.W. Tozer wrote about this quite eloquently, "The Spirit-filled life is not a special, deluxe addendum of Christianity. It is part of God's total plan for his people. When the Holy Spirit presents Christ to our inner vision it has an exhilarating effect on the soul much as wine has on the body. The Spirit-filled man may literally dwell in a state of perpetual fervor, amounting to a tranquil and pure inebriation. God's dwelling in you puts you in a mild state of continual enthusiasm."
* That certainly describes the life of the Moravians. They went to the mission field exuberantly. They had the fervor and vitality to meet up to eight times on a weekend for services and were eager to be selected for prayer vigils.
* The Moravians were not attached to their land, homes, and meager possessions. After leaving their homeland in Moravia and Bohemia, they didn't know for twenty years whether they could stay in Herrnhut. Like the Schwenkfelders, they always expected an edict from the authorities in Dresden, telling them to pack up and leave. They were sojourners on this earth and had something in common with Abraham. "It was by faith that Abraham obeyed when God called him to leave home and go to another land..." (Hebrew 11:8). David prayed in 1 Chronicles 29:14-15, "But who am I, and who are my people, that we could give anything to you? Everything we have has come from you, and we give you only what you have already given us! We are here for only a moment, visitors and strangers in the land as our ancestors were before us. Our days on earth are like a passing shadow, gone so soon without a trace."
* August Wilhelm Heyde and Heinrich August Jäschke left Herrnhut as young men to go to Tibet. After fifty years they returned, as old men. Jäschke translated the Bible into the Tibetan language. On his

gravestone in God's Acre are these words written in Tibetan, "Oh, you pious and faithful servant, go into the joy of the Lord." He lived like the Patriarch Jacob when he was a foreigner in the land of Ham (Psalm 105:23).

* The Moravians had no manual and attended no mission school before they were sent into the world. They were groping in the dark about how to be effective in bringing the "Light of the World" to the lost. The American Indian, Job, told Christian Heinrich Rauch about the other missionaries' failed attempts to convert him, but Christian Rauch was different. In the power of the Holy Spirit, he told Job about the cross and the blood of the Lamb, and Job's calloused heart softened.

* Like all true believers, the Moravians had the anointing of the Holy Spirit. "But you have received the Holy Spirit, and He lives within you, so you don't need anyone to teach you what is true. For the Spirit teaches you everything you need to know, and what He teaches is true – it is not a lie. So just as He taught you, remain in fellowship with Christ" (1 John 2:27). It was Zinzendorf's anointing by the Holy Spirit that inspired him to introduce the twenty-four-hour prayer vigil and the daily spiritual encouragement of the *Losung*.

* The Moravians were filled with a deep love and devotion for the suffering Lamb of God. The atoning blood of Jesus and the efficacy of the cross were the frequent themes of their teaching. During the Rococo period of the eighteenth century, it was popular to extol the blood of Jesus. This emphasis on the expiating blood spilled over to America. If you fan through old American hymnals, you will be amazed how many sacred songs eulogize the blood. When we joined a true church, joy resonated in our hearts as we sang, "There is power, power, wonder working power in the blood of the Lamb." Hymnology is very close to theology.

* Zinzendorf's deep reverence for the suffering Lamb began when he saw the painting, *Ecce Homo*, Behold the Man, in the city of Düsseldorf. The cross and the blood provide eternal blessings and privileges for those who are saved. For this reason they are subjects of wonder and awe for the angels in heaven. His sacrifice will be our central theme and heaven's song of the redeemed.

There are so many blessings we receive through the blood of Christ. Paul writes in Ephesians 1:7, "He is so rich in kindness and grace that He purchased our freedom with the blood of His Son and forgave our sins." Not only did the blood pay for our freedom from the slave market of sin, it also keeps us from God's judgment. "And since we have been made right in God's sight by the blood of Christ, He will certainly save us from God's condemnation" (Romans 5:9). The blood also gives us a wonderful God-given boldness. "And so, dear brothers and sisters, we can boldly enter heaven's Most Holy Place because of the blood of Jesus" (Hebrews 10:19). The blood continues to cleanse us, and because of its power, the devil cannot bring any accusations against the elect. The cross and the blood secure our resurrection and bring us safely home to God (1 Peter 3:18). The cross cleanses us from dead works, sets us free from God's curse, sanctifies us and brings forth fruit in our lives (Hebrews 13:12, Romans 7:6). There are 400 references to the blood and 1,300 references to the atonement in the Bible.

Here is an excerpt of Zinzendorf's prolific writings about the *"Blut und Wunden,"* blood and wounds theology: "The entrance to the *Grundwahrheit*, rock foundational truth that the Creator died for the creatures comes only through the revelation of the Holy Spirit, God himself. To receive this anchor deep in your heart you have to pontificate in drastic painted words before the eyes of the hearer that on the cross hung a wounded, bleeding Man who carried your sins. If the soul then receives a longing to get acquainted with her Creator, Savior, and Friend she will desperately know that she will have to cling to Him. Slowly, she will develop an intimacy with her Savior, a union with the resurrected Crucified One, who enabled her to have reconciliation with God.

"The Pietism in Halle [under the leadership of August Hermann Francke, Zinzendorf's school years] emphasizes mainly the wretchedness and sinfulness of mankind with an intermittently consoling look at the wounds of Jesus. My main preaching is to look continuously with eyes and soul upon His blood and wounds, and only look occasionally upon the lamentable state of a sinner. Pietism in Halle is like a limping Brother on his way to heaven, Pietism in Herrnhut is like dancing on the way to the Father's house. A Christian should not always brood about

The Moravian spirit

his sins, but his life should exuberate joy because of the forgiveness he received through his relation with the *Schmerzens-Mann*, afflicted Man."

* This joyful way in the lives of the Moravians was confirmed by John Wesley. He wrote in his diary in February 24, 1736 in Savannah, Georgia, "At our return the next day, (Mr. Quincy being in the house wherein we afterwards were) Mr. Delamotte and I took up lodging with the Germans [Moravians]. We had now opportunity, day by day, of observing their whole behavior. For we were in one room with them from morning to night, unless for the little time spent in walking. They were always employed, always cheerful themselves, and in good humor with one another; they had put away all anger and strife, and wrath and bitterness, and clamor, and evil speaking; they walked worthy of the vocation wherewith they were called, and adorned the Gospel of our Lord in all things."
* To summarize it, the Moravians put in plain sight the life of a converted child of God. Here is Zinzendorf's expression of his understanding of a true conversion: "The Word of God proceeds out of the mouth of the preacher or teacher. The love, the longing, the desire and the faith flows out of the heart of the listener. The Word and the yearning of the heart unite together. The Father in heaven holds His hand over this union. The Holy Spirit embraces and encourages it and in a moment the bleeding Man reveals himself deep in the soul and causes an inmost sorrow of the penitent's sins. The heart is full of Jesus, treasures His blood and wounds, and is filled with the merits of the Lamb. The Redeemer has cast Himself over the heart and soul, and the soul is saved now and for all eternity."
* The question may arise: Did the spirit of the Moravians have any lasting effect? The answer may come from William Carey who spent forty-two years in India and was known as the father of modern missions. While in Kettering, England, he read a detailed account of missionary work in a Moravian magazine. William showed his fellow Baptist ministers the magazine and said, "See what the Moravians have done. Can we not follow their example and go out into the world and preach the Gospel to the heathens as our heavenly Master commanded?" Shortly

afterward, the Baptist Missionary Society was formed. The Baptists had many specific questions about missionary know-how for the Moravian British secretary, La Trobe. He provided the Baptists with the proven methods for evangelizing that helped launch their missionary movement. In fact, one historian writes, "The first ambassadors of the London Missionary Society went out with Moravian wisdom in their heads and Moravian instructions in their pockets."

* Furthermore, the Moravians indirectly aided William Wilberforce, the British Parliamentarian who spent his life bringing down the slave trade in England. He used La Trobe's chronicle on the Moravian's work in the Caribbean islands to prove before Parliament that slaves, once unshackled and freed, could live peacefully. In this way, Moravian missionaries indirectly helped Wilberforce to end the vile practice of slavery.
* It was the Moravian congregation on Fetter Lane and men like Peter Böhler who greatly influenced John Wesley and George Whitefield. While these two men were with the Moravians, fire from above fell on them. During the eighteenth century, Wesley and Whitefield were instrumental in starting the Great Awakening in Britain and in America.
* Comenius prophesied before he died that the "hidden seed" of the *Unitas Fratrum* would blossom again some day. One hundred years later, the prophecy came to fruition when the Holy Spirit's empowerment fell on the Moravian remnant in 1727. The Moravian spirit was expressed in their motto:

> "Together we pray, together we labor,
> Together we suffer, together we rejoice."

* We all share the Moravian spirit if we have a *Spezialbund*, special bond with our Lord and Savior, Jesus Christ. This spirit wasn't just talk with them but was demonstrated by continued prayer vigils, their zeal to bring Christ to a dying world, their detachment from worldly possessions, and their discipline in living godly lives.
* May the Moravians' example kindle in our hearts the same joy for frequent fellowship and the singing of sacred songs by heart. May

The Moravian spirit

we be inspired to read and meditate on the Word and the '*Losung* of the Day.' And may we, as the Moravians, have the humility to be taught by those who expound the Word of God with anointing. Let the Moravians arouse in us a thankful adoration for the suffering Lamb of God. And let us mirror their devotion in celebrating the love feast, Holy Communion.

* We can learn from them to accept it as all joy when people ridicule and persecute us for Christ's sake. From them we can learn how to treat enemies, and all people, without slander or ill will.
* Let us follow their example to reach the lost through continued, fervent prayer. With the power of the Holy Spirit, may we tell the lost of the excruciating pain the Lamb of God suffered for the restoration of our relationship with Him. This we confirm with our lives; we are a new creation with a new lifestyle, trusting and obeying our Master. Let us agree with the Moravians as they still sing at funerals today, "My Savior's blood and righteous. That beauty is my glorious dress. Thus well arrayed, I need not fear. When in His presence I appear."
* Let us be in accord with Count Zinzendorf when he said, "I have but one passion, and that is Jesus, only He." Let us look at the seal of the Moravian church, which has in its center the white Lamb of God. He holds a staff with a victory banner displaying the cross. In a circular band on the outer edge it says,

Vicit agnus noster, eum sequamur

In England, the *Losung* was printed while Zinzendorf was still alive. A well-known printer by the name of James Hutton, a member of the Aldersgate congregation and a friend of John Wesley, published the first edition in 1746. Printer Johann Brandmüller published the first *Losung* in America, just seven years after Zinzendorf's death. Biblical texts for the *Losung* are still chosen in Herrnhut to this day.

As in every denomination, there are Moravians who have an outer appearance of Christianity as well as those who have the inner reality of the indwelling Christ by showing the fruits of a new man (2 Corinthians 5:17). There was and always will be a tension between those who are

Christians in name only and true disciples of Christ. On earth there will always be the tares and the wheat. In recent years, there have been minor tensions between the Moravians and the Spirit-filled Moravians. At an international conference in 1992, the Moravian bishops in Nova Paka, Czech Republic, gave their approval and blessing to the charismatic revival. However, in Herrnhut, the Spirit-filled Moravians, as mentioned before, have bought their own big building, named it *Jesus-Haus,* and worship the Lord in a more informal manner.

27

Helpful pointers for a victorious transformation

I believe Christian conversion has four main parts:

    Believing in Jesus as a personal Lord and Savior
    Repentance from a contrite heart
    Receiving the Holy Spirit
    Water Baptism

There are fifty-nine curses in the Old Covenant against law breakers. When I read them I felt quite smug for not having broken most of them. I've never been a kidnapper, practiced witchcraft, sacrificed a human being, or committed incest. However, many other actions of mine definitely fell under the curses that are mentioned in Scripture: I failed to give glory to God when people complimented me (Malachi 2:1-2); I robbed God of his tithes and offerings (Malachi 3:9); I trusted in men and not God (Jeremiah 17:5); I did not warn sinners (Ezekiel 3:18); and I was carnally minded (Romans 8:6). The Good News is, "But Christ has rescued us from the curse pronounced by the Law. When He was hung on the cross, He took upon himself the curse for our wrongdoing. For it is written in the Scriptures: 'Cursed is everyone who is hung on a tree'" (Galatians 3:13). No wonder that the display of Christ on the cross should be the centrality of our adoration and faith.

From my own conversion experience I discovered many things that do not have the power to make a person right with God. It may be redundant to say, but being a priest, a minister with ecclesiastical duties, or a faithful attendee of Sunday services cannot save anyone. People may hate the sin in their lives and make all kinds of vows, and still not have the assurance of heaven. Zealous service, praying, being baptized, living by the Golden Rule, agreeing with a lengthy creed, signing a statement of faith, praying routinely, or giving mental assent that God exists (many of these things I did all my life, but I was not saved), and even suffering for Christ will not give eternal life. It is belief in Jesus Christ as Lord and Savior that brings true conversion. His blood frees us from the penalty and consequences of sin, and the power of the cross frees us from the power of sin.

Each of us should come to a point in life where we abhor our sins. In my case, a time of weeping for my sins came after the baptism by the Holy Spirit. In some exterior conversions an "altar call" is an emotional event. "The seeds on the rocky soil represent those who hear the message and receive it with joy. But since they don't have deep roots, they believe for a while, and then they fall away when they face temptation" (Luke 8:13). Shallow roots speak of a lack of a commitment to God of the deepest level. When the wild, hot winds of testing (temptation) blow, their newly blossomed faith shrivels and dies. Also, true joy will only come after repentance and a deep sorrow for sins. If it is missing, it is not a true conversion. Jesus said in Luke 13:5, "I tell you again that unless you repent, you will perish too."

D. Martyn Lloyd-Jones writes in *Studies in the Sermon on the Mount*, "Repentance means that you realize that you are a guilty, vile sinner in the presence of God, that you deserve the wrath and punishment of God, that you are hell-bound. It means that you begin to realize that this thing called sin is in you, that you long to get rid of it, and that you turn your back on it in every shape and form. You renounce the world whatever the cost, the world in its mind and outlook as well as its practice, and you deny yourself and take up the cross and go after Christ. Your nearest and dearest, and the whole world, may call you a fool, or say you have religious mania. You may have to suffer financially, but it makes no difference. That is repentance."

Dr. H. A. Ironside wrote in *Except Ye Repent*, "Shallow preaching that does not grapple with the terrible fact of man's sinfulness and guilt, calling on 'all men everywhere to repent,' results in shallow conversions, and so we have myriads of glib-tongued professors today who give no evidence of regeneration whatever. Prating of salvation by grace, they manifest no grace in their lives. Loudly declaring they are justified by faith alone, they fail to remember that 'faith without works is dead' and that justification by works before men is not to be ignored as though it were in contradiction to justification by faith before God."

Saying a sinner's prayer may not always prove that a person is genuinely saved. A few tears, a pang of regret, a little fright amounts to nothing if it is not proven by an incremental walk in holiness, submission to the Lordship of Christ, and enjoying the fruits of the Holy Spirit. Do not let anyone assure you about your salvation. Only the Spirit through the Word can confirm to your heart and spirit that you are saved. "For His Spirit joins with our spirit to affirm that we are God's children" (Romans 8:16.) Paul expressed his concern on this issue in 2 Corinthians 13:5, "Examine yourselves to see if your faith is genuine. Test yourselves. Surely you know that Jesus Christ is in you, if not, you have failed the test of genuine faith."

A true Christian will also experience how dearly God loves him, because he has been given the Holy Spirit to fill his heart with God's love (Romans 5:5). You may call this the baptism of love. History shows that true martyrs had this love, even when they were tortured, they never made disparaging remarks about their persecutors and they also never approved the use of violence.

There are always people who accept Christ with joy, but for the wrong reasons. Excitement, emotions, and euphoria are not necessarily the distinguishing features of true salvation. Some may accept Christ in the hope of fixing their marriage, healing family relationships, or being cured from a debilitating or terminal illness. There may be a loss of a secure job, they may want to surround themselves with different friends, or they may just want to avoid the Lake of Fire.

Jesus is certainly interested in all of our problems, but our circumstances may or may not change once we are saved. That is why the parable of the sower tells us that people fall away when tribulations, afflictions, hardship, and sufferings come into their lives. If a cross in life discourages a person from following Him, that person is not disciple material.

People also fall away in Luke 8:14, when the evil one crowd God's Word from their minds with worldly concerns and interests, making them numb and spiritually dead with cares of this life, pursuing riches, enjoying worldly pleasures, such as coarse jokes, bawdy amusements, and sensual gratification. But endurance in suffering and distaste for worldly pleasures will differentiate the new man in Christ from one who has no true regeneration. These are important truths. Those who endure are secure, especially in afflictions.

We have to realize a few things about our state prior to accepting Christ as Savior and Lord. Before we are ready to hear the Good News, we have to hear the "dreadful news." The Word of God uses many adjectives to describe our natural, fallen heart condition. Apart from Christ we are wicked, evil, perverse, disloyal, deceitful, impenitent, hard, proud, foolish, stubborn, rebellious, idolatrous, covetous, dull of hearing, and enemies of God. Also, our tongue is a cataclysm of evil. It is foul, like a stench from an open grave. It is filled with lies, poisonous as a deadly snake, full of cursing and bitterness (Romans 3:13-14). In other sections of the Bible, the unmasking of our black-hearted root by the tongue continues. For it tells us that the tongue is corrupt, angry, crafty, backbiting, whispering, tale-bearing, slanderous, blasphemous, foolish, boasting, murmuring, contentious, sensuous, vile and foolish. That is why Paul wrote in Romans 7:18, "And I know that nothing good lives in me, that is, in my sinful nature. I want to do what is right, but I can't." He also gave a very dismal picture of our Adamic nature in Romans 8:7, "For the sinful nature is always hostile to God. It never did obey God's laws, and it never will."

Many people wonder, from where does this evil tendency come? It is entirely our own fault through exercising our free will. The flesh is man after the Fall, in contrast to man as God had created him. William Barclay, in his book, *Flesh and Spirit*, gives an interesting summary about flesh:

"No army can invade a country from the sea unless it can obtain a bridgehead. Temptation would be powerless to affect men, unless there was something already in man to respond to temptation. Sin could gain no foothold in a man's mind and heart and soul and life unless there was an enemy within the gates who was willing to open the door to sin. The flesh is exactly the bridgehead through which sin invades the human personality.

"But from where does this bridgehead come? From where does this enemy within spring? The flesh is what man has made himself in contrast with man as God made him. The flesh stands for the total effect upon man of his own sin, the sin of his fathers and of the sin of all men who have gone before him, starting with Adam. The flesh is human nature as it has become through sin. Man's sin, his own sin and the sin of mankind, has, as it were, made him vulnerable to sin. It has made him fall even when he knew he was falling and even when he did not want to fall. It has created in him a disposition that can neither avoid the fascination of sin nor resist the power of sin. The flesh stands for human nature weakened, debased, tainted by sin. The flesh is man as he is apart from Jesus Christ and his Spirit."

The Good News is that we do not have to live in the flesh, and we can live a victorious life. We can believe Paul's encouraging words found in Galatians 5:24-25, "Those who belong to Christ Jesus have nailed the passion and desires of their sinful nature to his cross and crucified them there. Since we are living by the Spirit, let us follow the Spirit's leading in every part of our lives."

The crucial factor is hearing the voice of the Holy Spirit. At the end of Romans, chapter 7, Paul gave the most agonizing, tormented cry, "Oh, what a miserable person I am! Who will free me from this life that is dominated by sin [this body of death]?" He then goes on to affirm being filled and controlled by the Holy Spirit over a dozen times.

The foremost question in Acts 19:2 is, "Did you receive the Holy Spirit when you believed?" (They believed and were saved). It is interesting to know that the sequence to become a Spirit-filled believer varies. In Acts 2 (among the Jewish believers) it was repentance, water baptism, and the baptism of the Holy Spirit. In Acts 8 (with the Samaritans) they first heard the Word, that is believing, and then there was water baptism, laying on hands, baptism of the Holy Spirit. In Acts 10 (with the Gentiles) the order was faith, baptism of the Holy Spirit, baptism in water. In Acts 19 (for the Ephesians) faith, re-baptism in water, laying on hands, baptism of the Holy Spirit.

As you can see, believing in Jesus and receiving the Baptism of the Holy Spirit may not be at the same time. In many cases, it happens simultaneously. Receiving the Holy Spirit is a definite experience with demonstrable evidence, and it should not be confused with water baptism. In my own case, reciting the sinner's prayer was not done with a deep conviction of a lost sinner, but shortly after the baptism of the Holy Spirit I experienced a deep contrition and I longed for water re-baptism by immersion. (I had been baptized as an infant).

In the early church, baptism with the Holy Spirit was always expected. After all, John the Baptist, gave the crowd the clue how to truly identify the coming Messiah by pointing out that "He will baptize you with the Holy Spirit and with fire" (Luke 3:16). It is interesting to notice that he did not say you would discern Jesus because He could heal the sick, cast out demons, raise the dead or calm the waters.

However, the doctrine of the baptism with the Holy Spirit has been allowed to drop out of sight in many congregations. The church today has little expectancy for its young converts along this line that many congregations are like the churches in Samaria and Ephesus. Someone had to call their attention to the Father's promise that He would send this power from on high. How wonderful it is when the Holy Spirit falls on a group of people, as occurred with the Moravians, and brings radical transformation.

The baptism of the Holy Spirit does not eradicate our carnal nature, cleanse us from an impure heart, or give us instant power and victory over the world, the flesh, and the devil. This happens progressively by our continued faith in the atonement of Christ, the daily washing with the Word of God and granting forgiveness to others. This is the lifelong **work** of the Holy Spirit in a believer, as we read in 2 Peter 1:4, "And because of His glory and excellence, He has given us great and precious promises. These are the promises that enable you to share His divine nature and escape the world's corruption caused by human desires." (See also Hebrews 10:15-16).

All Christians want to be saved from the fire of hell, but not all from the pleasure of sin. Salvation by works is an error, but salvation without obedience is also an error. Jesus told His disciples in John 15:10, "When you obey my commandments, you remain in my love..."

What should be the obvious signs of a true conversion? The fruit of the Holy Spirit will begin to be evident (Galatians 5:22-23). A hunger and a love for the Word will develop. "Let the message about Christ, in all their richness, fill your lives. Teach and counsel each other with all the wisdom He gives... (Colossians 3:16) The Holy Spirit will help us to grow in humility and the mind of Christ will slowly transform our own mind (Philippians 2:5). And what is the mind of Christ? It means that His selfless, serving, sacrificial mind slowly becomes ours.

We keep aloof from the world's behavior and detest more and more the sin in our life. The esteeming of the unholy trinity of me, myself and I will slowly be replaced with shouldering the cross, dying to ourselves, and losing our self-absorption. We sing and make melody in our hearts. Slowly, we feel the love of Christ in us radiating to other believers and we grow in our yearning to become holy and not to grieve the will of our Father in heaven.

You may ask, what is His will? Paul tells us in 1 Thessalonians 5:16-18, "Always be joyful. Never stop praying. Be thankful in all circumstances, for this is God's will for you who belong to Christ Jesus." In summary, to be a Christian is daily to become gradually more like Jesus. "For God knew His people in advance, and He chose them to become like His Son, so that His Son would be the firstborn, among many brothers and sisters" (Romans 8:29).

I discovered a few additional yearnings of the Father in heaven. He wants to become a parent to us. "God decided in advance to adopt us into His own family by bringing us to himself through Jesus Christ. This is what He wanted to do, and it gave Him great pleasure" (Ephesians 1:5).

The Father in heaven also wishes that all would weep over their sins and none would come to ruin. ... "No, He is being patient for your sake. He does not want anyone to be destroyed, but wants everyone to repent" (2 Peter 3:9). He also wants our lives dedicated to Him and to display much fruit by becoming more like His Son. "And so, dear brothers and sisters, I plead with you to give your bodies to God because of all He has done for you. Let them be a living and holy sacrifice – the kind He will find acceptable. This is truly the way to worship Him" (Romans 12:1).

Now, you may ask, what is the Father in heaven doing for us? The answer is put into words so beautifully in A. W. Tozer's writings:

"What is the supreme benefaction, the gift and treasure above all others which only God the Father can give? He gives Christ to be in our nature forever. This is God's supreme gift. Not the pearly gates, not the golden streets, not heaven, not even the forgiveness of our sins, although these are God's gifts too. Not a dozen, or two dozens, or a thousand, but countless gifts God lays before His happy people, and then bestows this supreme gift to us. He makes us the repository of the nature and person of the Lord. 'Christ in you'" (Colossians 1:27).

Ponder these guidelines to have a victorious and fulfilled lifestyle.

"He is so rich in kindness and grace that He purchased our freedom with the blood of His Son and forgave our sins (Ephesians 1:7). What a wonderful life, being forgiven.

"And I will ask the Father, and He will give you another Comforter" [Encourager, Counselor] (John 14:16). What a wonderful life, being indwelled by the Holy Spirit to empower us for holiness, worship and service.

"The Spirit is God's guarantee that He will give us the inheritance He promised and that He has purchased us to be his own people. He did this so we would praise and glorify Him (Ephesians 1:14). What a wonderful life to be adopted into His family and to have the guarantee to go to heaven.

* Seek the baptism of the Holy Spirit with a yearning and expectant heart. Stand on the promise that our loving Father in heaven will baptize you. "So if you sinful people know how to give good gifts to your children, how much more will your heavenly Father give the Holy Spirit to those who ask him" (Luke 11:13). Obey the call of God to renounce sin and the lures of the world. "We are witnesses of these things and so is the Holy Spirit, who is given by God to those who obey him" (Acts 5:32).

   Most of the time the Holy Spirit baptizes a seeker through the laying on of hands (Acts 8:14-17, 19:4-6). If you cannot find a brother or a sister in Christ who has the anointing and the Pentecostal experience, then by expectant faith and by lingering in the Lord's presence, by extended prayer and pressing into God, expect the Father in heaven to fill you with the burning and refining fire of the Holy Spirit (Acts 2:3). You are not alone. The scientist and pollster, D. Barrett (USA), determined that in 2004, 850 million born again Christians lived in the world and 550 million had a Pentecostal experience.

* Yield completely to the Holy Spirit's control. "And so, dear brothers and sisters, I plead with you to give your bodies to God. Let them be a living and holy sacrifice–the kind He will find acceptable. This is truly the way to worship Him. Don't copy the behavior and customs of this world, but let God transform you into a new person by changing the way

you think. Then you will learn to know God's will for you, which is good and pleasing and perfect" (Romans 12:1-2).
* Practice denial of self, empty self. "My old self has been crucified with Christ. It is no longer I who live, but Christ lives in me. So I live in this earthly body by trusting in the Son of God, who loved me and gave himself for me" (Galatians 2:20).
* Be sanctified by His Word, as it says in John 17:17, and also heed Paul's admonition, "Let the message about Christ, in all it's richness, fill your lives. Teach and counsel each other with all the wisdom He gives. Sing psalms and hymns and spiritual songs to God with thankful hearts" (Col. 3:16).
* Just as we have left the whole burden of our sins, and rest on the finished work of Christ, so let us leave the burden of our lives and service, and rest upon the inworking of the Holy Spirit. We give ourselves up, morning by morning, to be led by the Holy Spirit and go forth praising and resting, leaving Him to manage our day. Joyfully depending upon and obeying Him, expecting Him to guide, to enlighten, to reprove, to teach, to use, and to do in and with us what He wills. Count upon His working as a fact, altogether apart from sight or feeling. Cease from the burden of trying to manage yourself, then shall the fruit of the Holy Spirit slowly appear in us, as He wills, to the glory of Jesus (John 16:14).

The mind of Christ will slowly take hold. His mind was selfless all the days of His life. He was a servant and never sought to be served. He lived with a sacrificial attitude. For thirty-three years, He forfeited the glories and pleasures of heaven, lived on this miserable sin-cursed world, and He was willing to die a slow, excruciating death to pay for our sins. Through His death and resurrection, we have the power to become children of God, and progressively become more like Him. Spiritual satisfaction is the grave of spiritual progress.

Remember, fruit-bearing involves cross-bearing. As someone said, "True holiness is love hanging on the cross." It is measured by our willingness to love and sacrifice for one another and by abandoning selfishness and self-focus. Salvation includes faith, but also includes faithfulness to Christ. Someone said, "The widest thing in the universe is not space, it is the capacity of the human heart to love God and the ultimate test of our love to Him is **obedience**."

Finally, when there are times when cross-bearing becomes weary or lack-luster days fill the calendar with mundane things, do some serious thinking about our promised hope of glory.

"So be truly glad. There is wonderful joy ahead, even though it is necessary for you to endure many trials for a while" (1 Peter 1:6).

We have read those beautiful German words in Zinzendorf's sermons and letters. *Herzensfreund*, friend of the heart, and *Herzensgenuss,* relish or enjoyment of the heart.

Let us savor this poem about our *Herzensfreund* while we ponder this,

> Before you seek a blessing, seek Jesus first.
> Before you seek a feeling, seek Jesus in His Word.
> Before you seek a gifting, pursue Jesus the Giver.
> Before you seek a healing, seek Jesus the Healer.
> Before you try to become holy, trust Jesus He will do it.
> Before you become lukewarm, seek Jesus to the uttermost.
> Before you are drifting, make Jesus your anchor.
> Before you plan your day, trust Jesus with a prayer.
> Before you worry, trust Jesus for your care.

Helpful pointers for a victorious transformation

Before I say I want, ask Jesus what He wants.
Before you ask for something, give Jesus all your praise.
Before you seek riches, let Jesus be your treasure.
Before you attempt to use Him, let Jesus use you.
Before your lamp diminishes, let Jesus be your torch.
Before you seek signs and wonders, let Jesus be your wonder.
Before you seek an encounter, know that Jesus lives within you.

28

Addendum

When Count Ludwig Zinzendorf died, three of his daughters were present. Benigna was thirty-five years old at the time. Marie Agnes was twenty-five, and Elizabeth was twenty. When his first wife passed away, Henriette Benigna inherited the estate from her mother. She was married to Johannes von Watteville, the adopted son of his best friend, Friedrich von Watteville. Their marriage was blessed with four children, two of whom were born before their grandparents died. They were eight and six years old when their grandfather Ludwig died. The six-year-old daughter of Henriette Benigna, grandaughter of Zinzendorf, Anna Dorothee Elisabeth, immigrated to America and married an aristocrat, Alexander von Schweinitz. The book printed in the year 1900 for the 200th commemoration of Zinzendorf's birth mentions that descendents of that marriage were still living in America at the time the book was published.

The name Zinzendorf dropped from written records in 1817. It was mentioned for the first time in a deed dated 1114; so, the family lineage lasted seven hundred years. Although the German word *Dorf* means village, no actual village with the Austrian family name Sinsendorf has ever existed in Austria.

Addendum

Countess Henriette Benigna was Zinzendorf's oldest daughter. She had a noteworthy love for her dad and accompanied him on the trip to America. She was born in 1725, and departed in the Lord in Herrnhut on the 13th of May, 1789.

I was fortunate to find the original yellow-tainted eulogy, printed in 1789, in the old boxes from the attic. (Notice the unusual consolation at the end of the service about their grief).

Chorus:

"For the Lamb on the throne will be their Shepherd. He will lead them to the springs of life-giving water. And God will wipe every tear from their eyes" (Revelation 7:17).

Recitative:
[Rhythmically spoken by the congregation in poetic style].

"Henriette Benigna, you came through many tribulations. You are the daughter of our admired leader. He was more a father than a lord to you. His words and his name will not be forgotten. Benigna, just a short time ago we cried for your servant husband. You had a lovely marriage. You have been our mother for us servants more than thirty years. You loved us as your children. Benigna, you are God's faithful servant. You are a noble woman. Often in stillness, resting by the footprints of Jesus, you shed tears because His kingdom would not grow as fast as you envisioned. You felt great sorrow when a servant did not have salvation."

Aria:
[An accompanied melody sung by a single voice].

"How precious are those tears before our God. He gathered them all. The quiet weeping honored Him. He counted all the tears and did not forget them. The sighing of His chosen ones evokes His mercy in His heart. He knew your pain, even if your words felt inadequate. He was moved by your sorrow. Your tears brought eternal sweet fruits."

Recitative:

"Benigna is not crying anymore, the dear maid of the Lord. But we are crying now, out of love and thankfulness. She has finished her work on earth. She washed her dress in the blood of the Lamb of God. Because of her faith, we see her beautiful arrival. She is standing blissfully, bedecked with jewels. Immaculate, holy, dressed in a white garment. She arrived there where we long to be. Oh, we wish we could join her."

Congregation:

"Anticipation! That is the joy of life, up there, where many thousand souls are already surrounded with heaven's brilliance. They are standing before the throne of God, where the Seraphs are dwelling, singing the mighty chorus, holy, holy, holy is God the Father, Son and Spirit. She is full of joy resting in the lap of her Savior. She beholds her 'Precious Treasure.' Benigna, our beloved, looks around and beholds all the ransomed. She invites them to come to her mansion, father, mother, son, and husband. She is overwhelmed with a thankful heart. All her tears have been wiped away by the nail-pierced hands. She lives now in the city of her God, her joy is heavenly. God will care for her forever. What wonderful bliss!"

Chorus:

"For the Lamb on the throne will be their Shepherd. He will lead them to the springs of life-giving water. And God will wipe every tear from their eyes" (Revelation 7:17).

Recitative:

"She is resting, she is redeemed. Most jubilant in her Redeemer's lap. She beholds now her precious treasure. Benigna, our beloved, you see now the good Lord, who died for you. You look with joy upon the holy face of your Father. You see His brilliance, His light. You look around and see all the saints, who came already overjoyed before you into their mansions. You see father, mother, sons and husband. You appreciate the grace of God. All tears which flowed out of your eyes have been wiped away. Oh, yes, it was done by the nail-print hand. You are living in God's city. Your jubilation is exceedingly great. High is your status now. Eternally you will feast on untold ecstasies, glorious is your destiny."

Aria:

"When the hours are all counted, and the longing of the soul is over, you can rest in the wounds of Jesus. This is your hope when the tears on earth are flowing. One more tear escaped your eye, when you closed your eyes on earth forever. But oh, up there all sorrow will vanish, when you see Jesus as He is."

Congregation:

"This I know, these eyes of mine will see my Savior. I am not a stranger to Him; I am burning with love for Him. He will not remember my weaknesses, up there is only light and joy. We will be dressed in white silk, standing in purest holiness, adorned with crowns of gold. We will be seated on golden thrones and time will be no more.

"Now, stop lamenting, *mein blöder Sinn*, my dumb mind, where do you want to go from here? Be still, be still! Go with peace on your way, the time is also coming soon for you, when God alone will be your all in all."

29

Some important events in the life of Zinzendorf:

1700	Born in Dresden. Father dies a few weeks later.
1700-1710	Lived with Grandma Henriette von Gersdorf.
1710-1719	Student in Halle and Wittenberg.
1719-1720	Gentleman's journey through Holland and France.
1720	In love with Theodore von Castell.
1721	His friend Heinrich Reuss marries Theodore.
1722	Buys the estate from grandmother. Marriage to Erdmuthe Dorothea von Reuss. Christian David built first house in Herrnhut.
1722-1726	In Dresden as Minister of Justice.
1727	Baptism of the Holy Spirit on the Moravians. Establishes 24/7 Prayer meetings. Selects daily Bible text for devotion. Moves permanently to Herrnhut.
1729	Frequent journeys.
1732	Journey to Denmark for the coronation of the king. Meets Antonius, the free Christian slave.

	First two Moravians as missionaries to St. Thomas.
	Legally transfers his estate to his wife.
1734	Ordained as a Lutheran pastor and Bishop of the Brethren.
1736	Beginning of eleven years in exile. Travels to Holland, Switzerland, Berlin, St. Thomas. Establishes cell groups and congregations. Interrogation by King Friedrich Wilhelm in Berlin.
1742	Sailing to America with his daughter Henriette Benigna for 18 months.
1743	Prisoner in Riga. Rise and fall of Herrnhaag.
1747	Returns joyfully back to Saxony from exile.
1748	Relentless journeys through Holland, England, Germany.
1752	His son Renatus dies in England.
1756	His wife Erdmuthe Dorothea dies.
1757	Marries Anna Nitschmann, Journey to Switzerland and Holland.
1760	Count Zinzendorf and his wife Anna Nitschmann die.

Thanks to Sally Mickley for her countless hours typing my handwritten manuscript into the computer. Pastor Jason Hubbard for encouraging me. I also appreciate the help from my wife, Jean, who gave me continued encouragement to finish the book.

Lightning Source UK Ltd.
Milton Keynes UK
UKOW02f1817081116

287183UK00001B/65/P